SALES
MANAGEMENT

Sales Management
Principles, Process and Practice

Third Edition

Bill Donaldson

First published in 2007 by
PALGRAVE MACMILLAN
Houndmills, Basingstoke, Hampshire RG21 6XS and
175 Fifth Avenue, New York, N.Y. 10010
Companies and representatives throughout the world.

PALGRAVE MACMILLAN is the global academic imprint of the Palgrave Macmillan division of St. Martin's Press, LLC and of Palgrave Macmillan Ltd. Macmillan® is a registered trademark in the United States, United Kingdom and other countries. Palgrave is a registered trademark in the European Union and other countries.

ISBN-13: 978–0–333–99851–9
ISBN-10: 0–333–99851–0

This book is printed on paper suitable for recycling and made from fully managed and sustained forest sources. Logging, pulping and manufacturing processes are expected to conform to the environmental regulations of the country of origin.

A catalogue record for this book is available from the British Library.

A catalog record for this book is available from the Library of Congress.

10   9   8   7   6   5   4   3   2   1
16 15 14 13 12 11 10 09 08 07

Printed in China

Contents

Part I   The philosophy of selling

Part II   The selling process
(The mobilisation of resources behind a customer)

Part III   Selling in practice (the management of sales operations)

List of figures

List of tables

Preface to the first edition

This book is aimed at three potential groups of readers: first, students on undergraduate and postgraduate courses, or with the Chartered Institute of Marketing and the Institute of Sales and Marketing Management, where sales management is part of the curriculum; second, salespeople who want to learn and understand the wider issues involved in sales operations and sales management; and finally, existing sales managers who want to improve or update their knowledge of the subject.

The primary aim of the book is to provide students with a suitable UK text which enables them to understand the concepts involved in managing sales and salespeople. Hopefully, the book will also have some appeal to those currently involved in selling and sales management, particularly the practising sales manager well seasoned in the profession. The basis for this hope is that no matter how much is known, how successful or what the extent of their experience, sales managers never stop being students of their subject.

The book seeks to debate some of the key management questions as they apply to sales operations. For example, what is the role of selling in a marketing context? What effects do alternative sales strategies, salespeople and sales management practices have on company growth and profitability? How can the sales function be effectively controlled and evaluated? Can we improve sales effectiveness and, at the same time, reduce transaction costs? We evaluate previous work in this area, assess what does or does not work and present sound concepts and recent empirical evidence to assist and inform management. Although consideration of the sales function may not be an area neglected by practitioners, its true importance is not adequately reflected in most marketing courses. Personal selling is still the largest item in most companies' marketing budget and therefore worthy of critical attention as part of any marketing course.

In Part I, selling and sales management are discussed in a modern marketing context. Particular importance is attached to defining the role that salespeople are expected to perform, the different types of selling and a review of the characteristics of salespeople and selling as a career. Discussion of the importance of buyer–seller relationships and key account management is given special treatment. Part II examines aspects of the organisation of selling effort, including the impact of information technology and the Internet on sales operations, types of sales organisation, territory management, deployment and setting realistic targets. Special attention is paid to international and global issues. In Part III, the specific management topics are discussed, including recruitment and selection, training, leadership and coaching, remuneration, motivation and evaluation. Finally, we have expanded the section on ethics to include some legal issues that salespeople must be aware of in execution of their duties.

The book is intended to be followed in a sequential manner as a course but each chapter should be sufficiently robust to stand on its own as a self-contained learning unit. For this reason, each chapter opens with specific learning objectives and ends with a summary, a list of key terms, a selection of exam questions and a case vignette for discussion with additional questions. Further reading, useful web sites and full references are included for each chapter.

Preface to the third edition

Change is the one certainty. For selling, sales operations and for sales managers, changes in information technology (IT), in the globalisation of business and in the importance of key customers have had dramatic effects on sales operations over recent years. Understanding these changes and assessing their impact are the main ways in which this edition has been modified. The third edition of this book incorporates suggested organisational responses to these changes in markets, competition and customers. This requires new thinking on the role of salespeople. There is a new chapter on technology; the chapter on international selling has been expanded as has the chapter on relationship selling and major account management. Hopefully the layout is more reader friendly. Chapter objectives have been supplemented with definitions, key concepts and learning objectives. There are more exam questions, new case vignettes and new longer case studies. Supplementary reading and useful web sites have been added.

There are three new chapters and many others which have been substantially changed. The cases for discussion at the end of each chapter have been revised and updated, and three new larger case studies have been added. These cases can be used as the basis of more extensive class discussion, for training purposes or as assignments as part of student course work.

The text still aims to meet the needs of undergraduate and postgraduate students taking an elective in sales management and for those students studying with the Chartered Institute of Marketing. An instructor's manual with overhead examples, specimen answers and case study notes is available for teachers adopting this text.

I hope you find this new edition of the book both readable and worthwhile.

BILL DONALDSON
Aberdeen Business School
The Robert Gordon University

Acknowledgements

The author would like to thank a number of people for their help in the preparation of this text: Regis Lemmens of Sales Cubes; Professor Colin Wheeler, Portsmouth University; Professor Nikos Tzokas University of East Anglia; Gernot Resch; Tess Harris; and Lynn Parkinson.

The author and publishers are grateful to the following for permission to reproduce copyright material:

Ashgate Publishing for Figure 2.4 from Rackham, N. (1987) *Making Major Sales;* Gower: Aldershot. © *Making Major Sales*, Neil Rackham, 1987, Gower.

The American Marketing Association (AMA) for Figures 2.8 (Sheth 1973, reprinted with permission from the *Journal of Marketing* vol. 37, pp. 50–55) and 5.12 (Cravens 1972, reprinted with permission from the *Journal of Marketing* vol. 36, pp. 31–37) and Figure 12.4 (Walker et al. 1977, reprinted with permission from the *Journal of Marketing Research;* XIV (May): 156–168).

Emerald Group Publishing Limited for Figure 3.2 from Millman, A.F. and Wilson, K.J. (1995) 'From key account selling to key account management'; *Journal of Marketing Practice;* 1 (1): 8–21.

John Wiley & Sons, Inc. for Figure 2.5 from Howard, J.A. and Sheth, J.N. (1969) *The Theory of Buyer Behavior;* John Wiley: New York, reprinted with permission of John Wiley & Sons Inc; and John Wiley Ltd for Figure 2.10 from Hakansson, H. (1982) *International Marketing and Purchasing of Industrial Goods;* John Wiley: London, reprinted with permission of John Wiley & Sons Ltd.

Prentice Hall for Figure 2.9 from Webster, F.E. and Wind, Y. (1972) *Organisational Buying Behavior;* Prentice-Hall: Englewood Cliffs, NJ.

Every effort has been made to trace all copyright holders, but if any have been inadvertently overlooked, the publishers would be pleased to make the necessary arrangements at the first opportunity.

Part I

The philosophy of selling

1 The role of selling

1.1 Overview

The role of selling is to create value for a firm at the point of contact with a customer. Value, typically expressed as revenue or profits, may be from a single sales transaction or a lifetime of customer purchases.

Efficient and effective sales management is, therefore, critical to gaining the maximum value from each customer. Despite the use of advanced technology in other management functions such as manufacturing, marketing, distribution and communications, personal selling is often the principal factor in the sales process. The personal selling function however – as represented by the role of salespeople in traditional textbooks – has changed radically. Modern sales operations can combine face-to-face selling with other customer contact tasks such as technical consulting, telephone and Internet sales, and personalised or automated customer service.

Today's firms must find the best way to integrate these functions into an effective and efficient sales management process that will deliver continuous value, both to themselves and their customers. Surprisingly, courses in business and marketing sometimes marginalise this subject. By contrast, leading firms recognise its importance and constantly seek ways to improve its practice through process improvements and management training.

1.2 Learning objectives

This chapter aims to

- help you understand the role of selling in the business and marketing context;
- describe the environment in which modern selling takes place;
- explain the significance and costs of the sales process to the organisation;
- explain the role salespeople perform.

1.3 Definitions

Personal selling is the personal contact with one or more buyers for the purpose of making a sale.

Sales management is the process of planning, organising, directing, staffing and controlling the sales operations to achieve the firm's objectives through subordinates.

Salesmanship is a 'seller-initiated effort that provides prospective buyers with information and other benefits, motivating or persuading them to make buying decisions in favour of the seller's product or service' (Still, Cundiff and Govoni, 1988).

1.4 Selling in the business and marketing context

A firm lives or dies by what it sells. Sales are the engine of sustainability and growth and are usually defined as a set of objectives by the firm in its business and/or marketing plan. Achievement of these objectives depends on how well they translate into specific market and customer sales targets and then performed within the sales process.

To reiterate, the role of selling is to create the maximum value for a firm at the point of contact with a customer. The revenue and profits earned from this contact may derive from a single sales transaction or a lifetime of customer purchases. However, value maximisation may not be possible from every customer contact, and senior management must provide guidance to salespeople in the business plan regarding selling prioritisation by current and future profitability.

This guidance is often ignored in business planning. In later chapters on sales operations, we shall discuss how senior management can contribute to the accomplishment of the business plan objectives through a sales process that aligns selling with corporate goals.

Selling is an element of the marketing mix (readers are assumed to have studied at least the fundamentals of marketing before studying this textbook). Indeed, the traditional marketing mix, based on McCarthy's 4 Ps model (Perrault *et al.*, 2000), shows selling as a subsidiary function within the promotional mix, an adapted form of which is shown in Figure 1.1.

This hierarchy suggests a relegation of the sales function, which does not reflect today's competitive market context. Many firms spend more resources and employ more people in selling than in any other promotional activity. In some situations, the sales budget may exceed all other marketing activities added together.

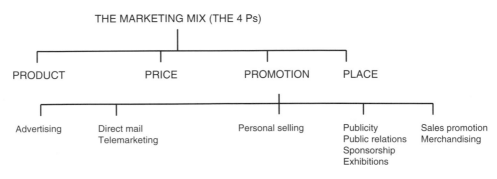

Fig 1.1 Elements in the marketing mix

Did you know?

Numbers of UK Marketing and Sales Professionals

Benson Payne Ltd, a management consultancy appointed by the MSSSB – a new government-backed body to set world-class standards in Marketing and Sales – estimates there were 545,000 full-time marketing professionals in 2003, an increase of nearly 80 per cent since 1993, and 766,000 full-time sales professionals within field sales operations, an increase of 9 per cent since 1993. This was greater than the number of teachers, doctors, engineers or accountants. Remarkably, MSSSB also estimates that over 2.5 million people have selling as a primary activity in their job.

(*Source: http://www.msssb.org/*)

A negative view of the subordinate role of selling in the marketing mix has an unfortunate outcome, which is to consider marketing and selling as differing functions rather than as complementary roles. This view is compounded by a persistent notion of firms as having either a 'production–sales orientation' or a 'marketing orientation', first expressed in 'Marketing Myopia' (Levitt, 1960). While there are firms that still operate with a production attitude, successful firms have since adopted a marketing customer orientation.

Viewing marketing and selling as opposing rather than complementary functions can also be a moral conceit. Marketing (giving customers what they want) is seen as virtuous, healthy and necessary, whereas selling (getting rid of something) is seen to be cynical, callous and indiscriminate. This view of selling is typified by the one-off, high-pressure sales approach, such as may be found in some telesales operations, where dubious techniques are used to induce people to buy. Selling, as a result, is sometimes seen as dishonest.

Professional salespeople know that repeat purchases and continuity of business are more important to the firm than an individual sale. Like most occupations there are good and bad salespeople, sales professionals and sales amateurs and, of course, honest and dishonest people.

1.5 Marketing and sales strategy

Once the business goals are set, it is the role of marketing management to develop an appropriate strategy. This could include (Jobber and Fahy, 2003)

- market and customer segmentation;
- market research to identify the needs and wants of prospective customers;
- decisions on products and services to be offered to each customer or prospect group;
- design and implementation of marketing communications programmes including the sales plan.

Sales planning involves a similar strategic approach at the individual customer level, typified by methodologies such as

- account planning (segmentation and targeting of key customers or groups);
- opportunity identification and value assessment;

- distribution channel management;
- territory management;
- personal communications with prospective and existing customers.

Effective managers will ensure that both marketing and sales strategies are consistent and coordinated by aligning people, process and technology. The sales strategy should derive from marketing, but sales should also provide input into the marketing strategy development. This integration is not easily achieved.

In many organisations, salespeople do not know what is expected of them. There is a lack of clarity from the top about objectives, which results in problems with individual sales plans, targets and remuneration. Conflict between individuals and management, or between sales policies and marketing policies, can arise. For example, the firm's policy on market segmentation can affect an individual salesperson's effectiveness. The extent to which the same product/service package is offered to the market or modified to suit specific groups of customers influences sales management decisions. Selling techniques and resources must be allocated according to whether marketing is undifferentiated (no segmentation), differentiated (different offerings to different customers) or concentrated (different offerings to several groups of customers) (Kotler *et al.*, 2001).

Changes made to the other elements in the marketing mix will have an impact on the degree of personal selling effort. At one extreme, a firm can offer the minimum product specification, cheapest price and rely on customers ordering by phone, letter, in person or electronically. Little or no personal selling is involved; overheads, such as selling costs, are minimal. At the other extreme, salespeople may seek their own leads, carry and deliver the product and collect payment.

We shall discuss how marketing and sales integration can be achieved in later chapters.

What do you think?

Salesperson: 'Marketing are OK at coming up with grandiose schemes and expensive advertising or PR stunts but it is the sales force on the ground, day-in, day-out that makes the customer contact and separates us from the competition. They all think they are customer driven but how would they know? They've never met one, far less having to deal with queries, complaints and a host of competitors in your face.'

Marketing/Brand Manager: 'The trouble with salespeople they only see their own target customers or area as important and if it doesn't suit they don't try to sell your product or brand no matter the overall strategy or the investment behind it.'

How would you resolve such entrenched attitudes?

1.6 Relationship marketing

However, the fundamental difference between the marketing and sales strategies is that the personal selling effort and the salesperson may determine whether a sale is made or not. This may depend as much on the individual salesperson's ability to build a relationship with the buyer, as on the intrinsic merits of the seller's product or service. 'Relationship Marketing (RM) refers to all marketing activities directed towards establishing, developing and maintaining successful relational exchanges' (Morgan and Hunt, 1994, p. 22).

Thus, RM predicates an intimacy between the firm and its customers, distributors, suppliers or other parties in the marketing environment (Sheth and Parvatiyar, 1995). Traditionally, owing to their boundary-spanning role, the field sales force of a company has been a vital link between the firm and its customers (Cravens *et al.*, 1992). They act as a platform for communicating the firm's marketing message to its customers and as the voice of the customer to the firm. Nonetheless, the sales management effort was firmly on 'closing the sale'. RM shifts this focus to creating the necessary conditions for a long-term relationship between firm and customers with the aim of building durable and successful sales encounters.

This shift necessitates a reappraisal of conventional sales management practices, in particular the philosophy and culture of 'aggressive and persuasive selling' (Donaldson, 1998). The new role of the salesperson is increasingly that of a relationship manager, advising and counselling, listening and helping (Pettijohn *et al.*, 1995). Each contact point and selling occasion becomes an opportunity to develop mutual trust and commitment, strengthen the relationship and build customer loyalty.

The role of salespeople can be considered as 'boundary spanning' since its purpose is one of coordinating sales activities within one organisation (the seller's company) and linking in a scamless manner with another organisation (usually the buyer or distributor company). The role is often extensive using team-based selling. For example, Proctor and Gamble have over 20 people working in Asda Headquarters in the United Kingdom. Likewise, a computer firm may have five or six in a team servicing a large bank customer and so on. As it was put to us by one senior sales manager at IBM 'my job is to mobilise resources behind customer solutions'.

We shall discuss RM in detail in later chapters.

Did you know?

In a recent survey of sales executives 88 per cent replied that relationships were essential in their sales process when asked 'How important are long term relationships to your sales effort'. Using a 7-point scale from not at all to vitally important the mean value was 6.18 (Donaldson and Wright, 2002). Many studies have revealed the importance of customer retention in adding value. For example, it is claimed that retaining 5 per cent more of your existing customers can increase profitably between 25 and 85 per cent (Reicheld, 1996).

1.7 The sales environment

As indicated above, the selling and sales management functions are transforming with the realisation of the value to the firm of customer relationships over individual sales.

The modern sales environment also poses complex challenges for salespeople.

Competitors. In today's economy every pound of disposable income competes with every other pound, and competitive activity is intense. Marketing and sales management must constantly appraise the strengths and weaknesses of competitors and modify their strategies and tactics accordingly to differentiate their firm.

Customers. Expectations continue to rise along with increasing dissatisfaction. Firms need to find ever more innovative and profitable ways to create and deliver value to buyers.

Technology. New materials, products and processes emerge at a seemingly ever-increasing rate. Product life cycles are reduced in length, affecting the way goods and services are manufactured, distributed and promoted. Technology also brings changes to the role and function of selling (more on this in later chapters).

Mature market economies and globalisation. Supply in many markets now exceeds demand. Pressure on prices and margins has resulted in cuts in sales forces and the level of sales support from their organisations. Globalisation has meant a shift towards global and key account management, requiring new and different knowledge and skills from salespeople.

1.8   The cost of selling

Table 1.1 demonstrates the relative importance of the main elements of the marketing mix by type of marketing.

The most significant difference between selling and other elements in the marketing effort is the personal contact, which varies depending on a variety of factors such as the type of customer and product, the frequency of purchase, the newness of the product and so on.

Sales and marketing directors should frequently ask the question: *What would happen if we halved (or doubled) the size of our sales force?* Would sales halve (or double), and what is the effect on profits in the short and long term?

Table 1.1   **Relative importance of each element of the marketing mix by type of marketing**

Type of marketing activity	Industrial goods and business to business marketing	Consumer durable	Consumer non-durable
Sales management and personal selling	Very high	High	High
Media advertising	Very low	Moderate	High
Special promotions	Low	Moderate	Moderate
Packaging, branding, other	Low	Low	Moderate

5-point scale: Very low, Low, Moderate, High, Very High

Table 1.2 Average cost of a salesperson 2005 (based on industry sources)

	Annual cost (£)
Salary, commission	21,000
Fringe benefits (pension, BUPA)	6000
Company car	12,000
Entertainment	2000
Telephone, postage, communications	4000
Accommodation and meals	4000
Samples	2000
Sundry costs	2000
Total	53,000

Table 1.3 Allocation of selling time

	Hours per day	Percentage of time
Pre-call preparation	1.5	15
Driving and parking	2.0	20
Face-to-face selling	2.5	25
Non-selling, e.g., display	1.5	15
Admin/reports	1.0	10
Meals and breaks	0.5	5
Telephone, meetings, other	1.0	10
Total	10	100

Seldom will the situation be as dramatic as this but the concern over value for money from the sales force is a continuing problem for sales management. Although there are very few examples of companies increasing long-term sales and profits by reducing the size of their sales force, senior management should consider the data provided in Tables 1.2 and 1.3.

Salespeople are expensive, and the time spent face to face with customers is low. These figures are, however, an average and will vary depending on the type of selling and other situational specific factors.

1.9 The role of the salesperson

Every sales situation is in some way unique. As shown in Figures 1.2 and 1.3 the extent of personal selling varies between different categories of goods and with the stage in the buying process.

The selling role of the salesperson can be expressed as a set of distinct stages, as illustrated in Figure 1.4.

These stages reflect stylised models of communication, the most familiar represented by the mnemonic AIDA, that is, Attention, holding Interest, arousing Desire and obtaining Action (Perrault *et al.*, 2000).

In some situations, the first stage can be achieved by impersonal means such as advertising. Indeed, the extent to which all or part of the sales process can be achieved

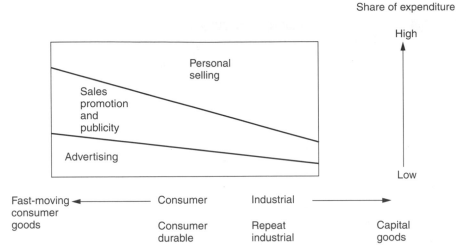

Fig 1.2 Importance of selling and type of product

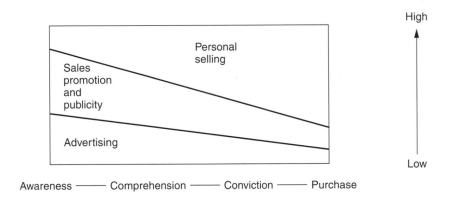

Fig 1.3 Importance of selling by stage in the purchase process

Fig 1.4 Flow chart of the selling process

Table 1.4	Communication methods comparison		
	Choice of type of communication		
Personal selling	Direct mail	Advertising	
Directed at the individual	Directed at the individual	Directed at a mass audience	
Personal direct contact	Impersonal direct contact	Impersonal indirect contact	
High level of adaptability	Medium level of adaptability	Less directly adaptable	
Working in depth	More broad than deep	Working in breadth	
Two-way	One-way	One-way	
Direct feedback	No voluntary feedback	Organised feedback	
Expensive per contact	Very cheap per contact	Relatively cheap per contact	
Push effect	Push effect	Pull effect	

at lowest cost and maximum efficiency is the 'holy grail' of sales management. A comparison of advertising, direct mail and personal selling is shown in Table 1.4.

Beyond the broad selling framework, salespeople will find themselves undertaking the following:

- customer problem solving;
- retaining (and increasing) existing business;
- obtaining new business;
- providing existing and potential buyers with adequate service such as quotations, advice and complaint handling;
- representing the company;
- providing information to and from customers, to and from management.

Salespeople will carry out a variety of specific tasks, ranging from

- taking orders;
- displaying products;
- advising distributors and users;
- after sales service;
- collecting payment;
- stock checking;
- training;
- monitoring delivery progress.

Increasingly, salespeople are required to use computerised technology, pointing to a need for continuing sales training and professional development.

Did you know?

Salespeople do spend a great deal of time on financial issues. The first one is actually trying to collect late payments and obtain cash from customers, but vetting the credit ratings of potential leads and new customers can also be part of the remit. According to one source, 12 per cent of a company representative's time on average is spent on such duties, with an incredible 8 per cent of firms spending over 30 per cent of a salesperson's time on this activity (Corcoran *et al.*, 1995).

1.10   The role of the sales manager

It is not unusual for a sales manager to be promoted from a sales position in the same organisation. This can give rise to performance problems. Salespeople who are promoted to first-line managers may fail to distinguish management tasks from doing tasks and continue to sell (doing) rather than managing salespeople (managing).

What do you think?

One of the issues facing many newly promoted salespeople and indeed some long-serving sales managers is that they are unable to separate doing from managing. Effective selling (doing) is what made them successful in the first place, and, understandably, they are reluctant to let go to others. Yet, it is the job of the manager to manage not to do the work of others.

Assume you are a sales manager and test yourself on whether you can readily identify the difference between managing and doing from the following list:

- visiting a customer with one of your salespeople to show a customer that the company values the account (doing);
- discussing new selling approaches with one of your salespeople (managing);
- making a presentation to a local community group (doing);
- contacting operations within your company to resolve a delivery problem for one of your salespeople (doing);
- deciding how to respond to a request to match a competitor on price (managing);
- telephoning the sales director to update her on progress in your markets (managing).

The role of the sales manager involves planning, organising, staffing, directing and controlling performance. The precise nature of sales management will be open to debate but should include

- defining the role and tasks of the sales function in relation to overall corporate and marketing objectives;
- selecting, training and delegating subordinates;
- using time effectively;
- allocating time to think and plan;
- exercising leadership;
- maintaining control.

This does not necessarily mean some selling tasks can or should be avoided. Large, important customers will expect to deal at director, often managing director, level with a supplier, and senior people must perform a selling role. Likewise, sales managers may be expected to address outside groups as representatives of their company. This does not invalidate the basic premise that sales managers should be primarily employed to manage salespeople. Table 1.5 summarises the amount of time different levels of management spend on different tasks.

Table 1.5 Allocation of management activities at different decision levels

	Planning	Organising	Staffing	Directing	Controlling
Top level – strategic	40	30	10	10	10
Middle level – tactical	10	30	20	30	10
1st line – operational	10	10	10	30	40

Source: based on an original idea by Ryans and Weinberg, 1981 and up-dated

The table divides management activities into three conceptual decision levels: (1) strategic, (2) tactical and (3) operational. In smaller organisations one person may embrace the three decision levels but the classification is a useful aid to understanding the nature of decisions in all organisations.

In the following sections, we look at each stage in more detail.

Strategic level

Strategic decisions are those concerned with definition of the firm's existing and future business to arrive at an appropriate marketing statement of

- the markets to be served now and in the future;
- the types of products and/or services which satisfy customers in these markets;
- the areas of business the company does not want.

The sales function will have an input into this process. The outcome of the process is to define the role personal selling will have vis-à-vis other elements in the marketing mix (advertising, sales promotion and publicity) and the tasks the sales force will perform. A failure to address these strategic questions will reduce the enterprise to a 'follow-my-leader' position or constant fire-fighting tactics. The strategic decision stage is crucial to a long-term business success.

Tactical level

Tactical sales management decisions are taken following marketing and sales strategy decisions. This means market exploration studies and market segmentation analysis have been done and decisions completed on product differentiation policies and promotional planning, that is, where the market and sales potential is known and the identity and location of customers and prospects have been established. Also, because of the sequential nature of this process, the balance between personal selling and other marketing variables is clear, the role salespeople are to perform is determined and management tasks fall into three areas:

1 structuring the sales force in terms of its size and organisational design;
2 developing the sales force such as recruitment, selection and training policies and programmes;
3 motivating the sales force by supervision, leadership, remuneration and by evaluation and control.

Operational level

Management concern at this level is to ensure that salespeople are doing an effective job. Managers must encourage salespeople to manage themselves and their territories as far as possible. Responsibilities include the type of person in terms of personality, knowledge, skills and motivation. First-line managers must also understand the needs and characteristics of the customers they serve. They must be able to evaluate and react to competitor's sales strategy and environmental factors. Finally, they must be aware of organisational policies and procedures as they apply to the sales organisation and implement rules and regulations applying to their salespeople. The way this is done can be a strong motivating factor in sales performance.

To implement sales policies at these three levels requires different types of skills:

1 *First-line managers*, for example, need strong person-management skills to lead a sales team. The emphasis is on product, company and customer knowledge, to be able to demonstrate selling skills and to select and train subordinates.

2 *Tactical decisions* require more organisational capability, setting job specifications and job descriptions, arranging the necessary training, payment, incentive packages and control systems.

3 The *strategic level* requires a much higher level of conceptual thought, superior organisational abilities and a corporate perspective. Sales managers should possess the capability to master all three levels of managerial decision-making. An important requirement within an organisation is to train salespeople in the technical, human and conceptual skills to prepare them for future sales management positions.

Finally, managers at all levels should consider their own management style in order to achieve the best results from subordinates in their organisation.

1.11   The study of sales management

The study of sales management presents several specific problems:

■ Traditionally, the emphasis in sales management is on implementation and tactical operations rather than strategic planning and policy, which tends to be the prerogative of marketing.

■ There is difficulty in isolating the sales response function and its causes. Many factors other than selling effort affect sales response.

■ There exists a myopic view that behavioural relationships and interactions in selling are not amenable to classification or that variables are impossible to measure.

■ Many principles of sales organisation, deployment and motivation are based on 'how to' principles, some of which are difficult to assess or understand; for example, how to overcome objections. Much of the data is highly specific and anecdotal.

■ The terrain on which operations takes place is continually changing (territories, personnel and customers).

- Much of the input on sales management issues comes from disparate areas of research, behavioural sciences, operations research and economics.
- Much study and evidence is US-based and these findings in empirical research do not necessarily remain intact across the Atlantic.

There are five possible ways to address these problems, by examining the sales function and its management.

1   View the position and role of selling as one element in the promotional mix, itself one element in the marketing mix. Management of each element is required to maximise both individually and collectively the effect on business performance as a customer-creation-satisfaction process more effectively than the competition. Moreover, the elements together used in an integrated and coordinated way have a synergistic effect greater than maximising the effect of each element individually and exclusively. Most marketing students address the subject with this approach, which in reality is the task only of senior executives who have responsibility for corporate and marketing strategy on which sales operation plans are based. Simple adaptations of this approach in consumer product marketing are inadequate when looking at the realities of industrial product markets or of services (see, for example, Gummesson, 1999).

2   Study the individual salesperson and attempt to understand the motives and actions that affect performance. Many sales management problems could be eliminated if a successful style could be established for a salesperson. If successful salespeople are born, or can be self-taught, then the sales manager's task is to find such people. Some writers have no problem in suggesting that the mysteries of the super salesperson are to be found in personality, psychological, even physical characteristics (McMurry, 1961; Lamont and Lundstrom, 1977). The search for critical traits is also seen to be important.

What do you think?

Are salespeople born or made?

If born, what are the attributes? Are they physical, psychological or behavioural?

If made, do you try to change people's behaviour, personality or what?

Does it make a difference in terms of age, sex, social class or other factors?

3   Adopt an interactive approach. All personal selling takes place with at least two people, a buyer and a seller, and it would be appropriate to study the subject around interpersonal situations. Early work in this field was an extension of individual physical and psychological elements into the perceived or real similarities and differences between two individuals (Evans, 1963). The outcome was that the greater the similarity between the characteristics of buyer and seller the greater the likelihood of transactions taking place. If the interaction effects are crucial to successful selling, then the wisdom of selecting a sales type in turn will affect the recruitment and selection of policies of sales managers and will affect the content of sales training programmes. The findings of the International Marketing and Purchasing Group have placed new emphasis on buyer/seller interaction by studying the active part played by both customer and supplier

and the negotiated nature of many transactions, which in turn influences resource allocation and organisational relationships (Hakansson, 1982).

4 Study the economics of selling. Various measures of establishing sales force size, the profit and sales from selling effort and the return on investment or value of the sales force can be made. For example, the lifetime value of customers can be measured, using standard cash flow discounting procedures. From this, new or modified organisational systems can be implemented, such as customer relationship management (CRM).

5 Observe the decisions sales managers are expected to make and explore means of assisting such decision-making based on sound theory and empirical findings. The uniqueness of product company and market circumstances may limit the applicability of such guidelines but better planning of territories, setting sales targets, recruitment, training and motivating salespeople will be important in making real productivity gains by management.

These approaches to sales management cover separate but interrelated aspects of the subject, which contribute towards a more complete theory of factors affecting sales force performance and its management.

1.12 Summary

Selling and sales processes have changed in recent years as companies have become more market- and customer-focussed. Sales management practices too have had to change, yet, despite the Internet, call centres and mobile communications, the cost and efficiency of the field sales force still accounts for much of the marketing budget in many companies. It is vital that sales operations reflect the corporate and marketing strategy of the organisation as well as specific sales management objectives. Today, more than ever, there is need to integrate sales, marketing and corporate objectives because of the high costs of personal selling and the limited time that salespeople spend with customers. The management requirement is for a clear definition of the role of selling, the tasks that salespeople must perform and the responsibilities of sales management.

Questions

1 Explain how the role of sales manager may differ between an organisation which is production-oriented and one which is marketing and customer-oriented.

2 In your own organisation, or in a firm you are familiar with, identify the main environmental influences which affect the sales operations.

3 What are the conflicts which arise between sales and marketing personnel in the same organisation? Describe how such conflicts can be resolved.

4 Describe some of the non-managing tasks that sales managers are expected to perform. Which of these do you feel can be delegated to subordinates?

5 Interview at least one sales manager and attempt to identify the time spent on different tasks and on different types of management activity.

Case study

Dell Computers

Dell is renowned for its direct sales to customers by phone, Internet and now through e-business enabling consumers to go through the whole sales process online. What is less well known is that Dell, in 2005, took on 150 salespeople to sell their products in United Kingdom/Europe. The reason for this change from direct selling to personal selling is that the cost of a salesperson for an individual customer makes no economic sense, but if you are selling many computers, printers, servers and other products and ancillaries to one customer then personal salespeople are required to understand the customer's needs, offer appropriate solutions and sell the correct package. In this regard, Dell must compete with HP and IBM for business customers on a more personalised service basis.

Yet Dell's background is interesting as the company pioneered direct selling and mass customisation. Founded in Texas in 1984, by 1992 Dell had made the Fortune 500 list and in 2004 was ranked 34 in *Business Week*'s Global list of the world's most valuable companies. In 1996, Dell began to sell computers on the Internet, and within 2 years, sales were exceeding $3 million per day. Much of this was due to the way Dell reduced transaction costs by cutting out expensive distribution and sales channels, including the high cost of personal salespeople. The Dell direct selling model gave the company infrastructure leanness, market agility, minimal inventory and high customer differentiation. Although relatively weak compared with competitors in R & D (Dell 1.3% of revenues; HP 5.8%; IBM 5.9%), the financial discipline using off the shelf components and assembly technology gave it a market-leading performance, quality and price combination.

Revenue figures and projections are shown in Table 1.6. Anticipating low growth in the future PC market, the company has refocused as an Internet-centric company (see Table 1.7).

Table 1.6

Dell revenues (in billion US dollars)

	2001 $	2004 $*	2006 $*
PCs	20	27	30
Servers/storage	5	8	10
Services	3	5	9
Software/peripherals	3	7	13
Total	31	47	62

estimate

Table 1.7

Dell's service products

Service	Name
Private Intranet sites: customer-specific pricing and paperless ordering	www.Premier.Dell.com
FAQs: diagnostics, customer discussion forums, parts ordering dispatch requests, service call status	www.Support.Dell.com
Web site hosting to provide small business with own website and web storefront	www.DellEWorks.com
Direct online auction for Dell customers	www.Dellauction.com
e-Commerce services including reselling	Gigabuys

►

Table 1.7	Continued	
Service		Name
Automated detection, diagnosis and resolution through Internet		Resolution assistant
Dell/Ariba alliance to create inexpensive tools for B2B e-commerce		Dell B2B marketplace exchange
Custom factory integration service and custom-built factory-installed solutions		DellPlus
'Brick to Click' works with dot.coms to improve business efficiency for SMEs starting in e-commerce		Dell consulting
Equity and incubation services for early-stage Internet companies		Dell ventures

Sources: 1. www.dell.com (accessed 12 Dec 2006)
2. *Business Week* 'What you don't know about Dell'(3 Nov 2003) 46–54
3. Dell, M. S. and Fredman, C. (1999) *Direct from Dell* London: HarperCollins

Discussion Questions

1 Given the company background above, are you surprised by Dell's move to personal sales-people and sales teams for business customers? Analyse the pros and cons in their strategy.

2 Draw a scenario of how you would perceive a working day for a Dell sales representative.

3 Discuss some of the issues integrating salespeople with other functions within the organisation.

Key terms

- market segmentation
- marketing concept
- marketing mix
- personal selling
- product positioning
- sales management
- sales force interfaces
- salesmanship
- selling environment
- strategy
- tactics

References

Corcoran, K.J., Petersen, L.K., Baitch, D.B. and Barrett, M.F. (1995) *High Performance Sales Organisations: creating competitive advantage in the global marketplace* McGraw-Hill: New York

Cravens, D., Grant, K., Ingram, T., LaForge, R. and Young, C. (1992) 'In search of excellent sales organisations' *European Journal of Marketing* **26** (1): 6–23

Donaldson, B. (1998) 'The importance of financial incentives in motivating industrial salespeople' *Journal of Selling and Major Account Management* **1** (1): 4–16

Donaldson, B. and Wright, G. (2002) 'Sales information systems: are they being used for more than simple mail shots?' *Journal of Database Marketing* **9** (3): 276–84

Evans, F.B. (1963) 'Selling as a dyadic relationship – a new approach' *American Behavioral Scientist* 6: 76–9

Gummesson, E. (1999) *Total Relationship Marketing* Butterworth Heinemann: Oxford

Hakansson, H. (ed.) (1982) *International Marketing and Purchasing of Industrial Goods: an interactive approach* John Wiley & Sons: New York

Jobber, D. and Fahy, J. (2003) *Foundations of Marketing* McGraw-Hill: Maidenhead

Kotler, P., Armstrong, G., Saunders, J. and Wong, V. (2001) *Principles of Marketing 3rd European Edition* Prentice-Hall/Pearson: Harlow

Lamont, L.M. and Lundstrom, W.J. (1977) 'Identifying successful industrial salesmen by personality and personal characteristics' *Journal of Marketing Research* **XIV** (Nov): 517–29

Levitt, T. (1960) 'Marketing myopia' *Harvard Business Review* **Jul–Aug**: 45–56

McMurry, R.N. (1961) 'The mystique of super-salesmanship' *Harvard Business Review* **Mar–Apr**: 113–22

Morgan, R.M. and Hunt, S.D. (1994) 'The commitment–trust theory of relationship marketing' *Journal of Marketing* **56** (Jul): 20–38

MSSSB – Benson Payne http://www.msssb.org [Accessed 26 Sep 2006]

Perrault, W.D., McCarthy, E.J., Parkinson, S. and Stewart, K. (2000) *Basic Marketing European Edition* McGraw-Hill: Maidenhead

Pettijohn, C., Pettijohn, L. and Taylor, A. (1995) 'The relationship between effective counselling and effective behaviors' *Journal of Consumer Marketing* **12** (1): 5–15

Reicheld, F. (1996) *The Loyalty Effect: the hidden force behind growth, profits and lasting value* Harvard Business School Press: Boston, MA

Ryans, A.B. and Weinberg, C.B. (1981) 'Sales force management: integrating research advances' *California Management Review* **24** (1): 75–89

Sheth, J.N. and Parvatiyar, A. (1995) 'The evolution of relationship marketing' *International Business Review* **4** (4): 397–418

Still, R.R., Cundiff, E.W. and Govoni, N.A.P. (1988) *Sales Management Decisions, Strategies and Cases* 5th edition Prentice-Hall: Englewood Cliffs, NJ

2 Theories of buying and selling

2.1 Overview

Selling and sales operations are considered practical, doing activities, and salespeople and sales managers can often be heard complaining that 'something is OK in theory but not in practice', implying that theory has no role in selling. However, even sales practices based on notions such as trial and error, or experience depend on the presence of a set of law-like propositions or theories. These typically exist as mental models that guide behaviour but they are, nonetheless, theoretical.

Therefore, in this chapter, we consider theories of selling, chiefly by studying the decision-making process of buyers. The models that emerge from these theories should help interpret a buyer's behaviour in different circumstances and therefore help predict likely future buying behaviour. This understanding should improve the effectiveness of the sales process.

2.2 Learning objectives

This chapter aims to

- describe theories of selling and buying;
- understand buyer behaviour;
- provide examples of theories in practice.

2.3 Definitions

Industrial Marketing is the traditional term now superseded by business-to-business (B2B) marketing. It still applies where marketing and selling takes place between those buying goods and services for use in the production and supply of their own products and services.

B2B Marketing involves the supplying of goods and services to businesses, intermediaries, government and public bodies for consumption, use or resale. B2B marketing therefore embraces industrial marketing and also *trade marketing* which involves the sale of goods and services to retailers for selling on to consumers. It also embraces the huge public procurement sector.

Direct Selling to consumers is still an important route to market. Avon cosmetics uses this approach as its preferred business model, but is more normal in relatively expensive products and services such as home improvements and financial services.

For Fast-Moving Consumer Goods (FMCG) sales are made through trade marketing teams, category managers and others as part of customer account management process.

2.4   Economic and behavioural theories

Theories of buying and selling are best studied and understood in chronological order. For this reason, readers should not be put off that some of the references in this chapter are dated but the history of buying behaviour also helps us understand the way that selling approaches have changed from a relatively simplistic process to highly complex and participative exchange. Also, many authors have separated theories of buying behaviour and their derived models between consumer and industrial/organisational buying situations, and, where relevant, this distinction is made throughout this section.

Traditionally, economic theory was used to analyse buying–selling activities. Purchasing was believed to be problem-solving behaviour undertaken by a rational individual whose goal was to maximise satisfaction (called 'utility' in economics) by choosing the ideal combination from a 'range of affordable commodities' (Arrow, 1951). The environment and process was one of atomistic transactions, that is, multiple, discrete and anonymous trades (Turnbull, Ford and Cunningham, 1996). Buyer would 'meet' seller in the market to engage in a rational 'exchange transaction' (Alderson, 1995). The final transaction was a complete price match between supply and demand, after taking account of all the influencing factors on each party's decision to buy or sell.

Alderson and others recognised the limitations of applying strict economic theory to buyer–seller processes. Katona (1995) combined behavioural sciences, namely psychology, with economic theory, aiming to study 'forms of rational behaviour, rather than the characteristics of the rational man' (ibid., p. 134).

What do you think?

Commodity trading is often said to be an example of a rational approach to buying and selling. Do you agree?

Marketers and salespeople were urged to 'take a closer look at the nature of the participants' and understand the overall behaviour of the 'system' (Alderson, 1995, p. 26). This system could range from well-organised groups such as firms and households to loosely structured networks such as trading centres. Social sciences were used to explain the behaviours of such systems, for example, sociology, psychology and cultural anthropology. In turn, this has influenced theories of selling, and it is to these we now turn. However, a word of warning, examination of theories of selling would suggest that while they may contribute to our understanding of the buyer–seller interaction process they are weak at explaining sales performance. What they do highlight is the importance of understanding the nature of the interaction between buyer and seller.

The sales process, whether in an industrial, B2B or consumer goods and services situation, commonly involves personal interaction between the participants. Unless attention is paid to managing the human aspects of the interaction, the sales process and the salesperson's performance will be ineffective.

Researchers have long tried to identify the buyer–seller characteristics that affect the outcome of a sales interaction, in particular focusing on buyer–seller similarity. Inevitably, some of these variables are not amenable to accurate measurement, for example, personality and physical characteristics. Brock (1965) found in retail paint selling that buyer–seller similarity was more influential in achieving sales success than seller expertise. This has subsequently been confirmed as important in life insurance (Greenberg and Greenberg, 1976) and for wholesale drugs (Tosi, 1966).

Lichtenthal and Tellefsen (2001) reviewed all the research literature on buyer–seller similarity in B2B situations and proposed two categories of similarity: internal and observable (see Table 2.1), comprising several characteristics. Lichtenthal and Tellefsen (2001) suggest that 'internal similarity can increase a business buyer's willingness to trust a salesperson' and that, in the main, 'observable similarity exerts a negligible influence' (ibid., p. 1).

Buyer–seller similarity has implications for sales recruitment and training. One concern, for example, is the preference sales managers sometimes show to hire people with similar characteristics to their own – which can raise ethical and legal problems. Other difficulties include the problem of evaluating how the characteristics suggested by buyer–seller similarity exert a positive or negative effect on a sales outcome.

What do you think?

The 'sports jacket and welly boots' image is thought to be needed to sell to farmers, Welsh-speaking salesmen in West Wales and so on. Davis and Silk (1972) suggested 'the greater the similarity between a salesman and a prospect the more the prospect will like the salesman and therefore, the greater the salesman's influence'.

This is contradicted by the study in Table 2.1 which suggests observable characteristics to be less important.

Do you agree?

Table 2.1 Buyer–seller similarity

Observable similarity	Internal similarity
Physical	**General**
Age	Education
Dress	Family status
Gender	Interests
Height	Personality
Nationality/race	Political/religious views
Behavioural	**Business related**
Mannerisms	Product usage and perceptions
Speech patterns	Perceptions about salespeople/ suppliers/companies

2.5   Stimulus and response

The premise behind this theory is that when a seller presents a buyer with a stimulus, for example, a low-priced product, he or she will act in a predictable manner. The seller's aim, over time, is for the buyer's behaviour to become automatic. This approach has traditionally been used in direct selling where the 'canned' presentation or conditioned response selling approach can be very effective. The assumption, based on psychology theory, is that since Pavlov's experiments worked with dogs, it should be good enough for the inexperienced buyer! The basis of this theory is that salespeople should say the right things in the correct order to stimulate buyers' needs and desires. This type of approach can be useful where the sales process is simple and straightforward, the outcome is sale or no sale, the product is low priced and the time available is short. However, the theory has weaknesses. In more complex purchasing where the emphasis is on supply chain integration and cooperation between teams, the persuasion process will be different. The sales organisation, whether an individual or a team, needs to identify a range of cues, both core and peripheral, which stimulate desire to purchase and show a willingness by the buyer to continue the interaction. Many readers will be familiar with the stimulus–response approach from telephone selling which if inappropriate for the recipient leads to negative views of both company and salesperson by the consumer.

2.6   Formula selling

Formulae are used throughout marketing to either describe or predict buyer or seller behaviour. The most famous selling formula is AIDAS (see Figure 2.1). This mnemonic and its variations are used to explain the sales process in terms of mental-states theory. First attributed to Sheldon (1902) as AIDR (attention, interest, desire, resolve) it was modified by Strong (1925) in his book, The Psychology of Selling, to AIDA (attention, interest, desire, action). Later the S, for satisfaction, was added.

The AIDAS formula is known as the hierarchy of effects and is often used in communication theory – although its relevance is widely debated on both theoretical and empirical grounds. However, the model does have an intuitive appeal because it can be matched to a series of distinct steps in the sales process (Figure 2.1).

	Hierarchy of effects	Steps in the sales process
A	Attention	Making contact
I	Interest	Arousing interest
D	Desire	Creating preference/specific proposals
A	Action	Closing the sale
S	Satisfaction	Retaining business

Fig 2.1   AIDAS selling formula

Many critics, in both advertising and personal selling, have questioned the appropriateness of this model. For example, Palda (1966), in advertising research, criticises the hierarchy for implying closer probability of an intended action as a potential buyer proceeds on this sequential process of mental states. Palda claims this is not necessarily the case (ibid., 1966). In other situations, the sequential order may be distorted, out of predicted sequence, telescoped or even omitted. Rackham (1987) accumulated data on numerous sales situations. He suggested that, particularly in larger sales, the hierarchy may be inappropriate.

Selling formulae aid our understanding but may not be typical of most selling situations. Most buying–selling transactions take place between participants who know one another and who are familiar with the products or services being considered. For example, it is difficult for a buyer to commit to a firm he has not heard of, to a salesperson he does not know for a product so far untried. What the model omits is the recognition of the buyer's need. Selling should be aimed at satisfying a customer's need or solving a problem not just persuading someone to buy available product by grabbing their attention. The model could therefore encourage inexperienced salespeople to 'assault' the prospect with a pre-arranged 'spiel' inappropriate to the needs of the buyer.

2.7 Needs–satisfaction/problem solving

Theories of selling which fail to incorporate the needs of the buyer are thus incomplete. Strong (1925) modified his AIDA model to reflect observed phenomena. Still presented as a hierarchical structure, the steps are shown in Figure 2.2.

Selling techniques developed from this formula are often popular with sales practitioners and trainers, the most famous being *FAB* – an acronym for features, advantage, benefits (Figure 2.3).

| Need | Solution | Purchase | Satisfaction |

Fig 2.2 Needs–satisfaction model (*Strong, 1925*)

FEATURE Example	ADVANTAGE Example	BENEFITS Example
Anti-rust paint with patented ingredients	Stops rust forming for up to 3 years	No need to apply paint annually, longer-term protection, lower maintenance costs

Fig 2.3 FAB sales training model

Smart salespeople know how to sell the 'benefits' not the 'features' of products and services. Benefits describe what the product or service will do for the customer, not what they look, feel, touch, smell or taste like.

To convert a feature or advantage into a benefit, use the term 'Which means that...' to the prospective buyer.

To convert a feature into an advantage, show how different the product or service is from the competition.

2.8 The SPIN model

As firms began to realise the importance of considering the buyer's actions before the seller's, models were re-oriented towards customer needs first, then benefits and features.

Rackham (1987, 1995) devised an approach, termed SPIN (see Figure 2.4). Basically, SPIN is an acronym for the order of questions raised by the salesperson during the sales process.

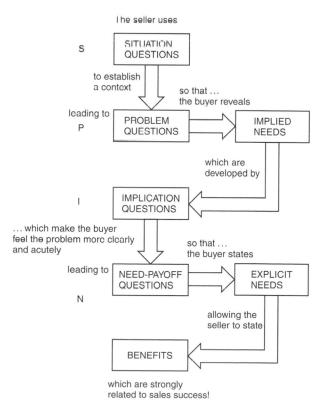

Fig 2.4 The SPIN model (*Rackham, 1987, p.67*)

In Rackham's model, the emphasis is on salespeople being more effective, working smarter and not just harder. Asking questions and getting the buyer to do most of the talking in a sales interaction is more powerful and more effective than a slick presentation. By identifying successful salespeople, Rackham found that these people ask questions which get the buyer talking, which in turn reveal both explicit and implicit needs and enable the salesperson to match their offer more closely to the customer's requirements. Furthermore, successful salespeople ask certain types of questions, as outlined in the model. For example, they ask situation questions to establish background facts but not too many, which may bore or irritate the buyer. They quickly move on to problem questions which reveal difficulties or dissatisfaction. The possibility of solutions may emerge at this stage but implication questions increase the scale of the problem and confirm the relevance of a solution. Need-payoff questions suggest benefits for the customer. While this may sound stylised, it has proved to be a powerful approach to fulfilling the salesperson's primary task – solving the customer's problem and revealing what has to be done to win the customer's business. Sometimes it may be necessary to provoke the customer to think through the issues to more fully understand what their problems really are.

2.9 Process and task models

During the 1960s to early 1970s, new theories and frameworks of buying and selling emerged. These concentrated on understanding the purchasing decision act by examining purchasing processes and tasks. Typical of the process approach was the complex, inputs–outputs model of buying behaviour (see Figure 2.5), first proposed by

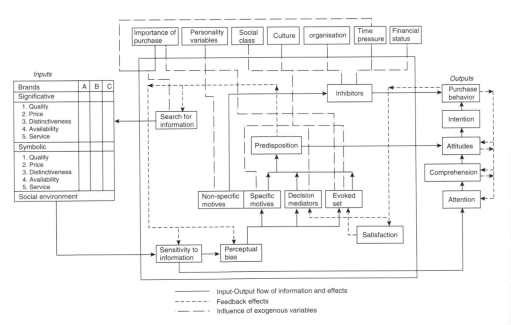

Fig 2.5   The Howard Sheth model of buying behaviour (*Howard & Sheth, 1969*)

Howard and Sheth (1969) as a means of understanding consumer behaviour. This model has been simplified to the buying-decision process (Wilson, Gilligan and Pearson, 1992), better known as the decision-making process or DMP, a hierarchical model closely related to the one in Figure 2.2 above.

What do you think?

Could you imagine using the Howard Sheth model in a sales process? What are the strengths and limitations of the model?

The DMP is a time-based sequential flow of activities, which represents the process a buyer follows from problem recognition, through identification of options, selection and purchase, then post-purchase evaluation. At each stage, there are internal and external influencing variables affecting the final purchase decision, including the type of purchase, for example, whether it is a product or a service (explored in more detail in the next chapter).

The length and complexity of a DMP will also depend on the characteristics and importance of the product to the buyer. This can be depicted in a matrix (Figure 2.6).

Complex Buying occurs when a product is purchased rarely, a mistake can be costly, product knowledge is low and there are significant differences between brands, for example, a car. The customer will tend to spend a long time at the search and evaluation stages.

Habitual Buying occurs when there are few brand differences and the product is of low importance, such as sugar at the supermarket. The customer is likely to make a quick decision and race through the DMP.

Variety-Seeking customers tend to indulge in brand switching. The DMP will not be long or complex.

Dissonance-Reducing behaviour occurs because some purchase decisions trigger feelings of dissatisfaction or dissonance afterwards. In these situations, the purchase tends to be important, but there may be little to choose between brands, for example, kitchen equipment.

In another research study, Robinson, Faris and Wind (1967) looked at the nature of the purchase task, from which they developed the Marketing Sciences Institute (MSI)

	High involvement	Low involvement
Significant differences between products/services	Complex buying behaviour	Variety seeking buying behaviour
Few differences between products/service	Dissonance reducing buyer behaviour	Habitual buying behaviour

Fig 2.6 Buying importance matrix

industrial buying model. This defined three separate tasks or 'buyclasses' in a buying situation, new task; modified rebuy and straight rebuy. Each task requires a different sales process and selling approach.

New task is where the buying centre members view the purchase as different or new. Significant information has to be collected, assimilated and evaluated. This is referred to as extensive problem-solving (Howard and Sheth, 1969). There is usually a lack of well-defined criteria for comparison and also a lack of strong predisposition to one particular solution. The implication is that marketing effort should be directed not to selling product but to customer problem-solving. Clear information, detailed proposals of benefits, cost/revenue evaluation plus evidence of previous and current successes have most effect. Sellers are required to monitor needs and respond accordingly.

Modified rebuy – in this situation, some or all of the members of the DMU/buying centre feel that reappraisal and re-evaluation of alternatives are necessary. This manifests itself in a need for further information and consideration of alternatives. Triggers for this may be the need for cost reduction, quality improvement, delivery performance, other sources of dissatisfaction or external forces. This is described as limited problem-solving with defined criteria needing reappraisal. Actions here depend on whether you are an 'in' or 'out' supplier. If 'in', attempt to move towards a straight rebuy, identify problem, correct it, and reinforce benefits. If an 'out' supplier, examine the source of advantage most appropriate to buyers' needs. Usually, individual responses are required through salespeople to match these customers needs.

Straight re-buy – for many organisations, there is a continuing or recurring requirement for the product or service. Buyers and buying organisations are experienced and require little or no new information. Decision processes in this case are routine: one or a few suppliers are used repeatedly. Marketing effort is geared to reinforcing the buyer–seller relationship and building, or at least maintaining, inertia. For a new entrant or 'out' supplier, life is very difficult. To change supplier or product requires a break in this routine, which involves uncertainty and risk for the buyer. An 'out' supplier must painstakingly research the market, assess buyers' needs and preferences and wait or create opportunities.

2.10   The buying centre or DMU

The role of buying centres, also termed decision-making units or DMUs, and their impact on the sales process have been studied extensively. The number of people involved in a buying decision would vary depending on the cost and complexity of a purchase. Therefore, it was judged important for suppliers to identify the most influential participants in a buying centre and understand the role that each played (Turnbull, 1987).

The participants in a DMU were classified by Webster and Wind (1972) as follows:

- users;
- influencers;
- deciders;
- gatekeepers.

User	Understands the benefit of the product
	May have initiated the DMP
	May assist in preparing specifications
	May provide opinions and advice
Influencer	May assist in preparing specifications
	May be involved in evaluation of suppliers and products
	Could be a subject - matter expert
Decider	Establishes purchasing criteria
Approver	Authorises the purchase, such as a Board of Directors, or Financial Director
Buyer	May be involved throughout the DMP or just the negotiation stage
	Usually selects suppliers and negotiates terms
	May be a trained professional
Gatekeeper	Blocks the DMP by controlling the information flow and access to DMU
	Can be anyone in the organisation, from a receptionist to an external specialist

Fig 2.7   Classic DMU used in industrial/B2B marketing

This simple model has since undergone several updates. It can be applied to both consumer and industrial situations. Figure 2.7 represents one version suitable for industrial purposes, with a description of the roles each participant normally plays. Several researchers attempted to combine all these theories into a single framework for describing buying behaviour – the most famous being Sheth's (1973) integrative model of industrial buying behaviour shown in Figure 2.8.

Sheth's model (1973) combined economic theory with behavioural sciences (sociology, psychology and culture) and demonstrated the complexity and dynamics of purchasing within organisations. However, it concentrated only on process, task and role, with little attention being paid to the nature or dynamics of the interactions or relationships between the component parts and the participants (Turnbull, 1987). As a result, models that included the interactive behaviour of buying centres emerged in the early 1970s.

Webster and Wind (1972) argued that organisational buying involved the aggregation of the decision-making purchasing process with both the behaviour and interactions

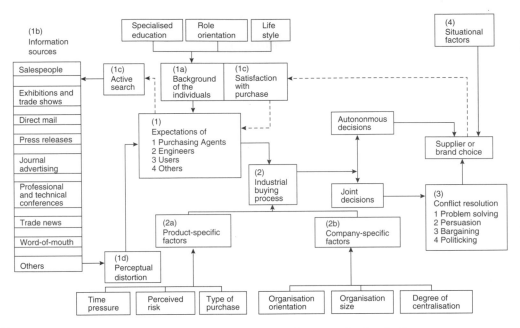

Fig 2.8 Sheth model of organisational buying behaviour (*Source: Sheth, 1973*)

of multiple persons in a buying centre. Their model for understanding organisational buying behaviour was considered 'truly comprehensive' by Turnbull (1987, p. 158) as it encompassed economic theory, behavioural sciences, organisational and management theories, and corporate politics (see Figure 2.9).

Webster and Wind's model (1972) described the psychological and sociological behaviour of the individuals in the buying centre. It omitted, however, any reference to what Turnbull (1987, p. 161) regarded as the 'fundamental' variables, that is, the personal relationships that occur between buyer and seller and the interactive context within which such relationships develop.

2.11 Interaction model (IMP)

The next phase in buying theory evolution came with the Interaction approach, proposed by the Industrial Marketing and Purchasing (IMP) Group in the early 1980s. The IMP Group was formed in 1976 to 'conduct co-operative research' into the nature of supplier–buyer business relationships, which were by then recognised as complex, multi-person phenomena (Turnbull, 1987).

IMP researchers emphasised buyer–seller interpersonal influences and relationships in the purchase decision over size, structure and DMP of the buying centre. The ensuing

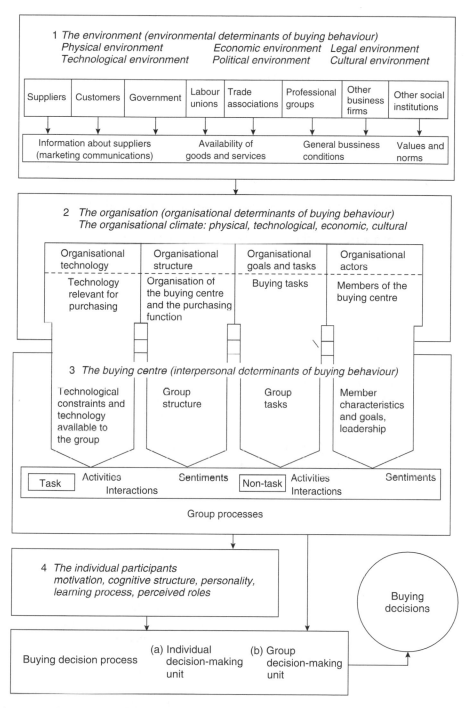

Fig 2.9 Webster and Wind model of organisational buying behaviour (*Source: Webster and Wind, 1972*)

IMP Interaction Model (Hakannson, 1982) described organisational buying as a function of four variables:

1 The *Environment* is the cultural/political/socio-economic conditions surrounding a trading relationship.

2 The *Interaction Process* is a series of active and episodic exchanges between the participants.

3 The *Participants* are the individuals or 'actors' involved in the exchanges.

4 The *Atmosphere* is formed from the expectations, balance of power, collaboration and cooperation in the relationship, a product of the exchanges between the actors.

The four areas of the model are interrelated. The origins of the interaction approach appear to have evolved from a dissatisfaction with the 4Ps paradigm as an adequate managerial framework when applied in an industrial marketing context and as a result of a series of empirical studies in a variety of industrial international situations. The main arguments against the traditional view centre on the idea that buying is not a single discrete purchase, that marketing management consists of more than the manipulation of the marketing mix to a generalised passive market operating in an autonomic way and that marketing and purchasing do not operate in separate and discrete ways. In industrial exchange, the relationship is more likely to be characterised by small numbers of buyers and sellers who are both active participants in the process and whose actions are identifiable by others and have long-term effects (interaction rather than transaction). There are likely to be specific investments in technical and organisational routines which result in a relationship characterised by stability, source loyalty and inertia. To explain marketing activity requires an understanding of the differences between buyer–seller relationships as they apply in concentrated and diverse markets. The IMP group refer to this as the interaction approach. Their focus is the relationship rather than the buyer or the supplier. This work is helpful in describing, understanding and classifying relationships but depends on the nature of the product, the number and degree of alternative sources of supply, the relative importance of the seller's product to the buyer and the distribution network (availability of product).

The interaction model shown in Figure 2.10 can be described as follows. In B2B market transactions, the parties involved, buyer and seller A and B, interact within their environment, the outcome of which depends on the characteristics of the parties, the interaction processes and the atmosphere surrounding their exchange. The interaction process consists of episodes and relationships. The episodes include the core product or service exchange, the information exchange (content, width, depth and formality), financial exchange and social exchange (reducing uncertainty, trust). The relationship embraces the degree of formality (institutionalised), the contact patterns and the adaptations of buyer and seller. The characteristics of the parties comprise both individuals and organisations and will reflect the technology, organisation, experience and individual personalities, experience and motivation. Impinging on this relationship are the effects of the external environment and the atmosphere surrounding the parties. The interaction environment encompasses the market structure, dynamism, internationalisation, channel structure and social systems. The atmosphere is 'the power-dependence relationship which exists between the companies, the state of conflict or co-operation and overall closeness or distance of the relationship as well as by the companies'

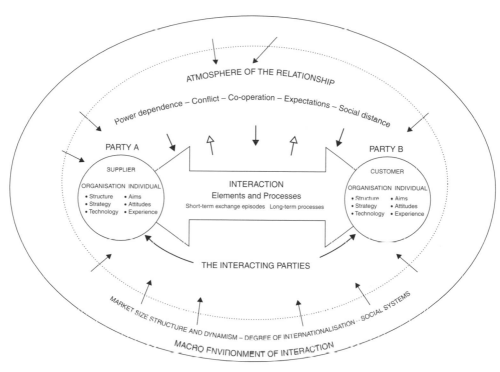

Fig 2.10   The IMP interaction model (Hakannson, 1982)

mutual expectations' (Hakannson, 1982). Such an atmosphere has both economic and behavioural dimensions.

In support of the model, a number of case studies and surveys have been conducted by the IMP group which add empirical support for the variety of relationships which can and do exist revealing variations in the relationship and the closeness between the parties (Ford, 1990). This empirical research suggests that the Interaction approach is a better approximation of the realities of organisational buying than the earlier DMP and buying centre models (Turnbull, 1987).

What do you think?

If relationships are a source of enduring competitive strength (Walter & Gemunden, 2000) should all firms practise relationship marketing?

2.12   Relationship marketing

Development of the interaction model has focused on the actors in the relationship, of which the salesperson is a primary player, on the activities undertaken by each party and on the use of resources in a relationship. By investing in relationships, companies and individuals achieve mutually beneficial outcomes. Hence attention has moved away from seller-initiated effort, focused on manipulating the elements of the marketing mix in a prescribed fashion, to one of an increased understanding of exchange processes where the buyer is more proactive and exchange is based on the joint efforts of different parties in the supply chain. Salespeople should welcome this change since the reasons for this new perspective include the adoption of total quality management (TQM), the need for cost reduction in finished goods to remain price competitive in world markets and the increased rate of innovation in not only products but also processes and systems. Innovations such as just-in-time manufacturing (JIT), computer-aided design (CAD) and information technology (IT) assist in the sales process as well as change it. More complex supply chains, the relative increased costs of labour and the global market economy contribute positively to the need for more efficient exchange systems between firms – again, selling is not redundant in this process but dramatically altered by it.

Evidence of these changes is most apparent in the motor industry, in electronics and in other industries where there is a complex end product of different raw materials, many components and a number of players in the supply chain, but this is a trend gathering momentum across many industries. These industries are characterised by collaboration rather than confrontation, by the joint involvement of participants rather than unilateral action, by interdependence rather than independence. In some cases, the positive results achieved have been persuasive in companies adopting this new relationship-based approach. For example, in the motor industry, consolidation and restructuring has reduced the number of major independent manufacturers from 36 in the 1970s to 13 in 2005 (Automobilproduktion, 2005). Within this rationalisation, purchasing has become much more concentrated. Renault-Nissan set up a purchasing organisation (RNPO) in April 2001 to handle around 30 per cent of their total annual purchasing in a centralised and structured way. By the end of 2002, this percentage had increased to 43 per cent and in 2003 to 70 per cent (Renault, 2005). Similar concepts have been adopted by Volvo and Siemens (Volvo, 2005; Siemens VDO, 2005). This drives a relationship imperative for suppliers in this industry.

Several writers have testified to the importance of relationships in organisational marketing exchange (Jackson, 1985; Dwyer et al., 1987). There is widespread recognition that trust, openness and fairness in partnerships have been increasing (Bhote, 1989), and this movement has been mirrored in the marketing literature, with the claim that the way to build superior market positions is to build relationships with customers based on trust, responsiveness and quality (McKenna, 1991). The importance to suppliers of retaining existing customers has proved more profitable than has winning new customers in a number of industries (Reicheld, 1996).

Greater openness and freer communications between buyer and supplier create an atmosphere which allows buyers to have a greater understanding of a supplier's plans, minimises surprises and permits them to be more responsive to the selling organisation. Relationships typically suit both parties but are not mutual admiration societies and often involve extensive negotiation, conflict and the desire for favourable outcomes, a process of negotiation. The salesperson, as an interorganisational link, is more rather than less important in this process. This is likely to be reflected in a change of title from salesperson to account manager, and this is more than semantic. These trends will continue.

What then are the rules, norms and operational dimensions of relationships between buyer and seller? Should they be based on human relationship ideas of friendship, caring and loyalty or on more managerial measures of previous performance,

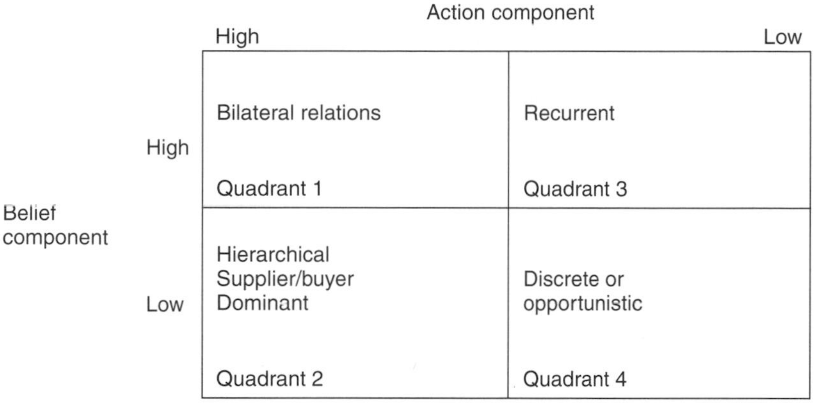

Fig 2.11 Contrasting relational forms based on belief and action

managerial attitude or corporate ethos? Morgan and Hunt (1994) have claimed that the key ingredients of relationships should be centred round relational commitment and trust as key mediating variables. The antecedents of these variables might include the anticipated benefits accruing from relationships, shared values, similarity, open communication, opportunistic behaviour and termination costs. Recent research in the United Kingdom (Donaldson and O'Toole, 2007) suggests that relationships can be classified using an assessment of the strength of a relationship, as shown in Figure 2.11.

The construct labelled relationship strength can discriminate between relationships on the basis that it measures the underlying motivation or assumptions guiding the relationship and the intensity of interaction between the partners to determine the structure of a relationship. The relationship strength construct discriminates between four relationship structures labelled bilateral, recurrent, dominant partner and discrete. It is supported by, but distinguishable from, other indices of relationship by combining behaviour and economic elements of relationships. Relationships can be classified as a function of belief, a behavioural element and action, an economic one. This belief in relationships is the force opposite to opportunism. The underlying motivation in a relationship is reflected in the level of belief. The definition of action in relationships also captures behavioural and economic components. The behavioural dimension (process) is reflected in expectations of partnership continuity and the economic dimension (content) in investment and adaptation patterns in the relationship. Action is a function of commitment to the future of a relationship (behavioural) and committed action (economic). The action element is a force opposite to the use of power in a relationship. Combined, these elements of belief and action reflect well the motivation and strength of a relationship and discriminate between the relationship structures shown in Figure 2.11.

Bilateral relations are high in both the belief and action elements to produce high relationship strength. In bilateral relations, partners cooperate for mutual advantage characterised by openness in communication and strategic collaboration. This is a unique and complex relationship not easily copied which would potentially offer the greatest potential in the context of performance of interfirm relationships. This does not mean that they are symmetrical but merely that they are dominated by a bilateral content and process.

Recurrent relationships is a hybrid form between discrete and bilateral. Elements of reciprocity and temporal duration creep into the exchange as belief in the relationship is built between the parties but committed actions are low. The focus is more on operational issues than strategic ones and purchases are likely to be transaction-based rather than relational-based. This form is characterised by matching sentiments in both parties, but the salesperson has to work hard to ensure that the operational performance of the supply organisation is equal to, or exceeds, the expectation of the buyer.

Dominant or hierarchical relationships are a common form of relationship and occur where a dominant partner specifies the nature of the interaction between the partners. The weaker partner faces a combination of low belief and high investment, a position experienced by many original equipment manufacturers (OEM) suppliers. Hierarchical decisions are resolved by the dominant partner who controls the transaction and may be common to own-label suppliers, which reflects the authority and power-dependency balance in the relationship. In certain situations, the size and power of the buyer may be served better in a bilateral rather than a dominant relationship, but the influence of environmental conditions, especially competitive forces, may strongly affect this position. The problem in this form is the asymmetrical views held by each party. The salesperson has to understand the power/dependence between the parties.

Discrete relationships are lowest in the relationship strength concept with minimal levels of belief and action. Opportunism can be expected to dominate this approach with few, if any, ties between the partners. Firms in this mode are assumed to make rational economic decisions as independent actors in the marketplace. It may be possible to build on belief and action, but it is not central to the transaction, and it would not be prudent to invest in the relationship. Again, salespeople have to focus on winning the business and being aware of the needs of the buyer over different periods of time.

2.13   Summary

For theories to be useful, they need to help marketers and salespeople understand what happens and why in a sales interaction or process. Next, they need to help the seller predict how the buyer will behave and act in the sales process, and what the outcome is likely to be.

Importantly, a theory can also help explain failure as well as success in a selling situation. Theories that have been developed from historical observations should be overlaid by other changes in the environment that also drive buyer behaviour: increased global competition, easily accessible information through the Internet and increased technology enabling e-auctions all have a profound effect, albeit on some businesses more than others, for example, automotive. This knowledge can improve the planning and management of future sales processes and in sales force training.

All the above theories and models were built from observation and research into how firms sell and customers buy. The ability to put them into practice will depend on the firm's marketing structure and processes, plus the actual selling situation.

Questions

1 Why is it important for B2B salespeople to understand the concepts of organisational buying behaviour?

2 Which factors in buyer behaviour are likely to be the most important to a consumer purchasing a home improvement product?

3 In what ways might the sales behaviour of a business development manager pursuing a large contract differ from that of a salesperson's repeat calling on retailers?

4 Invited to prepare a training programme for salespeople, how much emphasis would you put on helping salespeople understand buyer behaviour? Why?

5 Using the SPIN model, prepare a list of questions you would use if selling office furniture to professional firms (accountants, lawyers, estate agents and so on).

Case study

Jan Bronowski is a salesperson for Packard Bell (a computer company www.packardbell.com) and works exclusively in PC WORLD (www.pcworld.com) a retail company selling personal computers, printers, software and ancillary computer-related equipment. Working on a one-to-one basis, the job involves demonstrating the functions of hardware and software packages, answering any questions the prospect may have and solving problems by matching the appropriate products to the customer's needs. At the point of purchase, the prospect is 'handed over' to someone else who deals with payment, credit arrangements and invoicing. After six months, Jan has been relatively successful. He has worked hard and believes that his confidence, the ability to strike up rapport with prospects and his ability to 'read a prospect' have contributed to his success.

The company have decided to promote him to their direct business division, selling to local firms. As part of his new job, Jan has contacted by telephone the office manager of a local company which produces chemicals and employs 60 people, 12 of those in office and administrative positions. He is excited at the prospect of making his first sale. The office manager was interested in his products and has asked Jan to call and see him the following week.

Prior to his visit, Jan has been asked to post the relevant details of his products to the office manager. He has also been requested to bring some of the equipment to demonstrate to the office staff who would eventually use any such equipment. Thinking about his forthcoming visit, Jan is apprehensive; his background in retail has been with relatively inexperienced customers, and he is unsure of his ability to explain the product in these new surroundings to a more technical audience. He is also worried about demonstrating the product to the office staff since one of the advantages which will become apparent at any such demonstration is the potential staff savings of the equipment.

Meanwhile, back at the chemicals company, the office manager is trying to convince his managing director of the wisdom of his decision because of the capital outlay required. The purchasing manager is upset because he has not been consulted about the proposed purchase and rings Jan directly to complain of his annoyance at being bypassed, telling Jan that he is determined to block the purchase on principle.

Jan is dejected: 'Where did I go wrong?', he thinks and, more importantly, 'What do I do now?'

▶

Discussion questions

1 Compare the similarities and differences between the two jobs.
2 How might a knowledge of buyer behaviour help Jan in this situation?
3 Make a list of information requirements to assist Jan in his pre-call preparation.
4 Advise Jan on how he should now proceed.

Key terms

- Advantages
- AIDAS
- benefits
- B2B (business-to-business)
- buy phases
- buyer–seller similarity
- buying centre
- buying process
- DMP (decision-making process)
- features

- hierarchy of effects
- interaction model
- key account management
- needs-satisfaction theory
- OBB (organisational buying behaviour)
- problem–solution theory
- relationship marketing
- SPIN approach
- stimulus–response theory

References

Alderson, W. (1995) 'The analytical framework for marketing' in *Marketing Classics* Prentice-Hall: Englewood Cliffs, NJ, 22–32. From conference of marketing teachers from Far Western States, 1958

Automobilproduktion (2005) 'Konzentration der Automobilhersteller' [Online] Available at: http://www.automobilproduktion.de [Accessed 01 July 2005]

Arrow, K. (1951) *Social Choice and Individual Values* Wiley: New York

Bhote, K.R. (1989) *Strategic Supply Management: a blueprint for revitalising the manufacturer–supplier partnership* American Management Association: New York

Brock, T.C. (1965) 'Communicator-recipient similarity and decision change' *Journal of Personality and Social Psychology* 1 (6): 650–4

Davis, H.L. and Silk, A.J. (1972) 'Interaction and influence processes in personal selling' *Sloan Management Review* 13 (2) Winter: 59–76

Donaldson, B. and O'Toole, T. (2007) *Strategic Market Relationships: from strategy to implementation* 2nd edition John Wiley and Sons: Chichester

Dwyer, F.R., Schurr, P.H. and Oh, S. (1987) 'Developing buyer–seller relationships' *Journal of Marketing* 51 (Apr): 11–27

Ford, D. (ed.) (1990) *Understanding Business Markets* Academic Press: London

Greenberg, J. and Greenberg, H. (1976) 'Predicting sales success: myths and reality' *Personnel Journal* 55 (12) Dec: 621–7

Hakannson, H. (1982) *International Marketing and Purchasing of Industrial Goods* John Wiley: London

Howard, J.A. and Sheth, J.N. (1969) *The Theory of Buyer Behavior* John Wiley: New York

Jackson, B.B. (1985) *Winning and Keeping Industrial Customers* D.C. Heath: Lexington, MA

Katona, G. (1995) 'Rational behaviour and economic behaviour' in *Marketing Classics* Prentice-Hall: Englewood Cliffs, NJ, 125–36

Lichtenthal, J.D. and Tellefsen, T. (2001) 'Toward a theory of business buyer-seller similarity' *Journal of Personal Selling & Sales Management* **21**: 1–14

McKenna, R. (1991) *Relationship Marketing* Century Business: London

Morgan, R.M. and Hunt, S.D. (1994) 'The commitment–trust theory of relationship marketing' *Journal of Marketing* **58** (Jul): 20–38

Palda, K.S. (1966) 'The hypothesis of a hierarchy of effects: a partial evaluation' *Journal of Marketing Research* **111** (Feb): 13–24

Rackham, N. (1987) *Making Major Sales* Gower: Aldershot

Rackham, N. (1995) *Spin Selling* Gower: Aldershot

Reicheld, F.F. (1996) *The Loyalty Effect* Harvard Business School Press: Harvard, MA

Renault (2005) 'The supplier portal' [Online] Available at: https://suppliers.renault.com/gb/ [Accessed 10 July 2005]

Robinson, P., Faris, C. and Wind, Y. (1967) *Industrial Buying and Creative Marketing* Allyn and Bacon: New York

Sheldon, A.F. (1902) *The Art of Selling* Sheldon School: Chicago, IL

Sheth, J. (1973) 'A model of industrial buying behaviour' *Journal of Marketing* **37** (Oct): 50–55

Siemens VDO (2005) 'Supplier guide' [Online] Available at: http://www.siemensvdo.com/com/ xt_download/suppliers_guide_en.pdf [Accessed 09 July 2005]

Strong, E.K. (1925) *The Psychology of Selling* McGraw-Hill: New York

Tosi, H.L. (1966) 'Effects of expectation levels and role consensus on buyer–seller dyad' *Journal of Business* **39** (4): 516–29

Turnbull, P.W. (1987) 'Organizational buying behaviour' in *The Marketing Book* William Heinemann: London, 147–64

Turnbull, P.W., Ford, D. and Cunningham, M. (1996) 'Interaction, relationships and networks in business markets: an evolving perspective' *Journal of Business & Industrial Marketing* **11**(3/4): 44–62

Volvo (2005) 'Volvo group–supplier portal' [Online] Available at: http://www.volvo.com/ Suppliers/global/en-gb/supplierselection/sourcingcommittee/ [Accessed 07 July 2005]

Walter, A. and Gemunden, H. (2000) 'Bridging the gap between suppliers and customers through relationship promoters: theoretical considerations and empirical results' *Journal of Business & Industrial Marketing* **15**(2/3): 86–105

Webster, F.E. and Wind, Y. (1972) *Organisational Buying Behavior* Prentice-Hall: Englewood Cliffs, NJ

Wilson, M., Gilligan, C., Pearson, D.J. (1992) *Strategic Marketing Management* 1st edition Butterworth-Heinemann: Oxford

3 Types of selling

3.1 Overview

The fundamental purpose for which salespeople are employed is to retain existing business and win new customers. This purpose involves more than mere order-taking, and salespeople can be described and classified under a variety of job titles, for example, technical adviser, sales engineer, business development manager or marketing consultant. Today, the trend in closer relationships between buyer and seller organisations in industrial, consumer and service firms relies, to a greater extent than hitherto, on the knowledge, skills and abilities of the salesperson to create and sustain these relationships. Therefore, the way in which the selling job is conducted can vary greatly, and an evaluation of selling types will be studied in this chapter.

3.2 Learning objectives

The aim in this chapter is

- to examine the traditional classification of selling types;
- to describe a variety of sales jobs in today's business environment;
- to consider the types of selling appropriate for different markets, customers and circumstances.

3.3 Definitions

Key account management refers to the process of managing customers of strategic importance in a coherent and integrated way for the mutual advantage of both parties. This is linked to relationship marketing with the conscious aim to develop and manage long-term business.

Relationship marketing refers to all marketing activities directed toward establishing, developing and maintaining successful relational exchanges (Morgan and Hunt, 1994).

3.4 Why a classification of selling types is important

Selling tasks are often situation-specific. As a result, the weighting given to different tasks depends, primarily, on the customer and on the set of prevailing circumstances at

| Table 3.1 | Comparison of sales and marketing activity |

Stage	Salesperson	Marketing manager
Marketing research/assessment	Uses personal experience, customers' records and questions	Uses formal market research, target markets and defines segments
Strategy/planning	Emphasises relevant features which match company with customer	Establishes product/price/service position in the market
Marketing mix/implementation	Use of discounts, terms and credit	Price policy
Distribution	Use of back-up and collaboration when required	Sales policy
Promotion	Use of print, samples, factory visits and entertaining	Advertising and sales promotion

that time. Many 'how to sell' books elaborate on the stages through which salespeople must cross to close a sale. While such selling guides can work, and are certainly useful training modules, most sales situations do not easily conform to a stereotype. It is important to recognise that variations do exist between types of selling and that there are many forms of communication between a firm and its customers.

In a modern context, selling is the outcome of a marketing process. The salesperson is, by necessity, a marketing manager dealing at the individual customer level rather than with groups of customers or market segments. It can increasingly be observed that companies can no longer afford to separate marketing, as a strategic and planning activity, from the operational implications of customer account management. The implication is that salespeople will require marketing knowledge and skills and marketing positions will increasingly demand knowledge and ability in interpersonal relations and negotiations. In many companies, a re-emergence of a marketing/sales management position can be expected (Cuddihy, 1996). This similarity between marketing and sales is shown in Table 3.1.

It is to the traditional types of selling that we turn first.

3.5 Conditioned versus insight response

The sales process should be seen in the context of customer problem-solving rather than as merely selling available product. Any new salesperson or new sales situation is best approached by an initial assessment of the nature of the customer's problem, just as market research should be a prerequisite for evaluating a new market or a new product. This is particularly true of larger value sales, where continuity of business in the future is important. With some low-value and low-risk purchases, traditional salesmanship and a classic 'hard sales' approach may work for the company and improve its profitability (Chu *et al.*, 1995). However, in most organisational buying, a failure to assess customers' needs adequately will be a recipe for failure. Selling techniques must be made on the basis of an insight response rather than a conditioned response which may be effective in direct selling situations. These differences in approach will now be examined.

The *conditioned response* is where salespeople have been trained in advance to deal with problems and objections preventing a successful close. This relates to the stimulus–response theory outlined in Chapter 2. Examples of this are normally found in direct selling situations such as life insurance sales, double glazing and the infamous encyclopaedia salesperson. However, conditioned response techniques or canned presentations have some advantages for buyers as well as sellers. The sales story is the same, the answers to questions are known and usually directly answered, and the buyer's confidence is enhanced knowing that others have asked similar questions. The advantages mostly favour the selling company and the salesperson. The product/market position identified by the company is reinforced by the salesperson; the information given to customers is similar to all but can be as selective or as comprehensive as the company require. Sales training is more rapid and economical, and sales feedback can be directly related to specific rather than general problems. There may be disadvantages, one of which is salesperson motivation. If no allowance is made to vary the sales story for special customer requirements, if there is a lack of authority to vary the terms of a sale and if there is no room for initiative, salespeople may lack motivation. An equally serious disadvantage is that the customer may be persuaded or conned by superior sales technique but may later cancel the order or perhaps spread negative word-of-mouth recommendations. In extreme cases, these ultimately result in legal restrictions on overtly misleading sales presentations.

While direct selling is important for many companies, one-off sales situations are by no means the norm. Sales technique and presentation are more commonly based on an *insight response* in which salespeople must identify buyers' problems and objections as they arise and react with appropriate benefits. Greater skill is required to identify, understand and react to individual prospects, and this requires training in behavioural interaction rather than just product/market/company knowledge. For salespeople, it is a more challenging role but one giving greater satisfaction, more variety and less boredom. The benefits are customised to buyers' needs as the sales interview proceeds, which is a more marketing-oriented approach. Some difficulties arise in that training is more difficult in interpersonal skills and certainly longer and more expensive. This relationship-based selling creates difficulties in assessing the role of the salesperson in producing and delivering value for the customer and the firm. As problems arise with buyers, salespeople may not be able to answer these queries adequately and immediately. Conflicts may arise within the relationship and the salesperson may have difficulty in coordinating within their own firm, as well as between firms. Success will ultimately depend on the ability of salespeople to research individual buyer's needs, assess the problem and react accordingly (Sujan *et al.*, 1994). Research in industrial buying suggests a collaborative approach to be more productive (Doney and Cannon, 1997).

These extremes of conditioned and insight response are opposite ends of the spectrum. A better appreciation of variations in sales approaches can be obtained by viewing them as part of a continuum, as shown in Figure 3.1. The salesperson's skill is in identifying the most suitable position on this continuum to satisfy customer needs.

```
CONDITIONED ————————————————— INSIGHT
SALES-ORIENTED ———————————— CUSTOMER-ORIENTED
ORDER-TAKER ——————————————— ORDER-MAKER
DIRECT ——————————————————— INDIRECT/CONTINUING
TRANSACTION-BASED ———————— RELATIONSHIP-BASED
```

Fig 3.1   Alternative approaches in selling

What do you think?

Most of us have faced a pushy salesperson at some point of time. How did you react?

Have you been in situations where you were undecided then, as a result of a sales pitch, made a purchase which later you were glad you did?

Have you been in situations where you were undecided then, as a result of a sales pitch, made a purchase which later you regretted?

To what extent do you feel the salesperson was right or wrong in these situations?

3.6   New business versus service selling

Selling effort must match the requirements of customers and reinforce the marketing strategy of the organisation. Selling must also reinforce and complement policies relating to market segmentation, the role of distributors and intermediaries and the positioning of the product to its market. This idea of not only modifying selling effort but also structuring the sales force on the basis of large and small customers, new products or new markets has important organisational implications. The basic premise of such specialisation is that while salespeople may have many diverse tasks, there are two distinct jobs to be performed – *sales maintenance* and *sales development* (Kahn and Schuchman, 1961). Many salespeople are very competent at sales maintenance, that is, calling on existing distributors (retailers and wholesalers) and existing users. They are seeking to defend and retain existing business, where the emphasis must be on customer service, building inertia and ensuring that competitive advantage in product, price or service is maintained. The same salespeople are often reluctant, or unable, to win new business for fear of customer rejection or competitor reaction. They lack the necessary confidence, perseverance and perhaps selling skills to win new business. Large important customers, new products and developing markets require people with different skills from those who may be highly competent service salespeople.

According to Kahn and Schuchman, the development salesperson must proceed through a series of stages, such as making contact with the correct people in the buying organisation, building up rapport not only on a technical but also on a personal, psychological level, motivating prospects to change behaviour, facilitating such a change and finally building up confidence to be able to turn a prospect over to a service salesperson. The skills required to do this more difficult selling job can therefore be quite different to those required in service selling. Development salespeople must have exceptional communication skills, higher levels of creativity, higher intelligence, more resourcefulness and motivation to succeed. While there is still some argument about the types and kinds of skill required in development salespeople, the continuum from Figure 3.1 helps to identify development selling as lying to the right of the spectrum, that is, high insight, customer-orientation, being an order-maker and operating over a period of time. Selling new products or into new markets is certainly different from dealing with existing business in existing markets. If salespeople themselves cannot make this transition, separate organisational arrangements must be made to achieve marketing and sales objectives.

It is not sufficient therefore merely to cast doubt on a salesperson's ability to do both a development and a service selling job. It is incumbent on management first to identify the job requirements, second to match the best people with the most appropriate skills and personality type to these jobs and finally to provide the correct organisational system. It is 45 years since Kahn and Schuchman suggested an organisational split, and this may therefore be inappropriate to today's markets. Market research, the identification of prospects, generating awareness, making initial contact and generating realistic sales leads are seldom best achieved by one salesperson. The emphasis on development selling must shift to building relationships and activating change. In industrial situations particularly, business is not often won, it is only lost. It is not therefore the abilities of salespeople but the organisation's ability to react to a variety of environmental circumstances and to seek and develop competitive advantages which precipitate and encourage change. The effective salesperson is an agent in this change process.

3.7 Traditional classifications of types of selling

Extensive research by Derek Newton at Harvard led him to develop a four-way classification of selling types (Newton, 1969). These types were trade, missionary, technical and new business selling. Newton related these categories to measures of performance by salespeople and to turnover rates in personnel. In *trade selling*, Newton found that the high performers were older, used extensive reporting and were paid at least in part on commission. Less emphasis was placed on order-taking and selling could be termed low key, where objectives centred around the need to build and maintain longstanding customer relationships. This may explain why older (more experienced) salespeople perform better. The extensive reporting stresses the need for accurate and informed feedback, possibly as a surrogate for closer supervision. The commission element of pay seems to reflect a need by salespeople to relate effort and reward to retain the necessary motivation, which may otherwise decline. This is very much service selling referred to above. The sales force's main objectives are retaining and increasing volume with existing customers. This is often concomitant with a push strategy through distributors. Effort is concentrated on sales support activities such as promotional deals, service aspects and so on. In fast-moving consumer goods, the changing distributor's structure has led to merchandising salespeople and key account salespeople being separated. The emphasis is on development and service at head office level while the merchandiser at branch level is very much service selling only.

Traditionally, trade salespeople are seen as helpful, persuasive and service-oriented, but neither a technical expert nor a pioneer salesperson.

Missionary selling is typified by the pharmaceutical salesperson calling on doctors who specify the product but may neither stock nor use the product. Similar salespeople may be found in the building industry selling to specifiers such as architects. Here the emphasis is on good coverage and presentation to make sure that these influencers know of the product, its benefits and competitive advantages. These types of salesperson create different problems for management particularly in trying to relate selling effort and skill to performance. Newton found that this type of selling suited younger salespeople and performance related to the number of calls and coverage of a territory. Unfortunately, this also correlates with a high turnover of personnel. Sales managers must offer support through supervision and training.

In *technical selling*, more emphasis is placed on the professional level of salespeople who are technically competent with high levels of product knowledge most common in industrial goods and services. In certain industries, technical qualification or a degree may be a prerequisite upon which selling skills can be built. As a result, such people are paid higher rates, they are usually paid more on fixed salary and turnover rates are lower. More emphasis is placed on training younger people but supervision, at least initially, must be closer.

With *new business selling* and development work, salespeople need the security of stable earnings but tend to be older and less trained than average. The implication is that young people find it difficult to cope with rejection and the lack of regular call patterns and customer relationships. The enigma in this position is that it suits people who may enjoy cold calling and the challenge but do not necessarily seek the mature customer relationship sought by many salespeople. Sales management practices seem to confirm that such people are hard to find and retain.

With Newton's type of analysis, classification problems may arise in creating too many or too few categories. Newton suggested that sales managers are better at avoiding failure (low turnover of salespeople) than they are at producing success (increased sales performance). This work, supported by empirical research (Cravens *et al.*, 1992; Sujan *et al.*, 1994), offers some guidelines to aid management decisions but many factors such as market structure, marketing strategies and programmes, and management capability will also affect sales performance.

Various other classifications of selling have been suggested based on both theoretical and empirical grounds. One of the most widely quoted is that suggested by McMurry (1961), and McMurry and Arnold (1968). They built on the development/service spectrum to classify sales positions in terms of both the difficulty of making a sale and what they refer to as the creativity required by salespeople. Their nine categories, in order from 1 = easy/routine to 9 = difficult/creative, were

1 *Inside order-taker*, such as a retail salesperson, whose function is to serve the already committed customer. Critics might suggest that many customers for many products are not committed, and therefore salespeople have the scope to close a sale or inadvertently put off customers. Some firms, aware of the importance of this moment of truth, ensure they have their own salespeople within the store, for example, a bed manufacturer in a department store.

2 *Delivery salesperson*, where the prime function is the end result of the physical movement of goods. The importance of such a person will vary depending on the nature of the relationship between buyer and buying organisation and seller and selling organisation. In McMurry's first classification, this person was rated 'below' the inside order-taker. However, variations in the role of delivery salesperson often occur. These range from delivery with little or no other service, through delivery plus order processing or invoicing functions, to delivery salespeople who have a direct influence on the size of an order or even whether or not an order is placed at all.

3 *Outside order-taker*. In the previous category, the prime function was physical delivery of the goods. In this category, the salesperson takes orders but does not deliver and may also fulfil other services such as checking stock, merchandising and maintaining goodwill with retailers. In this case, their sales ability may determine the shelf space their product is given in a retail outlet, a major factor in sales success.

4 *Missionary salesperson*. In this case, orders are not normally taken but the salesperson is expected to educate prospects, generate goodwill and encourage the product to be used or specified. As referred to earlier, it can be exceptionally difficult to evaluate a salesperson's performance in these important but indirect selling activities.

5 *The technical salesperson* acts not only as a salesperson to the company but also as an adviser/consultant to the client. Again, it is difficult to assess how well the selling job is being performed, and this leads to a potential area of conflict between giving the customer professional help and achieving company sales. The two, it is hoped, are not mutually exclusive but there may be a conflict of interests.

6 *Creative salesperson – tangibles*. Included in this category is the direct selling of such products as double glazing, encyclopaedias and vacuum cleaners.

7 *Creative salesperson – intangibles*. Similar to point 6 for services such as insurance, advertising or sales training programmes.

8 *Political or indirect salesperson*, normally associated with large-scale contracts for raw materials such as coal to power stations, cement for road contracts or other 'big-ticket' items.

9 *Multiple salesperson* who is dealing with an organisation usually over a period of years such as selling aircraft or turbine engines or services such as management consultancy, auditing and other financial services.

It is perhaps inappropriate to criticise each classification in turn, and there should again be some intuitive appeal in such a categorisation. However, readers must appreciate that different products, markets and customers create situations requiring different levels of creativity and presenting different levels of difficulty. The salesperson's job can be quite varied while the scope for creativity and innovativeness in, for example, merchandising may be much greater than this classification would suggest. Certainly, the degree of difficulty in achieving additional shelf-space for the number three product line in a supermarket sales portfolio of soups, soaps or yoghurts should not be underestimated. Conversely, it is not unknown for sales contracts in excess of a million pounds to go to one supplier in preference to another on the most insubstantial of motives. No one type of person or uniform sales approach is universally applicable. Efforts should therefore be directed to classifying sales types into usable and understandable groups (Moncrief, 1986, 1999). In a recent survey, six clusters created a taxonomy of categories of sales jobs as follows: consultative selling; new business selling; missionary selling; delivery seller; sales support; and key account seller (Moncrief, Marshalland Lassk, 2006). Taking cognisance of these findings and new developments in today's markets, the following represents a classification of selling types.

3.8   Sales jobs in today's business environment

Direct selling to consumers

It has already been suggested that salespeople who deal directly with the public are the most visible and most familiar type of salesperson, but they do not represent the majority of people employed in selling jobs. Nevertheless, this is an important type of selling employing many people and also presents particular difficulties in their management and control. Direct salespeople are order-getters who rely on selling skills and use canned presentations and conditioned response techniques to close sales. They normally earn directly related to their sales effort/ability, and payment by commission or a results-oriented means is common. While word-of-mouth may be important in identifying and locating prospects, management support in generating sales leads and maintaining a positive image are also crucial to effective selling. Sales territories may be much less clearly defined.

There is much discussion on what contributes to success in this type of selling. It is often by watching or experiencing direct salespeople in action that the myth of born salespeople is generated. Clearly, those who enjoy meeting people and the challenge of making a sale and have a high level of persuasive skills seem best suited to this type of job. Also, since sales are one-off events, techniques of salesmanship can be particularly effective. The rewards can be high and very little in the way of formal qualification is demanded. With little or no entry control, it is an opportunity for people to make money and rapidly gain promotion and recognition. There is great variation in the type and quality of people employed. As a result, many books and training courses are offered by people who have been successful; for example, *Increase Your Sales the Tack Way* (Tack, 1989) and *How I Raised Myself from Failure to Success in Selling* (Bettger, 1949) are two best sellers.

Direct selling to organisations

In this category, salespeople are also order-getters, *hunters* rather than *farmers*, the difference being in the scale and value of purchase, the length of negotiation, the organisational nature of the buying decision and the use for which the product is required. Included here are industrial products such as machine tools, raw materials and component parts purchased on a contract basis. Other examples may be telecom systems, network computer solutions and customer relationship management (CRM) systems. High-level technical and negotiating skills are necessary, as are perseverance and business acumen. Lists of attributes may be rather glib since in this category there are a vast range and type of products and services. The ability to develop solutions appropriate to the unique product or organisation being dealt with by the seller is a crucial dimension of this sales job. Whereas in direct consumer selling, salespeople must learn 'how to sell', in direct B2B they must also learn 'how to negotiate'. The necessary skills must be applied over a period of months, even years. Again, the management skills and techniques required to manage such a sales force are by no means uniform. Companies A and B may both have a sales turnover of £50 million per annum. Both may be selling computer systems directly. Company A, however, employs five salespeople in the UK whereas Company B employs 50. The problems of management are quite different, with Company A selling directly to leading financial institutions while Company B is selling to small, medium-sized enterprises (SMEs). Salespeople in this category must add business acumen to selling skills. A knowledge of finance and the importance of cash flow and profitability will be high on the buyer's selection criteria for a supplier.

Did you know?

Selling in the B to B sector has become much more strategic. A major reason for this has been the growth in electronic(e) Procurement which includes eRFQ (electronic requests for quotations); eRFI (electronic request for information); catalogue procurement and eAuctions (Stein and Hawking, 2002). In 2003, almost half of large buyers had used electronic reverse auctions. Most however spend less than 5 per cent of purchases in this way although some had used them for up to 25 per cent of their total spend. (Fein, 2004).

Direct selling to the public sector

This category has some similarity to B2B but differs in the organisational buying processes and usually in the way in which business is conducted. Here again, the system of tender requires salespeople to have insight into the organisational complexities as well as the personal characteristics of buyers' needs. Included here are the purchases of central and local government, hospitals and health boards, schools, colleges and universities, who vary in their purchasing organisations and procedures, each requiring different and sometimes unique sales approaches. In some of these organisations, such as the Ministry of Defence, nationalised industries or large institutions and utilities, there are publications issued by the buyers on how to sell to their organisation. In some cases, the rules of business and the profits which can be made are specified. For salespeople, the selling job here involves much painstaking work into the rules, the committee procedures, the timescale for approval, the quality control checks and the criteria required to be considered as an accepted supplier. For the salesperson from a previously untried supplier, these create real problems before negotiations can even start.

Trade selling

Traditionally this has been one of the most common types of selling, in which salespeople are primarily employed on dealer/retailer service selling. However, the concentration of the retail trade into a small number of very large organisations who dominate their retail sector has changed the nature of this type of selling. Usually selling will now be conducted on a team basis with a combination of roles led perhaps by a customer account manager. In their team will be *logistics experts, merchandisers*, and *new product and special promotions representatives*. We return to the complexity of this role in key account management below. Others, who still maintain this type of sales force, require salespeople to carry out a variety of tasks in addition to taking orders. Selling is normally on a repeat basis to establish contacts. Salespeople must understand buyers' needs and emphasise adequate stocks of products, assist with point-of-sale displays, promote the company's advertising programmes to retailers and assist with merchandising tasks. This type of job suits younger salespeople who are achievers and see their job as the first rung on the management ladder. These people quickly learn about the business, the competitive position of their company and its products and the way in which buyers operate. It is an ideal training therefore for future management positions, but it can also create problems in terms of supervision and motivation. Too much emphasis on call rates and specific sales objectives may make 'Jack a dull boy'!

B2B trade selling

In this role the salesperson will have a dual role: first, to get the product or service adopted as the preferred option for the customer; and second, to ensure that the service via a distributor or installer is adequate. While merchandising and point-of-sale may be less important or even non-existent, the joint cooperation between intermediaries exists in different forms. Therefore, the building materials salesperson works with and through a builder's merchant on specific contracts for the house builder. The skills required are more on product knowledge and application but the objectives are to defend existing business, retain inertia between buying and selling organisations and promote service aspects to the selling job where the other elements in the marketing mix (product, price and distribution) are relatively fixed or equal between competing suppliers. Examples include oils and lubricants or small tools in addition to the building materials example already given.

Missionary sales

This category, identified by Newton, seems to warrant special mention. This is a difficult form of selling in which the sale is to have the product or service specified by a major influencer in the purchase decision, rather than by the user of the product. Architects and doctors are two such influences, as indeed would be lecturers who compile a reading list for students. Most prevalent in the pharmaceutical industry, missionary selling attempts to educate and train customers in the use of the product and therefore aims not at the one-off sale but at building relationships for future orders. The danger for a company is the commitment to high-overhead fixed selling costs for an uncertain reward. As a result, specialist sales organisations have emerged serving the needs not only of customers, doctors and health advisers but also the pharmaceutical companies themselves. Innovex is a specialist sales company, the advantage being that medical practitioners need to see fewer salespeople from many different companies and the pharmaceutical companies such as Pfizer, Wellcome and Glaxo can and do can employ a more flexible salesforce to achieve specific sales objectives with, for example, the launch of a new product.

Missionary or detail selling of this type is most effective where

- the product has clear benefits over the competition;
- the selling cycle is long term yet the information needs of the potential customers are many and urgent;
- other forms of communication, such as advertising, cannot convey the whole message the supplier wishes to communicate, and the buyer needs to know to specify the product with confidence;
- the buying process is complex and involves a number of influencers in the purchase decision.

Key account salespeople

Another category which warrants special mention but which would normally be part of either consumer or industrial indirect selling comprises the so-called key account salespeople. The changing structure of major retailers, distributors and others means, for many companies, that certain customers are of strategic importance. The Pareto rule, which states that 80 per cent of the business comes from 20 per cent of customers, necessitates that these important accounts are given the attention and service they deserve. Furthermore, since these are normally large organisations with buying groups, a more customised approach similar to the government direct category may apply. Where an organisation is attempting to open a new account, a different approach may be required (see the section on system selling). These issues of key account management are of such importance that a separate section on this management approach is covered later in the chapter. Suffice to say that some special skills are required in key account selling in which it is vital to keep these customers loyal by customising the product–service–information mix (Cespedes, 1996). Key account salespeople require competencies in a number of different areas of strategic formulation and implementation, systems and process design and relationship building (Millman and Wilson, 1995, 1996).

Retail trade selling

The design of your local supermarket store, the positioning of products and the mix of brands is no accident. Retailers, to maximise their sales per square metre, know that the product mix is a vital ingredient in maximising revenue and profits. Electronic bar coding can tell them exactly how many items of which type are being sold every minute of every day. Further, the combination of leading brands, specialised brands and own label products has a dramatic effect on their profitability. As a result, the role of food broker, category manager and merchandiser has emerged as part of the sales team in these outlets.

The food broker: The idea of an agent representing many principals or manufacturers is not new and has been used in small tools, publishing and other complex product markets. In the food industry, the growth of multiple chains to a dominant position and the importance of larger non-retail users have led to a problem in representation for the smaller company and the large buyer. One type of selling to overcome the problem of size is the use of the food broker who acts on an agency basis for several manufacturers selling a variety of products to retailers. The tasks mostly relate to merchandising and promotional offers in which the cost of individual salespeople for each company is too high and for each store manager too time consuming. The specialist in, say, delicatessen items, dairy products or confectionery is preferred to individual representation on individual lines. The retailer gets a 'mix' of product from one broker. The manufacturers get representation that they could otherwise neither get nor afford. The skill of such brokers is in balancing the items carried and matching these to customers' requirements. In retailing a new area, category management has emerged to handle the complexities involved in these situations.

The category manager: The efficacy of food brokers to add value in distribution has led to greater adoption of the concept of category management in the modern supermarket supply chain. An example of this approach is the Glasgow-based McCurrach's, which is one of the largest food brokers in the UK. Although founded over 100 years ago, this company has seen its sales grow rapidly in recent years. Representing over 30 clients such as Guinness, Campbell's and A G Barr, their role is to maximise customers' sales by getting products into stores and ensuring appropriate shelf-space and in-store promotions. McCurrach's at present employs over 100 people and have invested in new technology to provide the best possible service for client and customer. Such an operation involves specialist sales people competent in selling, merchandising, logistics and account management. This requires a product, information and service mix which meets the demanding needs of retail customers.

The merchandising representatives: As indicated by the success of food brokers, an important aspect of many companies' marketing success is to have available product, superbly presented and displayed at the point-of-sale to maximise distributors' margins and make it easy and a pleasure for the end customer to buy. For this reason, an important aspect of many salespeople's job specification is to merchandise their company's product or service in the most competitive way. For some companies, this is most effectively achieved by separating merchandising from other sales activities. Mars confectionery have for some time maintained a separate merchandise force from their conventional sales force, calling on large and small outlets to maximise the effectiveness of their point-of-sale displays. Others, such as Procter and Gamble, have their own employees in major supermarkets to more effectively coordinate their operations on behalf of their distributors. Such personnel not only sell but also operate merchandising planning and operations and a range of logistic activities. The title of salesperson has changed to customer account manager, which is much more than merely cosmetic. These managers have one of the most vital tasks than anyone in their organisation, namely solving their customer's problems and increasing the amount of business their customers do – a key task in the management of sales operations.

Telesales

Ever cognisant of the high costs of selling and the low face-to-face selling time, an important consideration is to balance sales with other elements in the marketing mix and to consider the most effective selling mix. Is a personal call necessary? Would a telephone call suffice or be of more benefit to the customer? Can groups of small or non-customers be approached by telephone? The use of the telephone in selling can be both a replacement for personal contact and a complement to personal selling. So pervasive has the telephone become, and so vital a part of sales operations, that much of Chapter 6 addresses the problems and opportunities of communicating with customers via the telephone and other modern communication systems.

Did you know?

The cost of customer contact

Industrial sales call	$300
Telemarketing	$35
Direct mail	$2.50
Internet	$1.25

(Source: www.e-marketinggroup.com/the_costs_content.htm)

Telephone selling, like personal selling, requires good communication skills, empathy and professionalism. Certain techniques will be different. On the telephone, it is essential to record details of the caller's name and number and the approach to asking questions is different since the call is very often in response to a request. The resources at the salesperson's disposal are also different in that a VDU is likely to be used, making information more readily available. Closing the call and follow-up are vital so that customers are satisfied with their treatment and their problem is resolved. Good telephone salespeople need to speak clearly and are polite and courteous so that rapport is established. They need to be careful that they are clearly understood by the customer and that they in turn understand the customer's request accurately. Telephone selling is most effective in a conditioned response mode, preferably with a script and a standardised response format. Also, if the request cannot be met in full, there needs to be a clear line of communication to a more senior manager who can deal with the problem. Telephone salespeople usually have the advantage of working in teams which can be supportive for the individuals involved. For this reason, the growth in teleworkers operating from home has proved less effective than the modern call centre operation as a sales and service operation.

Franchise selling

Another relatively old idea which has expanded in type and form in recent years is the franchise organisation. Franchising is a more extensive form of licensing agreement involving the transfer of intangible assets and property rights to another party. A company (franchiser) licenses the business system, products, services and promotional efforts to an independent company or person to trade under the franchiser's name using their trade marks and brand. In return, the franchiser receives revenue from fees, royalties and other payments from the franchisee. Although rarely used exclusively for sales reasons, the combination of sales and service provided by this type of organisation is a prime factor in organisations managing their business in this way. In some cases, the total operation is prescribed in specific detail and the sales approach specified and controlled. In other cases, significant freedom is allowed in sales generation activity. Franchisers usually have the right to terminate agreements if the franchise fails to perform to set standards or reach agreed sales volumes. The franchiser would normally provide the product or service, training, finance and management support. The relationship usually involves some form of financial commitment by the franchisee (purchase of the franchise rights) but is a lower-risk operation than trying to become established in an existing or new market. Franchising can cover a variety of formats such as car distribution, service outlets or wholesale systems. The type of selling may therefore vary greatly.

Did you know?

The turnover of the UK franchising industry has grown from £ 5.9 billion in 1995 to an estimated £10.3 billion in 2005, which represented a 13.2 per cent increase on 2004. The total number of non-dairy franchises was 19,700 in 1995 and estimated to stand at around 29,100 in 2005.

(Source: NatWest/British Franchise Association Franchise Survey 2006, Keynote 2006)

International selling

The complexities of the international selling job will be dealt with in depth in Chapter 8. The method of selling internationally will vary with the customer and culture in the market to be served, the organisational arrangements used, such as direct agency or joint ventures, and the marketing capability of the company. Therefore, some or all of the previously listed types of selling may be required. What is clear is that, in different countries, the criteria for success in the home market will not necessarily apply overseas. The tasks, responsibilities and methods must be tailored to suit the market and customers served.

System selling: team selling

The move from a sales orientation to a marketing orientation has changed the selling approach. Salespeople are more effective by understanding buyers' needs and providing and emphasising benefits in their product or service to satisfy such needs rather than by merely exploiting the selling technique. This has led to a more consultative role for salespeople advising buyers and decision makers. In the computer industry and industrial direct applications, it is common for three or more people in a team to advise customers. Such teams have product, technical or financial experts to assess customer needs and so tailor the product/service package to be most effective. In other businesses, salespeople, service engineers and teleworkers need to work together to create sales and maintain relationships. Again, the salesperson is a coordinator and orchestrator to promote collaboration within the organisation and maximise effectiveness between organisations. Team selling can create additional problems in terms of sharing rewards or assessing performance-related pay and is perhaps best suited to situations where payment is by salary or group bonus rather than commission or personal rewards.

The previous classification is not the only possible means of grouping types of selling. To reflect the changing role of salespeople, it has been suggested that other roles emerge, such as customer partner, buyer–seller team coordinator or customer service provider. In many companies, the role of sales manager and marketing manager is combined, and this trend may increase, as marketing becomes the essential coordination between a firm and its customers. This will require salespeople to have a much greater relationship orientation than hitherto, yet marketing people will require much greater interpersonal skills than that are found in planning-oriented people. This further confirms the variety and complexity of selling jobs and the possible variations in types of selling which must be incorporated into effective sales management policies.

What do you think?

Select three sales positions – one from a financial service company, one a mobile phone company and the other selling industrial machinery. Briefly consider what the job might entail and select an appropriate title other than salesperson for the position.

3.9 Key account and global account management

Key account management (KAM) enables a firm to manage the transition from transactional selling to relationship building between buyers and sellers. KAM is appropriate for industrial, B2B and consumer selling. KAM was a term first used in the 1960s for selling in the fast-moving consumer goods (FMCG) market but developed in the 1970s in line with the move towards centralised purchasing, outsourcing and supply-based rationalisation (Millman, 1999) which in turn influenced the marketing and sales behaviour of suppliers. Stevenson and Page (1979) noted the use of national account marketing by major sellers in concentrated industries to sell to major buyers in concentrated markets. An example of this was found in the automotive industry, which was dominated (and is) by a few large customers and heavily dependent suppliers. Sellers faced with such concentrated purchasing power had to find a different, non-routine way to deal with these accounts (Stevenson and Page, 1979).

Firms would therefore dedicate resources to a core portfolio of customers who represented the highest value, known as the *key accounts* (Pardo, 1998). This seller-initiated alliance became more widely known as key account management (KAM) or (among sales managers) key account selling (KAS).

The key account manager, also called national account manager, implies managing a sales team specialised in the account, although on many occasions this has been one person. A firm adopting such an organisational structure is aiming to improve the quality of the relationship with the customer, improve communication and help increase the coordination between the two parties. In this way, service is improved as the size of the account grows (Barrett, 1986).

Also, this sales-oriented approach required the supplier to be skilled at negotiation and deal making, thought by Millman and Wilson (1996) as somewhat adversarial competences that were taught and reinforced in the sales training courses prevalent in

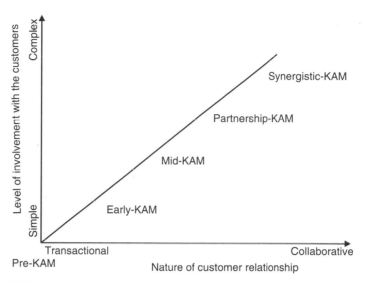

Fig 3.2   The KAM model (*Source: Millman and Wilson, 1995*)

the '80s. Eventually, writers and practitioners began to recognise that, to be effective, KAM depended crucially on the ability and willingness of individuals to build close, long-term relationships. As a result, the lifecycle model of KAM was developed by Millman and Wilson (1995), who identified six stages in the 'relationship development cycle' (see Figure 3.2).

Millman and Wilson (1995) noted a distinct shift among firms from a selling focus to the more sophisticated discipline of KAM. Their definition of KAM went beyond the targeted, sales focus seen in Barrett's earlier work (Barrett, 1986). Instead, they viewed KAM as a process of customer management in business-to-business markets.

Millman and Wilson's KAM model not only implied different relational strategies at each stage but also the need for differing and possibly unfamiliar skills and competences in both buying and selling firm.

What do you think?

Millman and Wilson (1995, p. 10) defined a key account as a 'customer the supplier considered to be of strategic importance'. *Strategic* does not necessarily imply economic worth – the account's brand image or its capability to aid market penetration may be more important to the supplier (Pardo, 1998). However, it is presumed that economic worth will ensue from a strategic account.

What criteria would you apply in selecting a key account in a firm you have experience or knowledge of?

Note that the model suggests that KAM is a process undertaken by the *supplier*. This involves identifying firms with key account potential, then deploying appropriate resources (people and structural) to develop relationships and manage each customer account over time. The primary aim of this model is to provide suppliers with incremental profits from large or potentially large and complex accounts (Shapiro *et al.*, 1987).

A more recent approach to KAM, however, stresses new degrees of *collaboration* between buyer and seller – at both individual and organisational level. This might, at the extreme end of the lifecycle (partnership or synergistic KAM) involve supplier and customer in joint business planning and goal sharing. Such an approach requires high levels of trust and commitment in both parties.

Should a firm tell a customer that it has key account status? Pardo (1997) questioned whether a customer wants to be regarded as a key account and thus is prepared to accept the supplier's KAM function and process. She observed that buyers would accept KAM provided it did not impose additional constraints. KAM may, however, necessitate an increase in organisational complexity (ibid. 1997) in both firms, for example, through functional coordination or new forms of departmental integration. In other situations, in project management and tendering, the customer organisation may proactively seek suppliers who have the ability to implement KAM efficiently at the partnership level.

3.10   Summary

No one theory or set of principles will apply universally to every selling situation. Care has to be taken to adapt to the product, company or market situation which creates the unique circumstances impinging on the sales interaction. The role and tasks of direct salespeople, retail salespeople or director-level negotiators are significantly different, creating diverse management problems and solutions. A classification of selling types is suggested in this chapter on the grounds of usefulness rather than infallibility. These similarities and differences in selling will influence the remainder of this book.

Questions

1   In what ways do the selling tasks differ between copier machines and selling the paper used in these machines?

2   Selecting two types of selling, examine whether the salespeople are predominantly male or female. What justification could be offered for this difference? Explain whether or not these differences are likely to continue.

3   In certain types of selling, for example, selling pharmaceuticals to doctors, so-called missionary selling, the sales force do not take orders directly. Consider some of the difficulties this might create for both the salesperson and the sales manager.

4   What problems might arise in the coordination of a telephone sales operation when used in conjunction with a direct personal sales force? How might these problems be overcome?

5   Select a business you are familiar with and recommend for the sales force the time they should spend prospecting for new leads versus the time they should spend developing business with existing customers.

6   What are the similarities and differences between selling cars to business users and selling cars to private consumers?

C R Smith

C R Smith (www.crsmith.co.uk) is a window and conservatory company employing over 1000 people in Scotland and now expanding in other areas of the UK. Although they have used telesales in the past, the company now operates two field sales operations, one a team of canvassers, the other salespeople to obtain orders and contracts. The canvassers distribute the company newsletter, a quarterly publication called C R Homes, and follow up with a personal call to ask house owners their views on the publication and, of course, whether any of the products are of interest now or in the future. The aim is to obtain appointments with genuine leads for the sales force. While this may be considered hard sell and intrusive, research has shown that most consumers prefer this to the unsolicited telephone call and in the majority of cases find the publication of interest. While the canvassers are set specific appointment targets, the work is flexible and hours can be made to suit part-time, mature people. The company is looking for individuals with a pleasant manner, experience and a certain maturity who can empathise with the customers on whom they call. The canvassing team is a combination of male and female, of different backgrounds, who range in age from 25 to retirement age. The canvassers, some of whom have previously been in telesales, say they prefer this approach. So far, separating sales prospecting from sales generation has proved innovative and successful.

1 Critically appraise C R Smith's approach.
2 Compare the above approach with other ways of expanding their business and generating sales.
3 Interview some (three or four is suggested) homeowners on their views of unsolicited telephone sales calls, the approach outlined above and door-to-door selling in general.

Key terms

- category management
- conditioned response
- development selling
- farmers
- food brokers
- franchise sales
- hunters
- insight response
- key accounts

- maintenance selling
- merchandising
- missionary selling
- new business selling
- retail selling
- system selling
- technical selling
- telesales
- trade selling

References

Barrett, J. (1986) 'Why major account selling works' *Industrial Marketing Management* 15 (1): 63–73

Bettger, F. (1949) *How I Raised Myself from Failure to Success in Selling* Prentice-Hall: Englewood Cliffs, NJ

Cespedes, F.V. (1996) *Managing Marketing Linkages: texts, cases and readings* Prentice-Hall: Upper Saddle River, NJ

Chu, W., Gestner, E. and Hess, J.D. (1995) 'Costs and benefits of hard-sell' *Journal of Marketing Research* **XXXII** (Feb): 97–102

Cravens, D., Grant, K., Ingram, T., LaForge, R. and Young, C. (1992) 'In search of excellent sales organisations' *European Journal of Marketing* **26** (1): 6–23

Cuddihy, L. (1996) An investigation of sales management practices in the Irish pharmaceutical industry. *Unpublished MBS thesis*, Dublin City University School: Dublin

Doney, P.M. and Cannon, J.P. (1997) 'An examination of the nature of trust in buyer–seller relationships' *Journal of Marketing* **61** (Apr): 35–51

Fein, A.J. (2004) Online autions are here to stay. Available at http://www.mdm.com/stories/fein3401.html [Accessed 12 July 2006]

Kahn, G.N. and Schuchman, A. (1961) 'Specialise your salesmen' *Harvard Business Review* **Jan–Feb**: 125–33

Lambe, J. and Speckman, R. (1997) 'National account mangement: large account selling or buyer-supplier alliance?' *Journal of Personal Selling and Sales Management* **17** (1): 61–74

McMurry, R.N. (1961) 'The mystique of super-salesmanship' *Harvard Business Review* **Mar–Apr**: 113–22

McMurry, R.N. and Arnold, J.S. (1968) *How to Build a Dynamic Sales Organisation* McGraw-Hill: New York

Millman, A.F. and Wilson, K.J. (1995) 'From key account selling to key account management' *Journal of Marketing Practice* **1** (1): 8–21

Millman, A.F. and Wilson, K.J. (1996) 'Developing key account management competencies' *Journal of Marketing Practice* **2** (2): 7–22

Moncrief, W.C. (1986) 'Selling activity and sales position taxonomies for industrial salesforces' *Journal of Marketing Research* **XXIII** (Aug): 261–70

Moncrief, W.C., Marshall, G. and Lassk, F. (1999) 'The current state of salesforce activities' *Industrial Marketing Management* **28** (1): 87–98

Moncrief, W.C., Marshall, G. and Lassk, F. (2006) 'A contemporary taxonomy of sales positions' *Journal of Personal Selling and Sales Management* **XXIV** (1): 55–65

Morgan, R.M. and Hunt, S.D. (1994) 'The commitment–trust theory of relationship marketing' *Journal of Marketing* **58** (Jul): 20–38

Newton, D.A. (1969) 'Get the most out of your sales force' *Harvard Business Review* **Sep–Oct**: 16–29

Pardo, C. (1997) 'Key account management in the business to business field: the key account's point of view' *Journal of Personal Selling and Sales Management* **17** (1): 17–26

Pardo, C. (1998) 'Towards a typology of key accounts in the industrial field' *The Journal of Selling and Major Account Management* **1** (1): 49–57

Shapiro, B.P., Rangan, V.K., Moriarty, R.T. and Ross, E.B. (1987) 'Manage customers for profits (not just sales)' *Harvard Business Review* **Sep–Oct**: 101–8

Stein, A. and Hawking, P. (2002) Reverse auction e-Procurement: a suppliers viewpoint. Available at http://ausweb.scu.edu.au/aw02/papers/refereed/stein/paper.html [Accessed 19 June 2005]

Stevenson, T.H. and Page, A.L. (1979) 'The adoption of national account marketing by industrial firms' *Industrial Marketing Mangement* **8** (1): 94–100

Sujan, H., Weitz, B.A. and Kumar, N. (1994) 'Learning orientation, working smart, and effective selling' *Journal of Marketing* **58** (Jul): 39–52

Tack, A. (1989) *Increase Your Sales the Tack Way* Gower: Aldershot

4 Salespeople and selling skills

4.1 Overview

Many sales management problems could be eliminated or at least mitigated if a successful sales type could be found. This would imply that successful salespeople are born, have acquired the necessary skills or possibly have been self-taught by experience. The sales manager's task is to find such people. Remember, sales situations are in some ways unique. The various roles, complex tasks and varieties of situations which can occur require some adaptability by individuals to any list of principles of selling which may be put forward. Not least, the problem of the measurement of personality and psychological traits is complex. The nature of the job (new business versus service calling; transaction versus relationship selling) may mean that entirely different characteristics are needed to be effective in different situations. The view here is that a unidimensional approach will be inadequate, and better explanations have yet to be found between the fit of certain jobs and the personality of individuals, and vice versa. The evidence on the characteristics of successful salespeople is inconclusive and contradictory. Indeed, the basic premise that there is an ideal sales personality may be unsound. Is it not the characteristics of buyers or sales managers rather than salespeople which needs to be examined for a better explanation of sales performance?

Sales managers, like marketing managers, must respond to changes in supply, demand or the framework in which business is conducted. People operating at the interface or boundary between different units in a dynamic environment need a wide range of skills, from strategic problem-solving and profit orientation to highly developed communication capabilities. The modern salesperson has had to acquire more qualities, more skills and a more flexible approach but, unfortunately for sales recruiters, people who have these skills may consider selling as low in status and unable to provide them with the necessary levels of job satisfaction.

In a marketing context, personal selling facilitates the matching of product or service offerings to buyer requirements. An important dimension of selling ability is the individual's competence in matching and influencing the variety of needs and behavioural complexities of the buyer. The factors that determine job success are not necessarily the intellectual dimensions which most selection devices are designed to measure. Instead, the result reflects a match between the prospect's and the salesperson's personalities and the knowledge, judgement and persuasive powers of both parties. The following discussion attempts to address the nature of these problems.

4.2 Learning objectives

In this chapter the aim is

- to review previous work on the desirable characteristics of salespeople;
- to separate reality from myth in the ideal sales type;
- to identify personality, knowledge and skills required in different selling jobs;
- to evaluate the status position and role conflicts inherent in sales jobs;
- to make assessments of the key determinants in higher sales performers.

4.3 Definitions

Contracts are legal agreements between buyer and seller to buy specified goods under agreed terms and conditions.

Negotiating is a process of resolving conflict to achieve a mutually acceptable compromise in buyer–seller situations.

Role conflict occurs when the salesperson believes that the role demands of two or more role partners are incompatible and they cannot possibly satisfy them all at the same time (Walker, Churchill and Ford, 1977).

Tender is a formal offer to supply goods or services to an agreed specification at a specific price.

4.4 Personal attributes of salespeople

Personality and physical characteristics are frequently cited as important (Churchill *et al.*, 1985). Personality is the sum total of all the behavioural and mental characteristics by means of which an individual is recognised as being unique. Because the costs of hiring and training new salespeople is high and the cost in lost business from ineffective salespeople higher still, sales managers and academic researchers have long been searching for the relationships between personal characteristics and personality traits and the measures of sales success. Examining previous literature on the characteristics of successful salespeople produces a mixed bag of one-off studies, anecdotal findings and some pure conjecture. Nevertheless, the search goes on, and it is worthwhile to review some of the literature in this area.

In a classic study conducted in the United States, mostly in direct selling, Mayer and Greenberg (1964) identified two basic qualities that a good salesperson must have. First is empathy, which Mayer and Greenberg define as the important central ability to feel as the other fellow does in order to be able to sell a product or service. Second, ego drive, which can be described as the need to conquer: a desire to want and need to make a sale. In many sales situations, life is tough against aggressive competition. Salespeople must be motivated by failure, not shattered by it. The ideal is the person who has both empathy and drive. Super salespeople have lots of both. Someone who has lots of empathy but is low on drive may lack the killer touch by being unable to close a sale. Someone with lots of drive but who is low on empathy is probably the sales caricature, brash and obvious. Someone with little empathy and low drive is in the wrong job.

Perhaps the most significant finding to emerge was that the link between personal factors and performance depends not on any one factor but on a combination of conditions and circumstances. The type of product, the market, the buyer or buying organisation, the characteristics of the firm, its culture and ethos, the type of manager and management style and the type of salesperson all have an influence.

What do you think?

In a serious academic study in the United States, published in the *Journal of Marketing*, Lamont and Lundstrom (1977) identified a number of personality and personal characteristics that better sales performers possessed. Among these were physical characteristics. In their words, part of the profile of the successful salesman was someone who is 'tall, physically impressive and energetic'.

What do you think? If the study were replicated today would you expect a similar result? If not does this mean that physical characteristics are completely unimportant?

The same authors also found better performers were those 'with good work habits and perseverance, who is willing to work long hours and enjoys solving problems ... who seeks and enjoys recognition from others for selling accomplishments ... has a broad range of interests but is not extensively involved in civic and professional organisations ... is not highly educated in a formal manner but is intellectually capable ... may be emotional and somewhat disorganised but adaptable and flexible in their work habits ... is not overly sensitive or perceptive to the reactions and feelings of others ... views selling as a professional career and has little interest in achieving status beyond the selling position'.

Evaluate the worth of these characteristics in a salesperson.

Personal characteristics and personality do matter but are not necessarily significant by themselves. In fact, it has been suggested that rather than look for more of the same, sales managers of traditionally male-dominated firms should actively recruit females and expunge existing stereotypes (Sigaw and Honeycutt, 1995). Regardless of age, sex or colour and by evaluating what buyers themselves say, sales managers and salespeople themselves believe (Donaldson, 1998), a number of desirable characteristics can be suggested as outlined below:

Enthusiasm

Salespeople must be enthusiastic about their job, their product, their company and themselves. One problem with this trait is the difficulty in defining and measuring an individual's enthusiasm. Enthusiasm is a fundamental personality trait exhibited by the person who, despite failures and rejections, attacks the next call or task as vigorously as the first. Although not the same as hard-working, the two are often found in combination. The current emphasis on customer satisfaction and long-term relationships suggest that job involvement can be related to enthusiasm but this concept has, so far, proved difficult to measure in a sales context (Ramsey *et al.*, 1995). People who work long hours, show perseverance and determination and enthusiasm, it is suggested, are more likely to be successful salespeople.

Did you know?

Frank Bettger was one of the first to produce a best-selling 'how-to-sell' book in 1949. He believed that enthusiasm was the major characteristic which turned failure into success in selling based on his experience as a baseball player in his youth. By paying attention to his appearance and adopting a positive mind-set and body language he claims this turned him from failure to success as a baseball player. By applying this to his career in selling, he became a star performer (Bettger, 1949).

Confidence

Those people who possess higher levels of self-confidence are more likely to enjoy selling and be successful. By itself, confidence is not enough but belief in one's own ability and belief in the product and the company are conveyed to buyers with positive effect. It can be agreed that there will be times and situations where salespeople will have to adjust their proposal or presentation and be able to make quick, important decisions. A lack of confidence can lose opportunities and ultimately sales.

Intelligence

While there will be some desirable minimum level of intelligence required for selling, there appears to be no evidence to suggest that higher levels of intelligence correlate with higher levels of sales performance. Conventional measures of intelligence may not be an appropriate means of assessment and higher levels of intellectual ability may create additional problems. Salespeople who overanalyse or criticise may lack conviction. In selling, mental and verbal agility, for example, would seem to be preferable to written or analytical skills.

Self-worth

The ability and desire to be motivated by non-pecuniary incentives such as status, self-esteem and sociability seem to play a part in effective selling. In a survey of industrial distributor salespeople, the most important motivating factors were rated as 'satisfaction with doing a good job' and 'meeting family responsibilities' (Donaldson, 1998).

4.5   Knowledge

The problem of trying to classify salespeople according to a prescribed list of necessary and desirable attributes has already been referred to, especially when a range of different situations may demand very different solutions. To some extent, these situations will always be product-, company-, market- and indeed customer-specific and therefore generalised theories concerning the necessary characteristics remain unproven. Knowledge of the products, company, customers, competitors, markets and territories will be important. Research in a number of areas suggests that product knowledge is rated by sales managers to be the most highly rated feature in successful salespeople.

Product knowledge

A product can be defined as a bundle of physical and psychological attributes which are capable of providing buyer satisfaction, be it a tangible good or a service. These attributes can be reinforced and differentiated by salespeople to create and sustain a competitive advantage. It follows that knowledge of the product, its benefits and how it is used and performs is essential to a salesperson. It is surprising therefore that various surveys of buyers reveal, among several criticisms of salespeople, that a lack of product knowledge was common. Detailed product knowledge by itself is not sufficient but is a necessary prerequisite and a major factor in effective selling.

Competitor knowledge

Combined with and part of product knowledge must be a detailed knowledge of competitors' products. In addition, salespeople must know and understand their competitors' sales policies, organisation, pricing and promotion tactics. Such knowledge is important, but experienced salespeople will almost always confirm that a golden rule is 'never knock competitors'. This is sound advice since success will come from strengths rather than from negative criticisms. A knowledge of competitors will enable positive benefits for a product to be identified and more closely matched with customers' needs and wants.

Market knowledge

It is a senior management responsibility to decide marketing strategy and policies on market segmentation, product positioning and the weighting given to individual elements in the marketing mix, but the individual salesperson should have the ability to understand and translate the application of marketing effort to individual customers and circumstances. An essential component of the selling job is to provide management with information on competitors, market conditions and trends. Salespeople may tend to be parochial in outlook but intelligently collected information from diverse sales areas can be used to form a composite picture.

Customer knowledge

Equally vital for the salesperson is the ability to develop and maintain ongoing customer relationships. Rochford and Wotruba (1993) maintain that the role of the salesperson has moved away from the traditional aggressive and persuasive selling to a new role of relationship manager (Crosby *et al.*, 1990). The specific tasks may vary but can include providing technical information, delivering information, handling complaints and providing other aspects of customer service as appropriate. Effective selling can be demonstrated as the ability to home in on the customer's choice space and therefore sell to meet a gap in buyer's needs and wants in preference to any competitor product. In a theoretical context, customer knowledge means being able to distinguish the buyer's preference correctly identified between two or more products and therefore the salesperson stressing the 'right' things in influencing a customer's choice. On a more practical level, customer knowledge may relate to credit-worthiness or potential credit problems, to dissatisfaction with existing suppliers or to internal organisational changes which may offer a potential route to being considered as an 'in' supplier.

Territory knowledge

Good territory knowledge is also important in effective selling. This requires management skills by the individual in the efficient allocation of time between customers, prospects and travelling. Good skills in planning routes and sales calls, together with an appropriate but not excessive time on non-selling activities, will be important determinants of sales force productivity. While some flexibility in the use of time will always be required, the ability to plan and manage a territory will be important determinants in effective sales performance. We will return to this topic in Chapter 6 as new technology has impacted on the salesperson's ability in this area.

Company knowledge

Salespeople should have an adequate knowledge of their own company, including its history, ownership, direction and aspirations of the owners. This helps to gel a united spirit of enterprise and commitment – a culture. In detail, this means knowledge of the organisation, its structure, personalities, rules, procedures and disciplines. The mushroom system whereby salespeople are kept in the dark and every so often receive a shovel of dirt can be neither effective nor desirable.

4.6 Skills

Skills are a combination of factors (personality and knowledge contribute to these) which can be used to practise the job more effectively. It seems both appropriate and useful to classify skills into three areas – communication skills, matching skills and persuasive skills. Rarely in practice can such a division into compartments be achieved, but it does provide a necessary understanding if not validity in what is required by salespeople.

Communication skills

Personal selling combines with advertising and promotion to form a communication link between sellers, intermediaries and end users. The more complex the distribution channel and the greater the number of intermediaries, the higher will be the cost of achieving communication objectives. No one single communication technique can be effective to all participants. Often, it is the combination of personal selling with other forms of promotion which is most effective. While the concern here is with personal selling, it should be acknowledged and understood that the effectiveness of personal selling can be increased and the costs reduced by support from other promotional expenditure.

Matching skills

The hypothesis put forward in this book is that there is no such thing as the ideal sales type in the abstract. The characteristics and skills required will be those which best match the role to be performed and the tasks which must be undertaken. Where this matching can be extended to the similarity between buyers and sellers, sales performance can be further improved. A study by Greenberg and Greenberg (1976), claiming to use information on 350,000 individuals, found evidence to question the wisdom of many sales recruitment policies. In their words,

> Youth, education, previous experience, maleness and whiteness simply are not real criteria to predict success. Despite all of the stereotype notions to the contrary, people over 40 produce as effectively as their younger competitors; people with no previous experience perform as well as experienced salespeople; people without even a high school diploma perform as well in sales as people with advanced degrees. Simply put, these external qualities, so long used as 'knock-out' or selection factors by industry, do not hold up. What counts are the dynamics within a human being that either make him or her appropriate or not appropriate for a particular job. When people are matched to a job in terms of these basic personality dynamics and not selected on superficial levels, job satisfaction, high productivity and reduced turnover can be expected (p. 627).

Effective selling also requires a selling style appropriate to the prospect, as was highlighted by Buzzotta *et al.* (1982). Their approach and recommendations on sales training suggest a procedure using a series of maps and sizing-up skills as being important in effective selling techniques. In outline, their approach uses perceptual mapping techniques to facilitate the matching of seller with buyer. Figure 4.1 describes patterns of selling behaviour. Most people's behaviour is consistent although not always appropriate. Identifying the type of behaviour is a first step to modifying it to

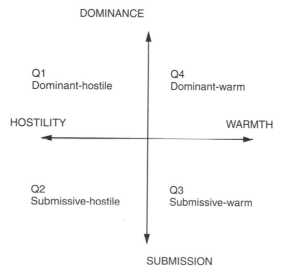

Fig 4.1   The sales behaviour model

be more effective. The first type of behaviour is dominant–hostile, as shown in quadrant 1 of Figure 4.1.

Some explanation of these dimensions is appropriate. Warmth is regard for others and involves awareness and understanding of the buyer's needs and sensitivity to their problems and circumstances. Hostility implies the opposite, being exhibited by a lack of regard for others, a lack of understanding of the other's position and almost contempt for their worth and self-esteem. Dominance is the desire to control interpersonal situations using techniques of force and leadership. At the other end of the spectrum, submission is exhibited by a passive, unassertive acquiescence in approach and a lack of assertiveness.

To return to quadrant 1 in Figure 4.1, dominant–hostile behaviour is exhibited by salespeople who see customers as people who seldom buy willingly and to achieve sales success the salesperson must have superior strength of character and determination to succeed. In quadrant 2, the salesperson views customers as people who buy only when ready to buy and the salesperson as impotent to change the situation. This means that salespeople have got to be ready when the customer is ready. In quadrant 3, salespeople try to ingratiate themselves with customers since people only buy from salespeople they like and every prospect is and should be a friend. Finally, dominant–warm sales behaviour views sales as being the result of customers being convinced of needs and benefits, and the sales process is a joint beneficial-type system.

These positions or map locations help understand different types of sales behaviour. This is only part of the picture, the other side of the coin or, more correctly with this analogy, the contour lines of the map being provided by a customer behaviour perceptual map, as shown in Figure 4.2.

The dominant–hostile prospect is someone who does not trust salespeople, who views them as getting rid of something no-one wants at prices higher than the goods are worth, and therefore the buyer must be tough, resilient and resist any sales

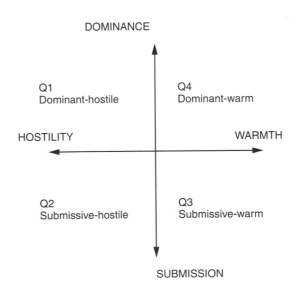

	DOMINANCE	
Q1 Dominant-hostile		Q4 Dominant-warm
HOSTILITY		WARMTH
Q2 Submissive-hostile		Q3 Submissive-warm
	SUBMISSION	

Fig 4.2 The customer behaviour model

'manoeuvres'. A submissive–hostile buyer does not trust salespeople or at least not very often and therefore will not see them or will try to avoid meeting them or make excuses not to be available for consultation. The submissive–warm customer can equally be a problem for different reasons. They see all products and sellers as very much alike and, other things being equal, will prefer to buy from people they like or feel at ease and familiar with in doing business. Finally, dominant–warm buyers want to buy and will generally purchase from those who demonstrate superiority and a proven competitive advantage for their product or company.

If these two maps are combined, different scenarios emerge concerning the nature of sales situations. For example, the dominant–hostile buyer meeting the dominant–hostile seller is a situation of friction, discord and unsatisfactory working or business relationships. However, the opposite problem can arise where a brash, overwhelming, extrovert salesperson meets a distrustful withdrawn introvert buyer. Again the business/working relationship, if any, probably confirms the worst suspicions of each party but a successful outcome is unlikely. A fuller discussion of these topics is explained by Buzzotta *et al.* (1982) in their book, *Effective Selling Through Psychology*.

These behavioural mapping models develop the matching skills of the salesperson to diagnose the true nature of buyers' needs and the complexities of sales interactions. Salespeople ask themselves questions on the type of behaviour they typically manifest and how prospects perceive them and the way they do their job, what types of behaviour the prospect manifests and their attitudes and actions in sales situations, and to what extent such behaviour varies with type of purchase, frequency of contact, risk and uncertainty in purchase decisions. Such analysis is an essential prerequisite to employing the correct skills in sales situations. Current advances in relationship marketing bring the firm closer to its customer, which manifests itself in the relationship orientation of salespeople (Donaldson, Tzokas and Saren, 1997). Evidence that more collaborative approaches to buyer–seller relationships are becoming the norm has been supported in a number of studies (Hakansson, 1982; Dwyer *et al.*, 1987; Donaldson and O'Toole, 2002). Developing this theme, Spiro and Weitz (1990) confirm that the ability to adapt sales behaviour is more important than personal or personality characteristics. Their work makes this important link between adaptive behaviour and performance. Salespeople who have scope to control or modify their behaviour to meet the needs of different customers, who are sensitive to customers' needs yet at the same time able to be positive in matching their offer to those needs, are the higher performers (Weitz *et al.*, 1986; Spiro and Weitz, 1990; Plank and Reid, 1994).

Persuasive skills

Understanding the communication process and the ability to appreciate the importance of matching the benefits of sellers to the needs of buyers are necessary but not sufficient conditions to complete the sales process. A third dimension of skill – persuasive abilities – needs to be added. No matter how well the company has conducted and managed the marketing process, the customer will still face a variety of options from competing suppliers. A key aspect of a company's performance is its ability to generate and close sales. Most often, this is done in person by the sales force. An essential part of this process is not only information about products, services or the company but the ability to persuade buyers against equally able competitors. The correct interpretation of buyers' needs and the application of selling effort is vital. While every sales call is unique and in some way different from every other call, the ability of the salesperson to make effective presentations in line with buyer's needs makes the difference between success and failure in selling. Experience is important in assessing what has previously worked, or in most cases failed to work, with prospects. Training, education and basic ability all contribute to what constitutes persuasive abilities, as does effectiveness in the selling process itself. It is to this we now turn.

4.7   The sales process

Despite what has been said about matching, technique in the sales job is still, and always has been, vitally important to effective selling. While cautioning against the idea of the one best or universal way to sell, there are nevertheless some appropriate guidelines which can be recommended.

What do you think?

A best seller, *McCormack on Selling* (1995) suggested a good salesperson needs to do the following:

Believe in your product.

Believe in yourself.

See a lot of people.

Pay attention to timing.

Listen to the customer.

Develop a sense of humour.

Knock on old doors.

Ask everyone to buy.

Follow up the sale with the same aggressiveness you demonstrated before the sales.

Use common sense.

How helpful is the list?

Generating leads and identifying prospects

Most salespeople create sales from existing customers, but the job also entails gaining new customers. The first step in achieving this is to identify suitable prospects. Many companies provide leads for salespeople from formal sources such as Glenigan for the building industry or perhaps from response enquiries as a result of trade shows, direct mailing, telemarketing or advertising. Salespeople will also generate their own leads from lists/directories, through personal contacts, newspapers or by telephone prospecting. However, a lead is a suspect which has to be qualified to become a prospect. To qualify a lead, it is important to ensure that the potential customer needs the product or service in question or has a problem to be solved and that they have the resources and authority to influence or decide on the purchase. Furthermore, the potential account will be profitable.

CES is involved in selling packages for major sporting events (e.g. Ascot, Wimbledon, the British Grand Prix and the Open Golf) to large corporate firms. Trade directories are used to identify companies, their size, telephone number and the names of the managing, marketing or sales director. They adopt a blanket coverage approach, telephoning 200 prospective customers per day, of whom 50 express some degree of interest, the outcome of this usually being 2 deals per week. All staff at CES work in teams to help to encourage and motivate one another and on the same area, such as selling packages for Royal Ascot. This is one possible approach which seems to work for this company in this market.

Precall planning

An old rule of thumb suggests that a good sales process is 40 per cent preparation, 20 per cent presentation and 40 per cent follow up. Regardless of the accuracy of these percentages, there is no doubt that success can be linked to preparation. All sales calls should have an objective, preferably with a specific outcome or action on the part of the prospect. Precall planning involves setting objectives, gathering information about the buyer and their company and deciding what questions to ask and what you intend to say. Remember that situation questions are important in the sales process but you do not want to ask questions you can and should have known from other sources. Information such as the size of the firm, their products and services, their competitors, the names of people in important executive positions and the current and previous sales history should be part of precall preparation. Further information, such as the customer's buying processes, their current suppliers and their future plans, can be identified in the initial stages of the sales interview. Ways to establish credibility and trust for the salesperson and their company with the buyer should be part of the precall preparation.

The approach

Getting an audience with a prospect can often be difficult and indeed harrowing for the inexperienced salesperson. Although the role of selling should not be technique-driven, there is a skill in getting to see the right people so that your message can be communicated and understood. It will ultimately rest on what you do and how you do it that builds long-term customer relationships but getting there in the first place can be difficult. Experienced salespeople will recommend the importance of getting past the gatekeeper (receptionist, secretary or personal assistant) and building a relationship not only with the buyer but also with their gatekeepers. Making appointments is, in most cases, essential to establishing a professional approach but letters of introduction and using third party references can also be crucial. As noted earlier, establishing rapport, whether on the basis of similarity or expertise, is necessary before exchange takes place. For larger sales and new products, where the risk for the buyer is greater, establishing credibility is vital. The well-known company has a distinct advantage in this stage and the salesperson from a less well-known company has to work doubly hard to reassure the buyer (Levitt, 1967).

The presentation

Rackham (1987) has shown that the ability to ask questions, and the right type of questions, differentiates between successful and less successful salespeople. Nevertheless, salespeople too often overemphasise the oral presentation and ignore the written sales proposal, the quotation or the subsequent follow-up, which can technically also be considered part of the presentation. It is vital to ensure that the buyer's needs have been correctly identified, that the solution offered is as expected and, if possible, that customer's expectations are exceeded rather than merely satisfied. Furthermore, in the right circumstances, the use of visuals can reassure the buyer and instill confidence in the salesperson, their product and their company. Most experienced salespeople rate canned and stylised presentations as much less important than the well-organised and individually tailored presentations (Hite and Bellizzi, 1986). Research in manufacturing has also shown that there is a need to segment customers and target your demonstration depending on the type of product. Many demonstrations were too long for the product and customer, in other words overselling (Heiman and Muller, 1996). Industrial buyers are looking for credibility, reliability, responsiveness and the ability to provide answers from salespeople rather than aggressiveness or persuasiveness (Hayes and Hartley, 1989).

Overcoming objections

It is human nature that a buyer may stall and raise objections to a sales presentation. Again, experienced salespeople will claim that objections are to be welcomed since they confirm the buyer's interest in the product or service, although the idea of questions is to reveal real needs so that surprises are kept to a minimum. Good salespeople differentiate between types of objection. Some objections are no more than clarifying questions and should be welcomed. However, there are also objections which express real concern. The advice here is to listen carefully to the problem, clarify that both parties understand the real issue and agree how it can be solved. Listening enhances trust in the salesperson and leads to anticipation of future interaction (Ramsey and Sohi, 1997). Salespeople have traditionally put too much emphasis on the ability to overcome resistance by technique instead of by sound solutions which meet the buyer's real needs and provide clear benefits. In other words, salespeople have been overly concerned with a performance orientation rather than a learning orientation but those who learn, and learn how to adapt, will increase their performance (Sujan *et al.*, 1994). Effective communication is helping the customer learn (Wernerfelt, 1996).

Closing

Since most selling is repeat business to existing and known customers, closing is a bad idea. Nevertheless, the salesperson has set an objective and achievement of this objective is necessary to progress the relationship. Salespeople very often just simply forget to ask for the order. They are so busy with their presentation that asking for commitment is neglected or forgotten. In some cases, adding on extra features and advantages, in which the buyer may not be interested, loses the sale by not asking for a decision

In the best-selling book *Increase Your Sales the Tack Way* several closing techniques are suggested including the following:

The alternative close (offer the buyer an option)

The summary close (emphasise the key benefits again)

The fear close (stress the risk of not purchasing)

Verbal-proof story close (tell a good story of another purchaser)

The isolation close (clarify or overcome the key objection)

'Influencing the mind' close (such as agreeing for the distributor to stock the product)

Closing on a minor point (agree one thing then the buyer will agree another)

The concession close ('If you do this then I'll do that')

The trial close ('What if I was to do this?')

(Source: Tack, 1989)

at the right time. Effective closing means agreeing on the objectives that both parties are trying to meet and which take the relationship forward to further integrated activities.

Follow-up

Vital to the customer-driven business is what happens after the sale. Most buyers object when promises are not delivered and the salesperson does not do what was expected. In modern business, this is fatal, where building relationships and the ability to deliver as promised, go the extra mile and delight the customer, are at the heart of what a business should be about. The most important question a salesperson can ask is 'What do I need to do, Mr or Mrs Customer, to get more of your business?'

4.8 Negotiation

One of the most popular words in the selling vocabulary today is negotiating. Everything is negotiable and everyone is a negotiator, or so it is claimed. The reason for the hint of cynicism is that these truisms, such as nothing happens until somebody sells something, is that they are neither very helpful to our understanding nor as a guide to behaviour. It is clear that in personal selling, the interpersonal nature of the exchange means that a process of negotiation takes place. Most authors suggest that negotiating and selling are different but in the relationship-based, nanosecond twenty-first century, negotiating is very much a part of selling.

Interest in negotiation has increased because of the importance of relationships. Repeat business and customer loyalty has increased, with both parties seeking to gain

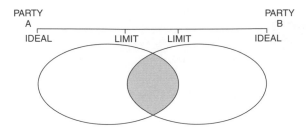

Fig 4.3   The basis for negotiation

an advantage. Despite the necessity of customer orientation, customers seek something more than a supplier can give them, whether it be a lower price, a faster and more reliable delivery or technical advice and efficiency. As a result, the need for negotiation, defined as a process of resolving conflict to achieve a mutually acceptable compromise, is usually present in buyer–seller situations. While there are many similarities between selling and negotiating, and the skills in one are very often applicable to the other, they are not the same thing. Negotiating involves compromise and manoeuvring between two parties who have something to offer each other and who are prepared to bargain to reach an outcome.

It is useful to consider the basis for negotiating as shown in Figure 4.3. As this figure shows, there is a degree of overlap but not total overlap. If you are giving something for nothing, you are not negotiating. Authority and ability are key aspects of negotiating. Negotiating can never be a substitute for selling but you can negotiate when something is scarce or limited in supply, and it may be prudent to think in the long term rather than as a one-off process. While you can con some people once, the second time is more difficult. With professional buyers, it is likely to be terminal.

Negotiating can be seen as a process of eight stages:

1   *Preparation* – This is essential to the good negotiator and separates the professional or competent negotiator from the amateur and incompetent. In this first step, objectives must be set. These cannot be unrealistic, and there must be room to manoeuvre. So set optimistic, realistic and pessimistic targets or, to put it another way, set an objective of what you would like to have, what you intend to get and what is the minimum you must have. What is important here is to be realistic, and this means collecting information so that you are well prepared. Detailed costs, revenues and profits arising from different options need to be worked out in advance. Another aspect in preparation is to decide, in advance, what negotiation strategy you intend to adopt, such as being robust and aggressive or submissive and responsive. Some salespeople are poor at negotiating because they continue talking and point-scoring instead of summarising the points agreed and reflecting. There are many times in a negotiating process when it is prudent to remain silent and consider an option rather than sell a point. Being prepared for these situations is crucial to success and high levels of mental agility are required.

2 *Discussion* – In the negotiating process, it is important to listen rather than tell and seek information by questions rather than point-scoring. Good negotiators plan a list of questions. Telling is non-persuasive whereas questions are persuasive. To prove this point, at the next meeting or lecture you attend, especially one of my own, you will find that people's attention wavers. However, if the presenter asks a question, particularly a direct question at a named individual, you find there is immediate attention. Questions demand attention; statements do not. Also, questions avoid disagreements whereas statements usually create them.

3 *Signals* – The art of negotiating is to look for movement and give help rewards by signalling. Label your own behaviour, for example by saying 'So you are saying . . . then I would feel that . . .'. This takes the process forward.

4 *Proposition* – In making any proposition, the negotiator must be fair and flexible. In any sensible negotiation, it is important to open realistically, move modestly and invite a response. Words such as fair, reasonable and generous are to be avoided since they convey insincerity and are usually resisted by the other person, who has a different perception of fair and probably does not believe you anyway. 'Can't say fairer than that, Guv . . .' means that almost any other way would be fairer!

5 *Presentation* – While part of this process is inevitably that you have to make claims which stress the positive and minimise the negative, it is more important to gauge the other person's objective. Negotiations very often break down because of a lack of appreciation of each other's situation. Each party's perceptions are often either inaccurate or incomplete. The skilled negotiator is practised in ensuring that perceptions are accurate. Finally, value your concessions in the other party's terms rather than your own.

6 *Bargain* – Central to negotiation is bargaining between the parties: 'If you do this . . . then I will do that.' In bargaining, unlike selling, everything is conditional – If you . . . then I . . . never give 'owt for nowt'. Likewise, do not match a proposal with a proposal. Research has shown that a person is least responsive to an idea when they have just put forward an idea of their own. A good negotiator listens to a proposal, acknowledges it, examines it and asks questions about it. They may then bargain on one or two points but not necessarily every one. When making a proposal, avoid too many points, features or advantages that may confuse the other party rather than increase conviction. If you ask salespeople whether there are any other advantages, they will in most cases find extra points to support their argument. Yet the skilled negotiator, well prepared, knows their own strengths and reinforces the argument rather than diluting it. Negotiate on only a few points but close only on the important ones.

7 *Close* – Negotiations must have some form of outcome and therefore agree your points, summarise your position but do not be aggressive.

8 *Agreement* – Don't just close, agree. Don't just agree, get commitment and if possible write out this commitment so there is no misunderstanding. While people may well shake hands on a deal, they may not interpret the deal in the same way. Get it in writing.

Good negotiating is never a substitute for selling, but if your customers are mostly repeat business on a contract or long-term basis, negotiating will be part of the process.

Did you know?

We can learn a lot from successful negotiators (Rackham, 1988):

Give signals to let the other party know your intentions, except when disagreeing, when you should act quickly.

Do not let misunderstanding occur. Test understanding by questions to get agreement and provide clarity.

Good negotiators understand the value of questions which provide information and control thinking rather than waffle.

Express feelings, which promotes trust and is more personal.

Don't use irritating words such as generous, fair and so on.

Do not be aggressive, and avoid spirals which escalate ending in acrimony. Behaviour breeds behaviour.

Counteract proposals by questions and problem-solving rather than by immediate alternative proposals.

Do not dilute your argument by adding on spurious plusses if asked for more reasons.

4.9   Contracts and tendering

A significant amount of business, and some very high value sales, is concluded as part of a contract or subject to a tendering process which has both legal and commercial implications. Contracts can be written, oral or a mixture of both. As with negotiation, it is advisable to have a written contract which avoids ambiguity and usually, although not always, to clarify the terms under which the transaction takes place. Building and construction projects, original equipment suppliers and government purchases are often conducted in this manner. Such a process may involve extensive prior negotiation, competitive and secret bidding and written and detailed quotations as part of the process. In the early stages, an open offer may be made by the purchaser inviting bids for the work or contract. In some cases, prequalification criteria may be set to limit the potential bidders and, if the process is likely to be expensive, may only invite a few, approved suppliers to tender for the work. Contracts which are large, high value and for complex work are best written, but even in one-off sales it is necessary for the company to protect itself from possible litigation. Terms and conditions of sales are therefore standard practice.

It is not the intention to cover legal aspects of contracts, but the sales manager needs to understand contracts and negotiations from a legal position as well as understanding issues concerned with the Trades Description Act, consumer protection, product liability and safety and rules governing promotional claims and finance arrangements. Furthermore, the sales manager has to ensure that sales and customer contact staff also know the rules, ignorance being no excuse under the law. A customer-driven company would generally only resort to legal action under exceptional conditions but in some areas, such as construction projects, disputes and contractual disagreements are the norm rather than the exception. In any business, staff need to know what they can and cannot offer customers and how to handle and resolve any disputes which do arise.

In particular, trades description acts and consumer protection and faulty goods legislation are important legal constraints. Furthermore, just because contracts or standard terms and conditions are printed on company stationary, it does not mean they are valid. Goods must be of merchantable quality, fit for purpose and in compliance with the description offered. Salespeople may be tempted to gloss over or exaggerate claims for their goods which are not supportable and the supplier may be liable for refund and/or compensation. On the other hand, the consumer may not be aware of differences in claims by suppliers. For example, a British Standard Kitemarked product (approved, tested and monitored by the British Standard Institute), a product made to BS specification and a product which meets the requirements of the relevant British Standard can be three different grades of product and reflect different quality performance. In the case of services, intangibility puts greater pressure on defining the product and its terms and conditions of sale. The need for additional consumer protection in financial services testifies to this problem. We will return to some of these legal and ethical issues in subsequent chapters.

Contract-based projects create their own set of sales management problems. For more comprehensive coverage of contracts and project marketing see Cova, Ghauri and Salle, 2002; Cova and Salle, 2006. Assuming that the marketing strategy has targeted certain types of business, by type, geography or other segmentation criteria, the initial problem may be to decide whether to go for all potential projects or whether and how to select the most likely to be successful and profitable. Resources may be wasted or diluted by submitting tenders or proposals with little chance of success. For example, one process company was achieving a success rate of orders to tenders of 1 in 8. The market leaders were achieving a 1 in 3 strike rate. On tenders taking several weeks labour time to prepare, this has a crucial effect on the cost base of the operation. The first priority is to analyse the market or market segment for the best and most profitable and appropriate prospects. The sales manager must then identify the best approach and the basis on which to bid for a contract. This requires detailed and painstaking work which solves the customer's problem in the most effective and cost-efficient manner, at the same time offering innovative and creative solutions. A difficult task. The preparation and presentation of proposals is also vital and requires high-level professionalism coupled with attention to detail. Furthermore, there may be extensive negotiation with a number of personnel from both sides, and the manager's job is to coordinate and mobilise staff in the appropriate way at the right time. This again emphasises the need for creating profitable relationships with customers. Those firms which work with their customers as part of the process will be more successful and more profitable (O'Toole, 1996).

4.10 Status of salespeople

One aspect of selling that is of concern to sales managers is the status of salespeople. Status is the relative standing of a person in a group and is measured by the prestige and esteem, real or perceived, that a person enjoys with associates. Today, occupation is a major determinant of status, replacing family background, ethnic origin and political affiliation. Surveys conducted among students, including business studies students, confirm selling jobs to be low occupational targets (Donaldson and Thomson, 1991). Many graduates seem to feel overqualified for selling jobs. Sales managers will have problems if the best people seek occupations other than selling and existing personnel may well be dissatisfied if the social standing of the job is low.

In a job context, power equates with authority or legitimate control over the behaviour of others. The responsibility without authority problem is apparent in many sales jobs, and salespeople must use their persuasive skills to coerce people to accede to their demands since the job itself does not legitimately enforce this. Some of these status problems result in higher staff turnover among salespeople and this is costly to the firm in recruitment costs, lost sales and goodwill. The best salespeople want to move into better jobs or selling better products with better companies. It appears that 'better' again equates with status. High achievers and sales performers may seek career moves from tangibles to intangibles, simple to complex, low-price merchandise to higher value goods. Indeed, selling is seen as temporary prior to promotion, prior to going into business alone or prior to getting a higher status job, for example, in a marketing/product manager capacity. Many salespeople are also prepared to trade income for status (Donaldson, 1998).

Selling careers can be viewed as positive in status by those less educated with no financial independence, and as a means to escape from manual occupations. Research evidence (Ditz, 1967) goes so far as to say that improved sales performance can be found from people who come from a social background which makes for strong status aspirations, where people have a need for achievement perhaps considered by others as unrealistic and compulsive and from people with insatiable ambition. Rather than take such analysis to unreasonable lengths, suffice it to say there is a need

- to increase the status of selling;
- to appeal to more qualified applicants;
- to reduce the cost of recruiting the 'wrong' people;
- to plan recruitment policies carefully.

4.11 Role conflict

The sales manager's primary task is to manage salespeople rather than sales. Since most sales managers are promoted from the ranks, they have an appreciation of the variety of problems that salespeople face. However, different attributes are now required for the management role, where key characteristics of good sales managers, such as a leader and a motivator, should now take precedence over selling skills. Some find this transition easier than others. Personal selling involves complex relationships with role partners. These partners include persons both within and outside the working environment who have a vested interest in how the salesperson performs in their job, including top management, the immediate supervisor, customers, family and the public at large. Relationships with these partners are dynamic, diverse and complex, requiring high-quality attributes in dealing with interpersonal situations. At times, contradictory elements will exist, resulting in what is termed 'role conflict'. The guidance given by management to subordinates on how to handle and resolve role conflicts will be a major influence on performance. Role conflicts exist in many jobs but are a major concern in sales positions where the salesperson operates on their own, deals at the boundary between different organisations and faces unique circumstances because there is no one best way of doing the job. These conflicts, together with other aspects of role behaviour, motivation and aptitude, affect the overall sales performance.

A salesperson's role stems from the activities or tasks that have to be performed and the behaviour required with role partners. The role concept is defined by the expectations, demands and pressures in dealing with role partners. The salesperson is susceptible to such pressures because of differing expectations by company and customers, by management and family, by their public attention. If these become incompatible, there is tension resulting in lower job satisfaction, which may influence job performance. It follows that sales managers must identify and anticipate potential or perceived conflicts and attempt to resolve them. For this reason, these issues will be considered again in both managing and motivating the sales force.

Specific problems that a salesperson may face in the job include

- the effects of the boundary position or 'pig in the middle': trying to serve two masters is a no-win situation involving compromise solutions;
- the effects of a large role set – salespeople have many points of contact and interfaces both within and external to the organisation;
- effects of a semi-innovative position with high visibility and low consensus.

The type of selling and the context in which the salesperson operates needs to be well understood. For example, those primarily involved in direct selling have to be efficient in the conventional sales process – contact, presentation, demonstration, overcoming objections and closing the sale. Energy, enthusiasm, empathy and drive are surely important. In other situations, the prospect's predisposition to buy and the similarity between buyer and seller may be more important. Such people strong on these traits may be less able to write reports, plan work and manage a territory if non-sales tasks are a significant part of the salesperson's role. Service-type salespeople need to be stronger in social skills, product knowledge and understanding of their customers.

4.12   Summary

The findings on the characteristics of successful salespeople are inconclusive. A priority list of desirable traits is frequently put forward but evidence of their worth is questionable. The best salespeople are those with the highest levels of product knowledge and the best communication skills, who understand their customers. In many cases, the ability to create and build lasting relationships with customers is a source of competitive advantage for the firm. The advice to sales managers is to recruit people who have the required orientation and skills or can be trained to be proficient. This is not the same as traits, intelligence, experience, age, sex, colour or any other similar factor. It is adequate intelligence, empathy and enthusiasm which are more important.

Questions

1   Given that many sales managers now accept that good salespeople are 'made' rather than 'born', does this mean personality and physical characteristics are no longer important in the type of salesperson employed?

2   Interview one (or more) salespeople to assess the characteristics they perceive to be important for their particular job.

3   What are the reasons for selling not being considered a more prestigious occupation?

4   Why might role clarity be a problem in selling jobs?

5   If your company is selling technical products to industrial markets, would you recruit engineers and train them to sell, or recruit those with proven selling skills and teach them technical expertise and product knowledge?

Case study

Clerical Medical

Clerical Medical (www.clericalmedical.co.uk), now part of the HBOS group, is one of the leading pension and investment companies in the financial services sector, arranging investment plans on behalf of their clients. As part of their evaluation of salespeople and in preparation for the training and managerial development of staff, they use a self-report questionnaire to be completed by new and existing staff. As a result of this a profile chart is compiled on the basis of the following:

Category	Dimensions (rated on a 1–10 scale)			
Assertive	Persuasive	Controlling	Independent	
Gregarious	Outgoing	Affilitative	Socially confident	
Empathy	Modest	Democratic	Caring	
Problem-solving	Practical	Data rational	Artistic	Behavioural
Radical	Traditional	Change-oriented	Conceptual	Innovative
Analytical	Forward planning	Detail-conscious	Conscientious	
Anxieties	Relaxed	Worrying		
Controls	Tough-minded	Emotional control	Optimistic	Critical
Energies	Active	Competitive	Achieving	Decisive

1   Critically appraise the elements in this questionnaire in terms of the characteristics and abilities that you feel are desirable in this selling job.

2   Which of the above dimensions do you feel a salesperson in this industry should score highly on?

3   What other information would you like to know if you were asked to select someone suitable for this type of job?

Key terms

- closing
- communication process
- contracts
- dominant–hostile behaviour
- ego drive
- empathy
- matching skills
- negotiation

- psychology of selling
- product knowledge
- relationship orientation
- role conflict
- self-esteem
- status
- submissive–warm behaviour

References

Bettger, F. (1949) *How I Raised Myself from Failure to Success in Selling* Prentice-Hall: Englewood Cliffs, NJ

Buzzotta, V.R., Lefton, R.E. and Sherberg, M. (1982) *Effective Selling Through Psychology* Ballinger: Cambridge, MA

Churchill, G.A., Ford, N.M., Hartley, S.W. and Walker, O.C. (1985) 'The determinants of salesperson performance: a meta-analysis' *Journal of Marketing Research* **XXII** (May): 103–18

Cova, B. and Salle, R. (2006) 'Introduction to the IMM special issue on Project Marketing and the marketing of solutions' *Industrial Marketing Management* doi:10.1016/j.indmarman. 2006.04.008

Cova, B., Ghauri, P. and Salle, R. (2002) *Project Marketing – beyond competitive bidding* John Wiley & Sons: Chichester

Crosby, L.A., Evens, R.K. and Cowles, D. (1990) 'Relationship quality in service selling: an interpersonal influence perspective' *Journal of Marketing* **54** (Jul): 68–81

Ditz, G.W. (1967) *Status problems of the salesman* MSU Business Topics Winter: 68–77

Donaldson, B. (1998) 'The importance of financial incentives in motivating industrial salespeople' *The Journal of Selling and Major Account Management* **1** (1): 4–16

Donaldosn, B. and O'Toole, T. (2002) *Strategic Market Relationships: from strategy to implementation* Wiley: Chichester

Donaldson, B. and Thomson, C. (1991) 'Recruiting graduates into sales: preparing Marketing for the New Millenium' *Proceedings of the 1991 Marketing Education Group*, Cardiff, pp. 340–53

Donaldson, B., Tzokas, N. and Saren, M. (1997) 'Project RELATOR: assessing the relationship orientation of salespeople' *Proceedings of 31st Annual Conference of the Academy of Marketing*, Manchester, pp. 1293–96

Dwyer, F.R., Schurr, P.H. and Oh, S. (1987) 'Developing buyer–seller relationships' *Journal of Marketing* **51** (2): 11–27

Greenberg, J. and Greenberg, H. (1976) 'Predicting sales success: myths and reality' *Personnel Journal* Dec: 621–7

Hakansson, H. (ed.) (1982) *International Marketing and Purchasing of Industrial Goods – an interaction approach* John Wiley & Sons: New York

Hayes, H.M. and Hartley, S.W. (1989) 'How buyers view industrial salespeople' *Industrial Marketing Management* **18** (1): 73–80

Heiman, A. and Muller, E. (1996) 'Using demonstration to increase new product acceptance: controlling demonstration time' *Journal of Marketing Research* **XXXIII** (Nov): 422–30

Hite, R.E. and Bellizzi, J.A. (1986) 'A preferred style of sales management' *Industrial Marketing Management* **15** (3): 215–23

Lamont, L.M. and Lundstrom, W.J. (1977) 'Identifying successful industrial salesmen by personality and personal characteristics' *Journal of Marketing Research* **XIV** (Nov): 517–29

Levitt, T. (1967) 'Communications and industrial selling' *Journal of Marketing* **31** (Apr): 15–21

Mayer, D. and Greenberg, H.M. (1964) 'What makes a good salesman?' *Harvard Business Review* **Jul–Aug**: 119–25

McCormack, M.H. (1995) *McCormack on Selling* Random House: London

O'Toole, T. (1996) *Relationship Governance: structure and performance in industrial markets.* Unpublished PhD thesis, University of Strathclyde, Glasgow

Plank, R.E. and Reid, D.A. (1994) 'The mediation role of sales behaviors: an alternative perspective on sales performance and effectiveness' *Journal of Personal Selling and Sales Management* **14** (3): 43–56

Rackham, N. (1987) *Making Major Sales* Gower: Aldershot

Rackham, N. (1988) *Account Strategy for Major Sales* Gower: Aldershot

Ramsey, R.P. and Sohi, R.S. (1997) 'Listening to your customers: the impact of perceived salesperson listening behavior on relationship outcomes' *Journal of the Academy of Marketing Science* **25** (2): 127–37

Ramsey, R., Lassk, F.G. and Marshall, G.W. (1995) 'A critical evaluation of a measure of job involvement: the use of the LODAHL and KEJNER (1965) scale with salespeople' *Journal of Personal Selling and Sales Management* **XV** (Summer): 65–74

Rochford, L. and Wotruba, T.R. (1993) 'New product development under changing economic conditions: the role of the salesforce' *Journal of Business and Industrial Marketing* **8** (3): 4–12

Sigaw, J.A. and Honeycutt, E.D. (1995) 'An examination of gender differences in selling behaviours and job attitudes' *Industrial Marketing Management* **24** (1): 45–52

Spiro, R.L. and Weitz, B.A. (1990) 'Adaptive selling: conceptualisation, measurement and nomological validity' *Journal of Marketing Research* **28** (Feb): 61–9

Sujan, H., Weitz, B.A. and Kumar, N. (1994) 'Learning orientation, working smart, and effective selling' *Journal of Marketing* **58** (July): 39–52

Tack, A. (1989) *Increase Your Sales the Tack Way* Gower: Aldershot

Walker, O.C., Churchill, G.A. and Ford, N.M. (1977) 'Motivation and performance in industrial selling: present knowledge and needed research' *Journal of Marketing Research* **XIV** (May): 156–68

Weitz, B.A., Sujan, H. and Sujan, M. (1986) 'Knowledge, motivation and adaptive behaviour: a framework for improving selling effectiveness' *Journal of Marketing* **50** (Oct): 174–91

Wernerfelt, B. (1996) 'Efficient marketing communication: helping the customer learn' *Journal of Marketing Research* **XXXIII** (May): 239–46

Part II

The selling process (The mobilisation of resources behind a customer)

5 Sales force organisation

5.1 Overview

In addition to establishing corporate and marketing strategy and formulating sales force objectives, one of the important tasks of management is organising selling effort. Before addressing the problem and the factors which influence management choice in organisational structure, two issues must be addressed and evaluated: first, the principles of organisational theory and practice as they relate to the sales force, and second, a re-examination of the role of salespeople in achieving sales, marketing and corporate objectives. Increasingly, new technology such as the Internet and telemarketing are forcing sales managers to reappraise the role of personal selling and how their function is organised. Nevertheless, decisions have to be taken on various dimensions of the organisational problem, such as the type of organisational structure, the degree of specialisation, the size of the sales force and how to deploy them.

5.2 Learning objectives

- to understand the principles of good organisational design and the difficulty with implementation in a sales context;
- to consider different types of sales force structure;
- to evaluate methods for calculating sales force size;
- to assess issues in sales territory deployment and prescribe sound principles for territory management.

5.3 Definitions

Agents are firms or individuals acting on behalf of another.

Telesales is the use of inbound and outbound telephone communication for the purposes of making and servicing a sale.

Sales territory is an area of responsibility for an individual or team of salespeople in which to develop sales.

5.4 Principles of organisation

Drucker (1968) suggested that 'Good organisation structure does not by itself produce good performance . . . but a poor organisation structure makes good performance impossible'. Consider how an organisation, in particular the sales organisation, may evolve from its inception as a small business to its maturity as a large organisation. This example, for an industrial product, should help to show the nature of the problems that sales managers face in organising selling effort and add realism by referring to a dynamic situation which demonstrates a means of applying the theory and principles discussed in this chapter.

In stage one (Figure 5.1), a business emerges, the owner acting as managing director employing a small workforce. Lines of communication are short and direct, with few organisational problems. As a result of product acceptability in the market, a period of rapid growth is experienced. Salespeople are employed to inform and persuade customers and distributors of the product's acceptability.

Problems begin to emerge with the control of operations, including the sales force, whose main task is to service intermediaries to sell on the product to users (Figure 5.2).

Further growth occurs both from internal expansion and by integration with other companies and a more formal structure now emerges to cope with the size of this business. Absolute size is still increasing, but the growth rate slows to a more moderate level. Salespeople sell to intermediaries but are increasingly expected to secure orders with specifiers and users of the product to protect the market share against competitors (Figure 5.3).

Fig 5.1 New business

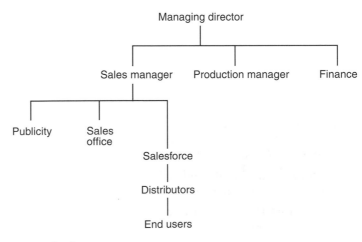

Fig 5.2 New business growth phase

Finally, the organisation, now with a 50-strong sales force, is established in the market. Growth, however, is comparatively low while sales costs have increased. Problems arise in maintaining control in a diverse multi-product organisation. The result is the organisation structure shown in Figure 5.4. At this stage, sales force organisation problems often depend on particular circumstances such as market conditions, product acceptability or competitive pressures. Consideration of organisational theory and the specific role of selling provides some help with this problem.

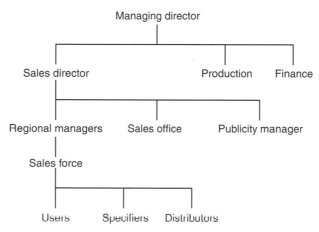

Fig 5.3   **Business maturity**

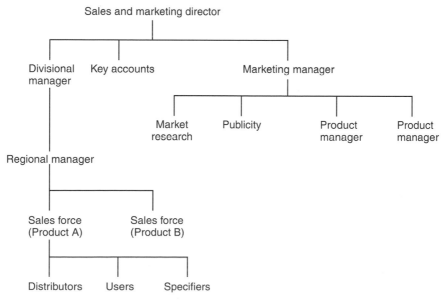

Fig 5.4   **Large organisation**

First, let us consider organisational theory. There are six concepts which are desirable in any organisation:

1 *Organisational structure* should be marketing-oriented. The previous example showed that, in a small company, the need to serve and service customers is fundamental, although resources may limit what can be done. Senior management in larger organisations become distanced from their customers, sometimes losing the close contact necessary for true marketing orientation. There is a danger as size increases of organising to suit the company's internal requirements or convenience rather than that of the customer. Such moves should be resisted at all levels and functions, and it is particularly crucial that this does not happen in the sales force.

2 Organisations should be designed for *activities* rather than people. The raison d'être of organising is to perform tasks, not to accommodate people, and management's task is to specify what is to be done by whom rather than who is available to do what. This is a more common problem in sales organisations where frequent changes in structure occur, the result being that jobs are created for certain people rather than people for the identified jobs.

3 *Delegation of authority* and defined *responsibility*. The rule here would be that the more authority and responsibility that can be delegated to subordinates, the more involved and committed individuals will be to the organisation. The size and complexity of the sales force will affect the ease and practicality with which this can be accomplished. It is, for example, easier to delegate pricing responsibilities to a stable sales force of five than to a more transient sales force of 50 with a turnover of 10 per cent, some of whom may join a competing firm. While such problems can never be resolved without some compromise, the job description in writing should convey clearly the extent of an individual's responsibility and authority. In this respect, management has a duty to allow salespeople to be more professional and more involved in the management activities of their firm.

4 Reasonable *span of control*. Much debate is given to define numbers which equate with 'reasonable'; somewhere between four and ten appears to be the consensus. The actual number will vary depending on the ability of the supervisor, the ability of the subordinate and the nature of the work. Certainly, a span of control such as 1:1 or in excess of 10:1 creates problems for both superior and subordinate. A shorter span of control has been found to reduce role ambiguity and may have a bearing on sales performance (Bagozzi, 1980).

5 Organisations should be *stable* and *flexible*. Internal pressures attempt to routinise and systemise activities in the interests of cost efficiency, but this can be myopic if the result is customer alienation. Firms who need to establish customer service departments may be exhibiting symptoms of this malaise since, by definition, other departments must be failing in customer care and liaison. Stability is necessary to ensure continuing viable operating conditions and procedures which are efficient, together with flexibility to enable the enterprise to adjust to dynamic market conditions or particular customer or competitive circumstances.

6 Organisations should be *balanced* and *coordinated* in the activities to be performed. As with the aims of stability and flexibility, so too the aims of balance and coordination of activities will tend to conflict rather than naturally complement each other.

One of the skills in management is to resolve differences, unifying the operations and personnel within complex organisations. This is more likely to be achieved where there is a unified purpose or corporate culture, where these principles of good organisation are considered and implemented and care and effort are given to the recruitment, training and motivation of employees.

A second issue to be addressed before deciding on the type and size of the sales force organisation is the role of salespeople in achieving marketing objectives together with the tasks that the sales force are expected to perform. The use of agents versus a direct sales operation, and the variations in types of selling, certainly impinge on, if not dictate, salesforce organisation decisions. Perhaps even more fundamental is to decide whether the sales force is the best or only way of achieving marketing objectives vis-à-vis using more automated ways of doing business.

5.5 Inside versus outside sales

Perhaps for too long we have been looking in a rather simplistic way at the activities and attributes of the individual salesperson rather than the sales function (Williams and Plouffe, 2006). A useful way to consider the decision is to compare both efficiency and effectiveness (Zoltners *et al.*, 2004). Generally, where products are easy to understand, accounts are small and activities are of moderate complexity and value, then the need for personal face-to-face contact will be less, and more efficient customer contact methods will be required. As the Dell example in Chapter 1 showed, where the reverse is the case then higher levels of personal selling will be required. Of course, sales managers want to do both by increasing efficiency and improving effectiveness. One way of achieving such gains may be to use an outside sales force, and it is to this issue we now turn.

Agents versus own sales force

Sales agents are independent businesses rather than employees of the company. They are given sales concessions, usually exclusively, to sell products and services in a given domain in geographic or product exclusive areas. Unlike wholesalers, they take neither ownership nor physical possession of the product and operate usually on a commission-only basis, although a retainer may sometimes be paid. Companies who used independent sales agents were traditionally considered to lack the resources to maintain their own sales force or were involved in import/export or in sales regions such as the Highlands of Scotland or Northern Ireland which did not seem to justify full-time salespeople. Increasingly, agents are recruited for their specialist market knowledge or their technical or sales competence. Changes and developments in food-brokers, franchise systems and independent sales agencies demand a rethink on the organisational choice of sales structure. There are several factors to consider, such as

- company resources;
- market potential;
- industries where agents may be the normal modus operandi;

- where one product complements other products from different manufacturers;
- where local market knowledge is important.

It is usually recommended to use an internal sales force where close control over the selling situation is required, goodwill to the company is important, detailed order-stocking or technical knowledge is required or special attention to specific groups is required (e.g. missionary selling and systems selling). Customer acceptance of agents may be a problem, for example, with government departments. Apart from cost, agents are used for their industry knowledge, professionalism and customer contacts. In economic downturns, cutting costs and overheads make independents a more realistic alternative where revenues and costs are directly related. The decision on whether to use outside agents or employ the company's own sales force has been researched by Anderson (1985). He tested several hypotheses and found that companies were more likely to use their own direct sales force where

- the greater the investment of company-specific resources (plant, equipment, promotional expense and so on) in a market;
- the more difficult it was to evaluate sales performance;
- the higher the combination of environmental uncertainty and transaction specific assets;
- the more favourable the price–quality combination, that is, the more attractive the product line;
- the greater the importance of non-selling activities (advice, service and so on).

Some characteristics, such as travel time, company size and nature of the goods, were less important in the decision than was predicted. The conclusion is that, while almost any marketing function can be contracted out to agents, there are circumstances in which it is imprudent to do so. Furthermore, it is wrong to think that sales managers can abdicate their responsibilities merely by using independents. Whether independent agents or company-owned salespeople, there is still a need for a coherent sales strategy, detailed sales plans and a need to train and motivate. In some respects, the motivation problem is not only different but also greater with independents.

Telesales

Another approach is to reduce costs by employing telesales people. While this approach is more efficient it is not necessarily less effective and such is its importance that we deal with telemarketing and call centres again in Chapter 6. Today telesales people tend to use multiple methods to communicate with customers and prospects including direct mail, e-mail and the Internet. It is generally acknowledged that telesales can make up to five times the number of contacts that an outside salesperson can achieve, and the cost is about half. Telesales overcome the problems of geographical distance and time since they can be used, if required, 24 hours per day, 7 days per week.

The decision on the use and extent of telephone usage is best considered in terms of the sales process. For presales the telephone can generate and qualify new leads as a precursor to a salesperson visit. Telesales can also handle information requests and schedule and make field sales appointments. During the sales stage, the telephone can be used to take orders and to offer advice and service support. Linked to an efficient computerised system, it should be possible to have on-screen customer information, in real time, of the order and delivery status, credit and other details of that customer. In the post-sales stage telephone back-up can provide technical and other service support for the customer to enhance their customer satisfaction.

Did you know?

A CARR report in 2001 found

- inside telesales, e-mail and direct mail accounted for 20 per cent of business to business sales;
- 57 per cent of telephone customers and 62 per cent of personal sales contacts make a purchase;
- the average sales value of face-to-face selling is up to five times more valuable than telephone sales;
- customers speak with an average 4.6 salespeople on the telephone per week but only 1.8 contacts in person.

(Source: Quoted in Zoltners et al., 2004, p. 195)

Relationship selling

Today it is necessary to consider using multi-channel routes to market and how the sales function can be integrated to maximum effect. Our research (Tzokas and Donaldon, 2000) in this area suggests that as a result of new technology, more demanding and expert customers and increasing competition, salespeople with direct, face-to-face contact with customers have a role to play in enhancing customer value. As a result, the sales job has become more strategic and requires a greater range of skills and abilities than hitherto. How this enhanced value is produced and delivered, how it is perceived by customers and how it affects the long-term performance of the organisation is the challenge for the modern sales manager.

What do you think?

IBM (www.ibm.com) is a fine example of opportunity management. As an IT director of a medical company put it to us in our research, the IBM salesperson was able to add value by providing a solution to his problem. The product supplied by the medical company was of relatively low unit value but crucial to operating theatres in hospitals. The IBM representative was able to bring in a company specialist, with experience in bar coding grocery products, to provide a similar solution for the pharmaceutical company. By linking the product to computerised stock control the product was always available when and where required. For the medical company the result is increased sales and few out-of-stock situations. For IBM they were able to offer other pharmaceutical companies a similar solution. Both the alertness of the salesperson to solve the customer's problem and the ability of the organisation 'to mobilise company resources behind customer solutions' provides a clear win-win situation.

Customer value will be enhanced if organisations consider three core issues. First, the relationship process. Customers perceive value in relationships and the role of salespeople multi-dimensionally, and we identified specific activities that salespeople need to undertake in order to increase customer value. These include respecting the priorities of the customer, enhancing the technical competence image of the firm and making promises that not only the supplying firm will keep but also seem 'sensible' in the eyes of the buyer. Being aware of the financial constraints and cost drivers of their customers also enhances the esteem of the salesperson in the eyes of the buyer, and salespeople need to look for ways to 'surprise the customer'.

Second, relationship selling behaviours. Results suggest that salespeople need to acquire new skills and competencies in order to perform in their role as relationship 'gatekeepers'. In short, these skills suggest that salespeople need to develop conceptual, managerial abilities, which, in the past, were associated with the middle and top-level management of the firm. In addition, they need to change their mentality from selling products and services to supporting competitive advantage and career paths of their customers, and from simply capitalising upon product and service characteristics to promoting differentiators emanating from the existing and planned competencies and capabilities of their firm. As such they need to understand their customers business and that of their own firm to a much greater extent than before. Furthermore, they need to develop the ability to 'orchestrate' their firm's capabilities for 'matching' a feasible promised offer with an objective, which is mutually agreed with the customer.

Finally, organisational support for salespeople. Management must provide support for their salespeople as shown in Figure 5.5.

We found three interrelated directions of this support, namely: educating internal personnel and changing processes in their own firms, educating and changing salespeople's behaviour and educating and changing customers' perceptions. Overall, we found evidence that both customers and suppliers recognise the need to mutually support the new role of salespeople. This joint recognition stems from the appreciation that contemporary salespeople operate in an extremely complex selling environment. To perform effectively in this environment they should be provided with greater access to the internal, yet previously remote, aspects of their own and customers' firms.

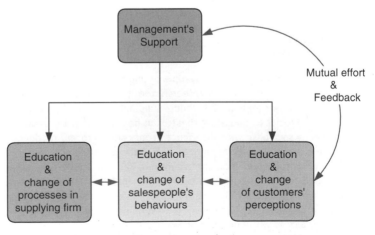

Fig 5.5 Management's support for relationships

The former requires changes in the training they receive and skills they develop, whilst the latter involves close collaboration with the customer and development of trust, honesty, commitment and continuous evidence of value creation. It is important to note here that in the cases of the suppliers we examined, the need was apparent for tools that can assist them to

■ evaluate the relationship orientation skills and capabilities of their existing salespeople and those to be recruited in the future;

■ qualify the relationship propensity of their customers (qualification of existing and potential customers was found extremely important to the effectiveness and efficiency of their salespeople).

Similar findings of this enhanced role for the salesperson have emerged from other studies such as the notion of entrepreneurial selling (Rackham and DeVincentis, 1998); precision selling (Zoltners *et al.*, 2004); consultative selling (Futrell, 2001) and key account management (KAM) (Millman and Wilson, 1995), strategic account management (SAM) and global account management (GAM) (Wilson, Speare and Samual, 2003).

5.6 Traditional types of sales force organisation

Sales managers have the task of determining how sales force effort should be allocated to specific sales tasks, to groups of customers, to geographical regions or to specific products or product groups. Traditionally, organisational solutions have been based on one of the following approaches:

Geography

Geographical specialisation is the traditional and most widely used type of sales organisation in British industry. In this type of structure, each salesperson is responsible for all tasks, all products and all existing and prospective customers within a geographical area. It is most appropriate in larger rather than smaller organisations, where there is a widely spread customer base rather than only a few, where regional variations are more important than national standards and where personal contact between buyer and seller is frequent rather than occasional. The advantages of a geographical split are likely to be that travel time and expense are less. Each salesperson can build good customer and area knowledge, which is itself a motivating factor in that salespeople manage their territory. There is less confusion since multiple calling on a single customer is avoided and customers know who is their point of contact. Finally, management control and evaluation are more easily administered. These advantages are important but reference has already been made to the complexity of today's selling job and the dynamics of the business environment. The need to specialise in product or customer, the need to use experts to meet customers' needs and the problem of using low-level personnel for key management decisions does exist. Furthermore, while control is straightforward, overhead costs may rise as more layers of management evolve (see Figure 5.4 above).

Product

Product specialisation would appeal where a company has product lines which differ in technical complexity, end user and profitability. Each salesperson can then attain the necessary expertise in product knowledge to handle different customer requirements more effectively. Companies who take over or merge with others sometimes continue to operate separate sales forces. Also, the case for expertise with a new product may require specialist development salespeople. With this type of organisation, problems arise with duplication of effort and multiple calling on one customer. This requires management to promote cooperation between salespeople with minimum conflict and confusion over who does what job.

Market

Implementation of the marketing concept would suggest that the most appropriate form of specialisation is that based on the customer. Where market segmentation policies can be applied, it is sensible to operate the sales force specialising in the respective segments. Grouping of customers into suitable classifications means that salespeople can develop customer expertise and implement marketing policy and programmes. This process can also work in reverse where knowledge of customers' customers can be used as a basis for differentiation (Smith and Owens, 1995). In dynamic, innovative markets, the information exchange process may require this form of specialism. In other cases, too much specialisation will result in excessively high selling costs.

Combination

The advantages and disadvantages of the three previous methods encourage many firms to seek combination systems of organisation which merge the benefits of specialisation with reduced selling costs. The increasing complexity of the selling job in dynamic, changing markets gives impetus to this organisational dilemma.

Figure 5.6, a pharmaceutical firm and Figure 5.7 a telecom company, show two innovative approaches to organising sales effort. Whichever approach is adopted it should incorporate the six concepts desirable in a sales organisation outlined earlier in the chapter and reflect the many specific factors affecting the firm operating in its environment.

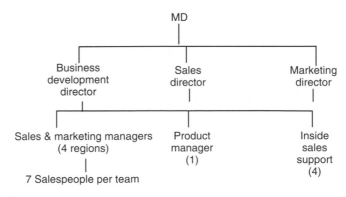

Fig 5.6   **Pharmaceutical company**

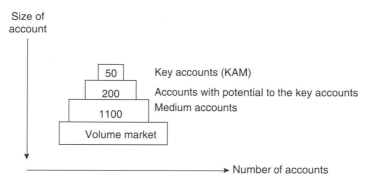

Size of
account

50   Key accounts (KAM)
200   Accounts with potential to the key accounts
1100 Medium accounts
Volume market

→ Number of accounts

Fig 5.7   Telecom company

No one organisational solution can fit all nor can it remain unchanged over time. For example, a product–market combination may be operated by separate divisions, groups or product managers as well as separate sales forces. A market organisation may split customers into key accounts, by different channel members or by industry type and is best served by multiple sales teams. There is no doubt in several markets, particularly food, DIY and household goods, that the disproportionate effect of major customers' control on the market necessitates specialist sales treatment. This in turn affects the job to be done by salespeople at branch level. A separate merchandising sales force may be used to call on branches rather than to sell to buyers. In some markets, such as office equipment, a junior sales force establishes contact and evaluates prospects. Similarly, an inside sales force or telemarketing operation may be used to complement the outside sales force for specific tasks. It should be borne in mind that, despite the theories, concepts and principles of organisation which can assist sales management to establish the 'one-best' system, marketing and sales management decisions apply in a dynamic and uncertain environment. As such, numerous diverse influences have to be considered in any organisational proposal and changing the way in which the sales force is deployed can provide an opportunity to increase sales force productivity.

5.7   Determining sales force size

It should now be accepted that problems in sales management are complex and solutions seldom permanent. In determining sales force size, the temptation to look for a simple, universal formula should be avoided. The type of sales organisation will affect the size of the sales force, particularly the degree of specialisation considered appropriate. The nature of the selling task between development and service selling will be fundamental. Other aspects of the selling task will be affected by the time required to be spent on activities such as

■ demonstration presentation;

■ negotiating on price;

■ explaining company policy;

- providing information on competitors and customers;
- dealer support programmes;
- stock-checking;
- display work;
- complaint handling;
- credit problems;
- prospecting for new business;
- report-writing.

These activities should be included as part of the salesperson's job description to reflect their importance to the firm. This importance will in turn affect whether 6 or 16 calls per day are possible. Questions about sales force size will also depend on company objectives, company resources and competitive or other environmental factors. Issues on sales force size cannot be divorced from the form of organisation, the method of specialising or territory allocation. With these concepts in mind, three methods of determining sales force size will be considered.

Workload method

The workload method is a composite figure made up from the total work time available, the allocation of this time to sales tasks and the time spent with each customer or prospect. It is usually based on the sales revenue per account. It is the most commonly used technique in UK sales management and calculated as follows:

(i) Determine the total work time available by each salesperson. This is likely to be a maximum of 35 hours per week × 46 weeks (excluding holiday) = 1610 hours.

(ii) Determine the work time allocated to selling activities. A salesperson's time may consist of

travel	25%
food and breaks	12%
waiting	15%
selling tasks	30%
administration	18%

Selling time available is 1610 ×30% = 483 hours.

(iii) Classify customers on the basis of sales volume potential or profitability. This might be, for example,

A – large accounts, say	500
B – medium accounts, say	2000
C – small accounts, say	4000

(iv) Decide on the appropriate length of call and call frequency per account type. On average this might be:

Type A – 60 minutes per call every 2 weeks
Type B – 30 minutes per call every 4 weeks
Type C – 15 minutes per call every 8 weeks

(v) Calculate the company workload to meet the required calls:
    A = 500 × 60 mins × 24 calls per year = 12,000 hours
    B = 2,000 × 30 mins × 12 calls per year = 12,000 hours
    C = 4,000 × 15 mins × 6 calls per year = 6000 hours
    TOTAL = 30,000 hours

(vi) Calculate the number of salespeople required:
    30,000/483 = approximately 62 salespeople

With this approach, each salesperson should have a similar workload in terms of size of accounts, number of calls and travel time. It is rarely the case that accounts can be distributed evenly so that travel time in some areas will inevitably be much greater than in others. Other weaknesses in this approach may be that larger accounts may not be those with the highest potential in the future. If potential is used, these may not be the most profitable if costs of servicing the account are higher or a less profitable product mix is taken. The most serious problem is the simplistic assumption that quantity equals quality. Each account and each salesperson will be different in quality, a factor not incorporated in this method. Put simply, different call frequencies (and time per call) may yield higher sales and profits.

Sales potential method

In this method, an estimate is made of sales potential for the company's products (sales forecast) based on management objectives and a desirable market share. If each salesperson performs to their job description, an average productivity level per person can be calculated. Some allowance should be made for the loss of someone leaving, for example, 10 per cent per annum, and the sales force size can be calculated using the formula

$$N = \frac{S}{P} + T\left(\frac{S}{P}\right)$$

or

$$N = \frac{S}{P} + \left(\frac{S \times T}{P}\right)$$

This is the same as

$$N = \frac{S}{P} \times \left(1 + T\right)$$

where N = number of salespeople
    S = sales forecast
    P = productivity level per person
    T = turnover rate in sales force

Assuming that S = £20 million, T is 10 per cent and P is £500,000, the sales force size can be calculated as
    20/0.5 × (1 + 0.10) = 40 × 1.1 = 44 people

Part of the problem with this method is the accuracy in estimating each variable, particularly P (productivity) and the accuracy of T (turnover) where the lead time in recruitment, the effect of lost sales and the desired level of productivity per person will vary. Also, it assumes a rather static market position when most companies will experience growing or declining sales productivity and perhaps regional variations within an overall sales forecast.

Incremental method

In order to overcome weaknesses in both the previous methods, the incremental method is suggested. Intuitively, this makes good business sense since the sales force should be expanded if additional sales revenue exceeds additional costs. The difficulty of estimating incremental revenues and costs can be quite daunting. This formula oversimplifies the economics of selling by assuming that the product mix is uniform and extraneous factors can be correctly assessed in advance for each area. The costs of selecting, recruiting or dismissing salespeople can seldom be accurately predicted. Other forms of promotion, such as advertising, may have unequal effects on different prospects. The simplicity of sales responding to personal selling effort where all other factors are constant is not tenable. The dynamic nature of markets, coupled with economic growth or decline patterns, distorts the calculations of the effectiveness of salespeople in terms of a sales response function. Seasonal, cyclical and competitive fluctuations create market uncertainty with a possible danger of overstaffing leading to cost inefficiencies. Companies may compound these problems by adding salespeople as long as profits are positive, that is,

$$S(P) - C > 0$$

where S = sales volume; P = profit margin on sales; and C = cost of maintaining salesperson.

The important weakness here is that salespeople become the result of sales rather than the creators of sales. Furthermore, it fails to take account of the effects of differing abilities, knowledge, skills and aptitudes of salespeople.

Consideration of these three methods should confirm that no one method will be perfect in establishing sales force size. The dynamics of the marketing environment increase the complexity of this problem. The best solution will be one which incorporates individual time and territory considerations as well as organisational expediency. Shapiro (1979) suggested that a rational process for structuring a sales organisation should follow a six-step process:

1　Analyse the needs which the organisation must meet. Remember that organisations should be based on tasks to be accomplished. A clear statement of sales strategy should be specified. The customers to be approached, call frequency and selling tasks help to focus the organisational purpose.

2　Structure the sales force at the bottom level. This way, the organisation will be designed to manage the sales force rather than the sales force being designed to fit a management structure.

3　Once the salesperson-level structure is established, keep shifts to the management level. This is because the basic level is task-oriented – the prime purpose of the organisation.

4　Integrate units and staff support into the structure. If possible, this can be done concurrently but not prior to previous levels.

5   Develop control systems (measurement, evaluation and rewards) to support the organisation structure.

6   Allocate people to fit the job to be done.

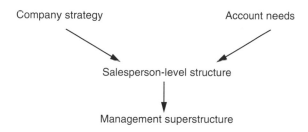

Shapiro points out two problems occurring in operationalising this process. First, implementation has to follow marketing decisions on the role of personal selling in the marketing mix since these decisions determine objectives. The second problem is that organisations are seldom formed from scratch on a blank sheet. Most decisions concern restructuring, which is often costly, unpalatable or both.

5.8   Territory management

Territory management is one aspect of sales management and a key determinant of organisation, performance and control. It would be wrong to isolate organisation, especially sales force size, from territory management or to suggest that suitable territories can be determined and evaluated without studying other determinants of performance, such as salesperson ability, distribution, economic conditions or marketing effectiveness. A related problem is to establish which comes first – the sales territory or the sales. Interaction effects between sales force size and design plague measurement of the disparate elements which contribute to sales performance.

Sales territories are established to facilitate effective sales force operations. This is achieved by allocating a number of present and potential customers to a particular salesperson within a given area, usually, but not always, a geographical area. The reasons for establishing territories and the basis for their allocation can vary greatly. It is not always the case that sales territories are necessary or desirable. Reasons for not having territories may be where selling is to friends or social contacts or through referrals from existing clients, such as many life insurance or financial investment companies use. Other reasons for not having territories may be where the market is small, the customers few or the sales force size itself does not justify such divisions. If information is not readily available about prospects, or where the acceptability of a new product is not yet known, management may want to withhold the establishment of territories until the position is clarified.

Most companies do establish territories for one or more of the following reasons:

■ To gain thorough coverage of the market. Territories permit identification of existing and prospective customers in a given area, thus reducing the possibility of missing business or duplicating calls, which can create excessive travelling time.

■ To define the salesperson's responsibilities more accurately and specifically, if possible, by account name, number and call frequency.

■ As a means of performance evaluation. Sales against the previous period, against the plan or against some measure of potential is both easier and more specific within a defined territory. The sales manager can in turn make comparisons between territories, which may in itself suggest improvements for all sales force personnel.

■ To improve customer relations. Salespeople with a specified territory can learn more about their customers and build up rapport with them through regular contact, itself a possible source of time-saving. However, the possibility of overcalling or time wasting on too many courtesy calls should also be avoided.

■ To reduce selling expense. Travel and expenses are much less in a given sales territory. For this reason, most companies would insist that salespeople live in their territory.

■ To match selling effort to fit customer's needs. This may be for parochial reasons such as a knowledge of local conditions or customs. Again, similarity between the salesperson and prospect may be important.

■ To help the salesperson. This facilitates coordination with other functions of the business, specific marketing and publicity effort while contributing in a positive way to the morale and motivation of salespeople whose job is enhanced by being managers of a territory.

The most compelling of all reasons is that territories facilitate implementing the marketing concept by contributing to better identification of customer needs and permitting more suitable actions to satisfy those needs. However, consideration of the new types of selling outlined in Chapter 3 and referred to earlier in this chapter suggest that new, innovative approaches are required for 'the territory management problem'. Again, we will compare the traditional approach to sales territory design with some new, innovative ideas.

Traditional sales territory design

The generally agreed procedure for establishing sales territories follows a five-stage process:

Stage 1: Selecting the basic unit

The starting point for defining suitable territories would be on the basis of economic planning regions or possibly television areas. The inequalities of population, income and industry spread do not necessarily make this equal in terms of potential. Where possible, the smaller the start unit, the better, since sales areas can then be built up from a compilation of more equal districts. Market characteristics, the distribution systems and the particular standing of the company are likely to have more influence than simple geographical lines.

Stage 2: Evaluating accounts and sales potential

The market information system should provide the necessary input to assist in this decision. Where there is accurate market and customer information, the compilation of territories should be relatively easier. This means listing all potential into categories such as unqualified lead, existing, past or potential customer. The advantage of a computerised system is the ability to select potential accounts by a relevant characteristic very rapidly. Information can also be stored on account status, value and prospects. Most firms use some form of A B C classification of accounts: A = most important, B = average importance, C = least important.

Stage 3: Analysing salesperson workload

Salesperson workload is an estimate of the time and effort required to cover a geographical territory. This means the number of accounts of different types, the frequency of calls required, the time at each call, the travel time between each call plus other time spent on non-selling activities. To suggest that workload is a matter of arithmetic disguises the complexity of the problem. Consider some of the difficulties which can arise in calculating the workload figure:

- The type of selling. Salespeople may be involved in developing and establishing an account, which requires on average much more time than servicing existing accounts. Calls may have to be made on several people in each account; in others, only the buyer needs to be seen. Some types of selling require more missionary or development work while in others extensive merchandising activity may be required.

- The type of product. Fast-moving consumer goods require less explanation or demonstration than more technical products. Business is repeated on a regular, mostly routine pattern. Certain industrial products or speciality goods require more explanation of benefits, requiring more time per call.

- The newness of product or market. With market or product development, more time per call and lower sales per account are expected than with existing products or accounts. Each account has to be built up over time. More accounts mean a higher workload in a developing territory than for the equivalent sales in an established territory.

Did you know?

Call rates vary across product categories

Product category	Average calls per day
Office stationary	20
Repeat consumer goods	10
Durable/intermediate	6
Repeat industrial	6
Capital equipment	4
Services	6
All	6

■ The market share, standing and competitiveness of the firm in the territory. If the competition is well established, the salesperson's task per account is more difficult, usually more time consuming. Most firms enjoy a stronger market share in their own locality and the salesperson's task is considerably harder in other more distant regions. Other salespeople may be more successful, but this may be due to the effectiveness of distributors in that territory rather than to individual selling skills.

Stage 4: Designing basic territories

The objective in this stage is to establish the sales potential for one salesperson in a given area. This must in turn relate to sales force objectives. As with sales forecasts, two different approaches can be used: the build-up method and the breakdown method. The build-up method is similar to the workload method for establishing sales force size described in the previous chapter. The procedures are

1 Establish the number, size and location of customers, including current, past and prospective accounts. If desired, these accounts can be graded and grouped on a suitable basis such as size or whatever segmentation criteria may be used by the company.

2 Determine the number of calls per account, the time required at each and the call frequency.

3 Calculate how many accounts can be handled by each salesperson. The use of some A B C classification may be helpful. In particular, there will be an average number of calls per day, an average frequency and, if possible, an average allocation of selling time which can be calculated.

4 Draw boundary lines around a realistic load per person commensurate with the geographical base unit. For example, one salesperson covering all of Scotland might be more realistic despite not having exactly the same average as other sales areas.

Did you know?

Average time allocation

	Hours per day	% of time
Pre-call preparation	1	10
Driving and parking, waiting	2–4	20+
Face-to-face selling	2	20
Non-selling, e.g. display	2	20
Administration reports	1	10
Lunch and breaks	1	10
Telephone, meetings, others	1	10
Total	10	100

The build-up method can be calculated using a computerised information system. Customer knowledge from data acquired through sales calls can be used to maintain a customer information file. It does, however, require up-to-date accurate information on accounts and the assumption that sales performance can be standardised to get the right outcome. These assumptions are often difficult to justify. Alternatively, management can adopt the breakdown method for territory planning. Given a countrywide assessment of market potential and target share, the sales potential can be estimated. This estimate then has to be allocated to the number of salespeople available (or to be recruited). Each salesperson is then allocated accounts which equalise workload and potential. Realistic geographical boundaries can then be drawn. The difficulty with this approach is that, when sales potential is equalised, workload will vary and geographical boundaries may be unrealistic. The problems of different market conditions and the varying effectiveness of distributors combine to complicate this rather simplistic approach.

Good territory design is achieved where

- territories are easy to administer;
- sales potential is relatively easy to estimate;
- travel time and expenses are minimised;
- equal sales opportunity is provided across customers and prospects;
- workload is equalised.

Stage 5: Assigning salespeople to territories

When territories have been established, the task of assigning individuals to a territory must be completed. Salespeople vary in knowledge, ability and skills, making some people more effective than others. The evidence suggests that matching salespeople to customers is important but many factors contribute to the effectiveness of salespeople. Management's task is to prioritise these variables in search of an improvement, if not an optimum solution. Variations in ability as well as the desire or inclination for individuals to move to other territories may create less than optimum but at least workable compromises.

Improving time and territory management

Geographical improvement

The high proportion of time that salespeople spend travelling is an obvious area in which to look for time-saving. Whether this saving can be achieved by management-imposed routes is more doubtful, except in the most routine forms of selling, such as the delivery salesperson or merchandiser. The widespread adoption of satellite navigation systems is an obvious help in avoiding wasting time on incorrect routes. The advantages of a properly designed system will be lower costs, improved territory coverage and better communication between management and salespeople and between salespeople and customers.

The first way in which time can be saved is by utilising the most appropriate shape pattern for the territory. Three possibilities are

1 *the circle system*, which is useful when customers are of similar size and type, being evenly distributed: the salesperson's base should be as near the centre as possible (Figure 5.8); variations within this enable a mix of size and type of call to be planned, together with a reduction of journey time;

2 *the hopscotch system*, which might help to reduce overall journey times if the distance from home is great; that is, travel to the furthest point and work back (Figure 5.9);

3 *the petal system*, which establishes a minimum working time, for example, a day's or week's work, the journey time being minimised (Figure 5.10).

Within these overall shapes, more efficient routes are sometimes possible as the features of motorways and call schedules are adjusted. In Figure 5.10, the route shown by the dotted line is shorter than the route shown by the continuous line. It is almost certain that a more efficient route could be found for an existing sales call pattern on a given territory. However, the difficulty of not calling on one customer in the same area as another may be considered rude rather than efficient. Extra travelling to some calls may yield higher sales than more calls.

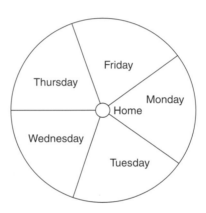

Fig 5.8   The circle system

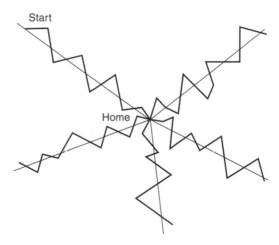

Fig 5.9   The hopscotch system

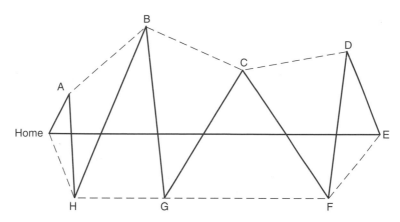

Fig 5.10 The petal system

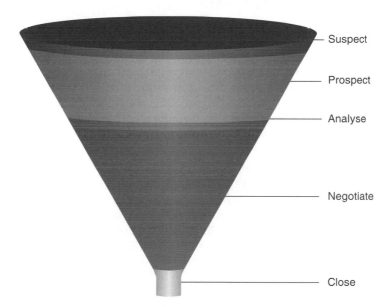

Fig 5.11 Sales funnel

Pipeline quality improvement

The idea of measuring the sales process is one that is also spoken of in the commercial literature, and it is often referred to as a sales funnel, a version of which is shown in figure 5.11

According to Heiman *et al.* (1998), the sales funnel enables the manager to evaluate the current sales situation and the sales strategy. They claim that the use of sales funnel or process to report sales opportunities provides

■ more clarity in terms of where each opportunity really stands;

■ better communication as it provides a common way to view opportunities;

- clearer perspective as it enables to see how different opportunities are linked together;
- better forecasting as it provides a detailed view of how far each opportunity really is from being closed.

They also argue that this overall process would enable a sales manager to detect problems related to sales skills and to time and territory management. Low conversion ratios would reflect sales skills problems, and unbalanced amounts of opportunities at each stage would reflect time and territory management problems.

Bosworth (1995) shares those views and extends it by arguing that statistical analysis should be used to measure and manage the sales process. In Bosworth's view historical process measures, combined with average sales cycle duration and average order value enables the development of process objectives needed to accomplish the sales targets.

Activity-based improvement

Several authors have provided classifications of selling types based on the actual activities performed by the salesperson (Newton 1969; McMurry,1961; Moncrief 1986, 1999). The latest and perhaps most complete list of sales activities is that of Moncrief (1999) which lists the following main activities: selling, working with orders, servicing the customer, working with distributors, travelling, entertaining clients, information management, servicing the product, attending conferences and meeting, training and recruiting new salespeople, managing customer relationships, using new technologies and team management. Chonko *et al.* (2000) argues that the sales manager must identify the relevant sales activities and for each of these activities define its goals, objectives, performance standards, what behaviours are needed to complete the activity and the relevant importance of each behaviour.

The problem of time allocation, not to mention the opportunity for profit, has attracted the attention of IT vendors and others in devising models which optimise on such factors as sales calling effort, number of salespeople, location and journey planning. The aim is to find the position of the optimum line between the extremes of maximum coverage and minimum cost.

Territory sales response improvement

To be effective, models require quality input data and a conceptually sound, empirically valid model. Review of the literature and the limited studies which are available can help with the territory design problem. Answers should be sought to questions about the factors which influence territory sales and the relative importance of each factor. Cravens *et al.* (1972) expressed the important variables in a relationship where $T = f (P, W, S, C, O)$. That is, T (sales territory performance) is a function of P (territory potential), W (territory characteristics or workload), S (salesperson's characteristics), C (company standing in the territory) and O (other factors). Factors which influence these variables can be classified into groups, as shown in the conceptual model in Figure 5.12.

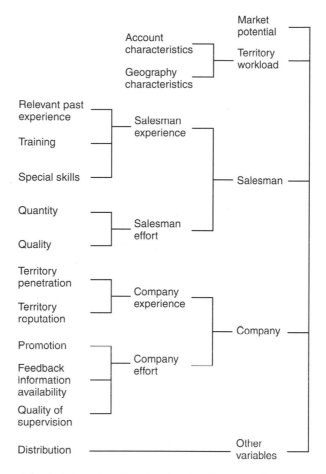

A conceptual model of determinants of sales territory performance (*Source: Cravens et al., 1972*)

The recommended solution to the analysis of sales territories is a six-stage approach:

Stage 1: Select one or more appropriate measures of performance such as sales or profit per salesperson.

Stage 2: Develop operational measures of the factors considered to be determinants of sales territory performance. These were considered to be

■ market potential (forecast industry sales);

■ territory workload (measured by annual purchases and concentration of accounts);

■ the salesperson's experience (length of time employed);

■ the salesperson's motivation and effort (management rating scale);

■ company experience (historical market share and change in market share);

■ company effort (advertising expenditure).

Stage 3: Analyse criteria and predictor variables using empirical data in a multiple regression model, for example,

$$T = a + b1P + b2W + b3A + b4Sc + b5Sp + b6M5 + b7Mc + b8Ad$$

Stage 4: Determine the relationship: evaluate the above multiple regression model.

Stage 5: Determine performance benchmarks for each territory to spot poor areas requiring attention.

Stage 6: Evaluate individual territory performance. This can be achieved by comparing actual sales with target sales and the response predictors using the multiple regression model between two different territories (Table 5.1).

Before claiming success with these models in predicting territory sales response, the problems and difficulties of measurement should be reiterated. Remember that the impact of other variables is likely to be large and significant. This occurs where markets undergo rapid change. Also, the ability to assess market share on a territory basis can be particularly difficult in many markets for different products. What is likely is that companies with much of this information as part of a sales or marketing information system can find alternative and improved ways of setting targets and improving sales performance evaluation. Indeed, there is no general agreement on the factors to be included. Consider some of the possible variables which are omitted rather than measured or relegated to the 'other' category, for example, environmental factors (economic, technological, social or political), competitive activity, the company's own marketing strategy and tactics, the salesperson's motivation and rewards, sales manager characteristics and particular customer factors.

These limitations to models of territory response should not disguise the fact that they provide a better explanation and measure of performance than traditional 'sales versus target', 'last year plus 10 per cent', or other rule-of-thumb methods. They also provide a better framework for the student to understand what contributes to territory

Table 5.1 Comparison of two territories

	Sales (units)	
	Territory A	Territory B
Constant		
Number of accounts		
Industry sales		
Market share change		
Workload per account		
Performance of salesperson		
Market share		
Length of employment		
Advertising expenditure		
Total	units	units
Actual	units	units
Actual to benchmark	%	%

sales and a ground for further empirical studies. It is the author's contention that any company can improve its territory allocation, management and evaluation by adapting these conceptual models to the specific company conditions in which they operate to yield improvements in sales force productivity. The limited evidence available so far confirms this to be the case. Ryans and Weinberg (1979), in reviewing the limited evidence, found territory potential and geographical concentration to be much more important in sales performance than measures of workload. This confirms part of the folklore which good salespeople know or learn quickly yet sales managers often forget. That is, put the effort where potential is greatest and take the necessary actions to achieve it by, for example, working longer hours or travelling further. Sales follow potential rather than historical sales or workload. Top sales performers work harder to overcome workload problems.

Predominant in the discussion of territory allocation and management is the more effective use of salesperson's time. Most of the improvements can be achieved by salespeople themselves being more disciplined and more professional.

More disciplined time-management improvements include

- starting earlier;
- finishing later;
- cutting down on social chit-chat;
- fewer breaks;
- less entertaining, fewer lunches and less drinking.

More professional time management would include,

- better planning of work;
- less calling on unqualified or unimportant prospects;
- a systematic travel plan;
- better use of travel and waiting time;
- more use of the telephone, including for appointments;
- systematic paperwork.

Factors that salespeople have to assess in their time allocation include the following:

- when to deal with paperwork;
- how long to spend at each call;
- travelling time;
- number of calls;
- order of calls;
- new business development;
- non-selling activities;
- social conversation.

Desirable though it may be to leave time-management problems to individual salespeople, managers have a responsibility not only to monitor but also to control time inefficiency and promote more effective sales practices.

5.9 Summary

Organising the sales force attempts to reconcile the principles of good organisational design with the dynamic needs of markets. Personal selling does not operate in isolation. Clear guidelines are required on corporate, marketing and selling objectives, the sales tasks and the degree of specialisation in selling activities. Methods of calculating sales-force size must be used with caution. These methods suffer from a failure to distinguish between quantity and quality in personal selling. Designing sales territories and allocating people to these areas is a key task of sales management. While established procedures can be helpful, the conventional approach is often much less than the optimum. Models of territory response and call-planning schedules offer some improvement over traditional approaches but have not yet been widely accepted. The key factors to consider in designing territories are market potential, account concentration and dispersion.

Questions

1   In what ways might changing market structures and market conditions necessitate a review of the organisational structure of the sales force?

2   Reasons can be given for organising a sales force without using a geographical split? Give examples of where alternative means of specialisation could be used.

3   Critically assess the workload method for determining sales force size.

4   Strathclyde Cutting Tools manufactures industrial products. Until recently, they employed 12 sales-people to call on accounts and prospects. Dissatisfied with the results, the sales manager discharged all 12 in favour of nine independent agents who were self-employed and sold a number of other products to the same customers. Sales immediately began to increase, and new accounts were obtained. Analyse the possible reasons for this improvement, and point out the possible drawbacks in the scheme.

5   A sales management consultant arrives at your organisation with what she claims is a user-friendly software package to assist in the design of sales territories and the improvement of calling sched-ules. What questions need to be asked and answered before deciding on the adoption of such a package?

6   If potential is the major factor in sales performance, what restricts the sales manager in allocating more accounts to the best salespeople?

Case study   ### Scotia Ltd

Scotia Ltd (name disguised) have been suppliers of packaging materials, that is, cardboard boxes, paper board and carding, for 50 years. Their works occupy a site owned by the company adjacent to vacant land also owned by the company and cleared for industrial development. At present, this land makes no contribution to the income of the company.

Analysis of the company's present sales show a dominance by traditional customers in a 50-mile radius of their works. Market penetration tends to decrease noticeably as distance from the base increases. There are no exports.

Although the company has a large turnover in its own regional area, this is relatively small compared with other UK suppliers. Scotia does very little advertising, what is done being confined to Yellow Pages and a once every two years small stand at the Printing and Packaging trade exhibition. There is no publicity manager, and any promotional activity is handled by the managing director or sales director. The company has no branding, all material being supplied printed for the particular user or unmarked.

Sales representation is well below that of competitors of equivalent size, but the company considers that this is offset by the regional location of the representatives. Of the ten-strong sales force, about half are within ten years of retirement, and all are male. The company has no systematic programme for training salespeople, sales manuals as such do not exist and new inquiries are dealt with by the sales manager and inside service personnel using the salesperson as liaison. Any contact after the initial enquiry is usually made informally between the representative and inside production personnel.

The firm has never been a product leader, and there are no unique product advantages. There are relative weaknesses in that the company is unable to produce the newer packaging materials sought by many of its customers, although an investment in shrink-wrapping machinery lies underutilised. Competitors have always led on innovations in materials and printing techniques.

The company's products are competitive on price and sales have been increasing steadily in absolute terms. At present, the competition seems to be increasingly active, and in the last financial year sales volume for Scotia fell. The current managing director, son of the founder of the business, has called you in for advice on their sales operations:

1 In your evaluation of the sales function of Scotia, what would you wish to know in addition to what is stated?

2 Consider the strengths and weaknesses of this company, and discuss how Scotia can hold its own and even increase sales. Consider how the company can meet the challenge it now faces.

3 In particular, what are your proposals for improving the effectiveness of the salesforce?

Key terms

- agents
- breakdown methods of territory design
- build-up methods of territory design
- circle pattern
- clover pattern
- combination methods
- delegation of authority
- direct sales force
- geographical method
- incremental method
- organisational structure
- potential method
- product organisation
- sales force size
- span of control
- specialisation
- territory sales response
- wedge patterns
- workload

References

Anderson, E. (1985) 'The salesperson as outside agent or employee: a transaction cost analysis' *Marketing Science* **4** (3): 234–54

Bagozzi, R.P. (1980) 'Performance and satisfaction in an industrial sales force: an examination of their antecedents and simultaneity' *Journal of Marketing* **44** (Spring): 65–77

Bosworth, M. (1995) *Solution Selling* McGraw-Hill, New York

Chonko, L.B., Low, T.W., Roberts, J.A. and Tanner, J.F. (2000) 'Sales performance: timing and type of measurement make a difference' *Journal of Personal Selling and Sales Management* **20** (Winter): 23–36

Cravens, D.W., Woodruff, R.B. and Stamper, J.C. (1972) 'An analytical approach for evaluating sales territory performance' *Journal of Marketing* **36** (1): 31–7

Drucker, P.F. (1968) *The Practice of Management* Pan Books: London

Futrell, C. (2001) *Fundamentals of Selling Customers for Life* McGraw-Hill: New York

Heiman, S., Sanchez, D. and Tuleja, T. (1998) *The New Strategic Selling* Kogan Page: London

McMurry, R.N. (1961) 'The mystique of super-salesmanship' *Harvard Business Review* **39**: 113–22

Millman, A.F. and Wilson, K.J. (1995) 'From key account selling to key account management' *Journal of Marketing Practice* **1** (1): 8–21

Moncrief, W.C. (1986) 'Selling activity and sales position taxonomies for industrial salesforces' *Journal of Marketing Research* **XXIII** (Aug): 261–70

Moncrief, W.C., Marshall, G. and Lassk, F. (1999) 'The current state of sales force activities' *Industrial Marketing Management* **28** (1): 87–98

Moncrief, W.C., Marshall, G. and Lassk, F. (2006) 'A contemporary taxonomy of sales positions' *Industrial Marketing Management* **36** (1): 55–65

Newton, D.A. (1969) 'Get the most out of your sales force' *Harvard Business Review* **Sep–Oct**: 16–29

Rackham, N. and De Vincentis, J. (1998) *Rethinking the Sales Force* McGraw-Hill: New York

Ryans, A.B. and Weinberg, C.B. (1979) 'Territory sales response' *Journal of Marketing Research* **XVI** (Nov): 453–65

Shapiro, B.P. (1979) 'Account management and sales organisation new developments in practice' in *Sales Management: new developments from behavioural and decision model research* American Marketing Association and MSI Proceedings, August: Atlanta

Smith, D.C. and Owens, J.P. (1995) 'Knowledge of customers' customers as a basis of sales force differentiation' *Journal of Personal Selling and Sales Management* **XV** (3): 1–15

Tzokas, N. and Donaldson, B. (2000) 'A research agenda for personal selling and sales management in the context of relationship marketing' *Journal of Selling and Major Account Management* **2** (2): 13–30

Williams, B.C. and Plouffe, C.R. (2006) 'Assessing the evolution of sales knowledge: a 20-year content analysis' *Industrial Marketing Management* [Online] [Accessed 24 Jan 2006]

Wilson, K., Speare, N. and Samual, R. (2003) *Successful Global Account Management: key strategy and tools for managing global customers* Kogan Page: London

Zoltners, A.A., Sinha, P. and Lorimer, S.E. (2004) *Sales Force Design for Strategic Advantage* Palgrave Macmillan: New York

6 Technology and sales

6.1 Overview

Information technology (IT) is the set of technologies related to the processing and communication of information, including computer and electronic databases, advanced telecommunications, the Internet and electronic commerce. These technologies have led to new and powerful ways of reaching customers and are changing the way in which firms interact. In this chapter, customer relationship management (CRM), database marketing, sales force automation (SFA) and electronic commerce (eCommerce) will be discussed. The use of new technology in the sales process is clearly having a significant impact on how sales operations are implemented and managed and will continue to do so. This chapter considers these developments, the problems and opportunities arising from them and the implications for sales management.

6.2 Learning objectives

The aims for this chapter are to

- explain CRM and the importance of information in the sales process;
- develop an understanding of sales information systems and sales force automation;
- assess the efficacy of database marketing, telemarketing and the Internet;
- comment on the development of e-commerce.

6.3 Definitions

Customer Relationship Management (CRM) is the integration of technology and process in the acquiring, retaining and growing your profitable customers.

Sales Force Automation (SFA) is the automated integration of front and back office activity to facilitate an information-empowered sales force that can improve the sales process and enhance the relationship.

Sales Information system (SIS) is a collaboration of data technologies that facilitate the collection and processing of information to assist the sales and customer management process.

Database Marketing is the process of using and maintaining customer and other sources of information to create, develop and improve customer transaction and exchange.

Electronic commerce (e-Commerce) is the use of web-based tools and other forms of business solutions such as electronic request for quotation (eRFQ), electronic request for information (eRFI), catalogue procurement or eAuctions, to conduct transactions and provide business solutions.

6.4 Customer relationship management (CRM)

Sales managers need to know and understand the changing environment in which they work, both internally within their organisation and in their external environment. Much of this change in recent years has been in IT which is continuing to present problems, challenges and opportunities in the sales function. Most academics and practitioners now agree that information systems should be focused on the customer, customer-centric, hence the prominence of CRM. CRM is the integration of technologies and business processes used to satisfy the needs of a customer during any given interaction. CRM involves acquisition, analysis and use of knowledge about customers in order to sell more goods or services and to do it more efficiently (Bose, 2002).

While there are many variations to definitions of CRM most analysts agree that CRM is a business strategy for using customer information to maximise the long-term value and profitability of its relationship with its customers, and not merely a software suite.

Did you know?

Investment in CRM software has been significant in recent years. Figure 6.1 shows the type of application software was being used for in 2004. (Source: AMR Research http://www.amr.com [Accessed 24 July 2006])

Customer service 21
Call-centre infrastructure 19
Sales-force automation 16
Marketing automation & analytics 12
Order management 9
Web self-service 7
Field service 6
Online sales/E-commerce suites 6
Pricing management 1
Other customer-management apps 3

Total 2004 revenues (projected): $10.8 billion

Fig 6.1 **The CRM market 2004 projected revenue share by type of application (in percentages)** (*source: AMR research http://www.amr.com [Accessed 24 July 2006]*)

CRM has been described as representing 'an enterprise approach to developing full-knowledge about customer behaviour and preferences and to developing programmes and strategies that encourage customers to continually enhance their business relationship with the company'. (Parvatiyar and Sheth, 2001 p. 1–2). To achieve this means successful integration of customer-facing personnel and front-office tools and data with the back office support functions. When this is achieved then it presents a unified view of each customer to everyone in the organisation. The result is a better understanding of the customer, better service at lower cost and improved sales performance.

As Figure 6.2 indicates, a major part of CRM is sales activity. In response, SIS and SFA are increasingly used as part of the CRM solution. SIS is a collaboration of data technologies that facilitate the collection and processing of information to assist the sales process. SFA is concerned with the integration of the front and back office to facilitate an information-empowered sales force that improves sales force productivity and enhances the customer relationship (Payne, 2000). At present, the interactive communication of the salesperson with customers is high in the sales management agenda of customer orientated firms, nevertheless 'closing the sale' has been the main driving force behind the sales management efforts of the firm in the past. Today, relationship marketing (RM) and CRM has shifted attention from 'closing' the singular sale to creating the necessary conditions for a long-term relationship between the firm and its customers that breeds successful sales encounters in the long run.

Traditionally, the role of salespeople has been perceived as crucial for the implementation (delivery) stage of the firm's operational marketing plans. However, the complexity of the relationship process necessitates a more advanced role for salespeople. Clearly, salespeople need to develop specific abilities as to which accounts to target, who to focus on within that account and which combination of products and

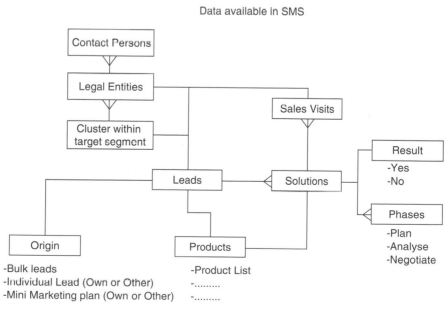

Data available in SMS

Fig 6.2   Data available in SMS

services to promote and sell And, in addition, how frequently should they call or support the account and how to divide their attention between service and developmental selling? For example, one study in the banking industry found that internal management procedures caused more than 90 per cent of relationship breakdowns (Perrien and Ricard, 1995). This outlines the importance of planning sales practices with a relationship orientation in mind and the importance of the need for integration and communication flow between the different functions as well as between the buyer and seller in the relationship.

There is some help in the literature on these issues. Burns and Stalker (1961) and Lawrence and Lorsch (1967) developed the contingency approach whereby a mechanistic system is most appropriate for firms operating under stable conditions but, in contrast, an organic system is most appropriate for firms operating in a less stable environment where the need for additional information and interpersonal communication is very important during task execution. This presents us with a conundrum. This is at the initial stages of the relationship, where the two sides (buyer and seller) try to know each other; an organic system seems most appropriate. Yet in view of possible conflicts, the need arises for clear rules and procedures for handling conflicts; the latter is closer to a mechanistic system rather than organic. At the later stages of the relationship process, it can be suggested that trust and commitment reduces uncertainty, a fact which can give rise to economies by means of a well-regulated mechanistic system. Yet in view of the high trust and commitment, the relationship partners embark on tasks of high complexity, a fact which gives rise to the need for an organic system. In future research there is a need to overcome this conundrum by examining what Mintzberg claims 'although we can characterise certain organisations as bureaucratic or organic overall, none is uniformly so across its entire range of activities' (Mintzberg, 1983, p. 37).

Yet, in both mechanistic and organic relationship management/development the demands on the sales manager are essentially the same. What do I expect my sales team to achieve? How do I deploy their time allocation and how to increase both effectiveness and efficiency?

6.5   Sales force automation

IT enables easier communication across time and location, more rapidly and with greater accuracy and to the people that need to know within the network. Moreover, salespeople and sales managers have a greater need than most in the organisation for mobility. Anytime, anywhere information collection and dissemination is important within the sales function which should enable salespeople to work smarter (Sujan et al., 1994).

Sales automation and sales information databases should provide the salesperson with up-to-date customer information regarding orders, deliveries, invoices and all business between supplier of the product and service and their customers and prospective customers. Salespeople can also work smarter by more efficient time management, call routing and targeting of customers and prospects. Indeed sales planning in terms of call preparation, customer information and sales presentation are all enhanced if the account history is accurate, buyer profiles are complete and information is personalised.

Adaptive (smart) selling behaviour can be improved with accurate and timely customer account information (Sujan *et al.*, 1994).

The trend within organisations to be both flexible and responsive has accelerated in response to the increasing demand for customised products/services and rapid response to satisfy the requirements of custom-focused markets. Inevitably, there is conflict between this requirement for flexibility and the need for automation in systems and processes in order to reduce costs yet maintain service. Businesses are realising that to improve shareholder value whilst satisfying customer needs requires a re-conceptualisation of strategy, technology, people and systems. As a result, there has been an increasing investment in IT – focused on new, low-cost customer channels and on customer management information systems (Engel and Barnes, 2000). Part of this investment has been in sales automation systems that drive a more efficient and effective sales-customer interaction. To facilitate this, companies have invested in these systems and processes to deploy a superior CRM system. Thus, leading firms have a multi-faceted system of data mining, data warehousing, salespeople, call centre staff and others who interact with the customer. The current challenge is to manage this process both effectively and efficiently.

More recently, the strategic focus of information technology applications has moved from transaction efficiency to a relationship orientation that embraces customer-focused technology (Peppers and Rogers, 2004). The fundamental drive is to reduce transaction cost while providing better service. The emergence of relationship marketing and CRM focuses on a need to reduce transaction costs yet be aware of the need to invest in advertising, marketing research and sales investment. A major objective is to develop relationships with customers and use new sales processes – with use of IT and database marketing as the primary strategy to achieve this objective. According to DeVincentis and Rackham (1998), the sales function has moved from a focus on transaction to a new focus on 'enterprise' selling – requiring different sales skills and abilities. In today's markets, it is now important to be able to identify low and high relational groups (Garbarino and Johnson 1999) and focus on realistic variations of the old 80/20 rule.

SFA systems have been defined, variously, as (1) centralised database systems that can be accessed through a modem by remote laptop computers using special software – hence focusing on information-handling capacities (Parthasarathy and Sohi, 1997), or (2) as the converting of manual sales activities to electronic processes though the use of various combinations of hardware and software (Erffmeyer and Johnson, 2001). However, several authors have noted that there is a lack of a clear definition of SFA (Rivers and Dart, 1999). Perhaps the best compromise is to adopt a broad, practice-based, approach to SFA and SIS usage (Widmier *et al.*, 2002), and utilise a definition incorporating the automated collection of information to assist the sales and customer management process. However, adoption of SFA has not been as widespread, uniform or as successful as early use predicted (Rivers and Dart 1999) but, as Jones, Sundaram and Chin (2002) note, the academic community '. . . remains silent in terms of reporting factors associated with SFA adoption and use' (p. 145). In fact, the majority of research that has been conducted has focused on individual-level factors – that is, at the level of the individual salesperson – leading to technology adoption and use amongst the sales force. Jones, Sundaram and Chin (2002) demonstrate the importance of salespeople's attitudes towards the new systems – including perceived usefulness and perceived compatibility with existing systems. Similarly, Venkatesh (2000) identified the importance of individual-level factors such as perceived ease of use and perceived usefulness – attitudes which themselves are shaped by general beliefs that the individual holds about computers – in the initial acceptance of SFA technology. Venkatesh and Davis (2000) extended this latter investigation by using three points of measurement – (1) pre-implementation, (2) immediate post-implementation and (3) three months post-implementation. These authors found that factors such as social influence – whether an individual perceived that other individuals who were important to him/her thought he/she should perform the behaviour in question – were also important as were factors such as job relevance, perceived quality of the output of the technology, and perceived ease of use. Taken together, Venkatesh and Davis found that these factors accounted for about 50 per cent of the variance in usage intentions.

Widmier, Jackson and McCabe (2002) focused on the usage of adopted SFA and found that the major sales use was for sales calls and expense reports. However, fewer than one-half of the salespeople that they sampled used the technology for calendar reports. In addition, the majority of the applications of the SFA reporting technology were initiated by companies rather than by salespeople. This was because, Widmier *et al.* argued, the sales managers saw the SFA technology as a 'very useful tool in managing the sales force'. Keillor, Bashaw and Pettijohn (1997) found that less-experienced salespeople indicated a significantly more positive attitude toward this corporate technology than more-experienced salespeople – who thought that adoption of the technology would result in a loss in employees' privacy. For Keillor, Bashaw and Pettijohn (1997), the solution to this issue was clear-cut: 'Experienced salespeople may need to be explicitly shown the connection between technology and productivity, and perhaps learn of the threat associated with less-experienced salespeople who may have the ability to become competitive faster than in the past' (p. 217).

What do you think?

Despite the investment in sales automation, Donaldson and Wright found that in financial services companies most sales automation systems were being used for little more than mail shots. What reasons would account for these sophisticated systems not being taken up, far less used to their full potential, by salespeople? (See Donaldson and Wright, 2002)

In contrast to this, simplified, management-focused advice is the work of Speier and Venkatesh (2002), who collected survey data from 454 salespeople across two firms that had implemented SFA tools in the United States. They found that, immediately after training in the tools, salespeople had positive perceptions of the technology but, six months after implementation, the technology had been widely rejected by the salespeople and, at the same time, salesperson absenteeism and voluntary turnover had significantly increased. Interview data indicated that the SFA tools were a primary driver for those salespeople choosing to leave the two firms. Speier and Venkatesh conclude that SFA technology may alienate successful salespeople in that the technology may change the salesperson's role by generating 'greater internal conflict and power redistribution when competence – destroying technologies are implemented . . . managers can quickly and easily assess the number of, frequency of, and time allocated to sales call, which results in increased monitoring . . . which increases the power differential between manager and salesperson in favour of the manager' (p. 110). The implication is that successful SFA implementations need to be carefully thought through in terms of the 'knock-on' implications. Speier and Venkatesh (2002) thus develop the issue of the 'logic of opposition' raised by Robey and Boudreau (1999) in their analysis of the organisational consequences of information technology interventions. Sviokla (1996) investigated the use of an expert system designed to support the insurance sales process at four insurance companies. Before the system was introduced sales agents 'often "owned" the clients and successfully took their business as they moved from one firm to another'. After the system was introduced, all the detailed client data were fed straight to the home office and so 'the company adopting the system could track its salespeople at a higher level of detail' (p. 32). Sviokla concludes that successful implementations were considerate of political ramifications of the adoption of technological innovation (Sviokla, 1996).

If CRM is about acquiring, retaining and growing profitable customers, then the process must be not only closely linked with sales but should ideally be merged and integrated in a seamless process.

Handen, 2000 identifies four types of CRM programmes which highlight the need to mesh with sales force activity:

1 *Win back or save.* Selling to new customers is important but retaining existing profitable business even more so. To save a customer that you have failed to deliver as promised, or to one who is defecting because of some competitive weakness, is difficult and time-sensitive. Information, in the correct form as part of a customer database file can identify declining sales, less frequent ordering and changing customer habits. On the positive side, the file can identify the most profitable and worthwhile customers. A customer once lost may be lost for good and difficult to recover. To win back lost customers requires excellent sales and negotiating skills coupled with good data, the ability to analyse such data and to package this into a saleable customer proposition.

2 *Prospecting.* For most businesses repeat business is more important and more profitable than winning new business, but new customers are also the life blood of any enterprise. Figure 6.2 showed that leads from central databases, from individual salespeople and from various marketing plans and targets need to be input to the information system and used judiciously. Put simply, winning new business requires good leads. Focusing on leads which are unlikely to grow or which will be unprofitable is wasted effort; therefore it is not the number but the quality of leads that matters. A good CRM system can categorise leads, assist in evaluating credit ratings and assess the potential customer's future value to the business.

3 *Loyalty* is a much used and misused term in business, but as many utility companies know to their cost customer churn is a real business problem. Most telecom companies now categorise their business in terms of revenue assurance given that customer churn can dramatically affect their future profitability. As a result, CRM is a profit centre rather than a cost overhead, and information that can identify and control subscriber churn is a critical source of competitive advantage. Such information

may also create new opportunities such as affinity marketing, loyalty cards, customised billing and target specific, cross-selling opportunities.

4 *Cross-sell/up-sell* opportunities are created by information that can identify customers' needs more specifically. As a result, complementary products and services can be offered which provide better solutions for the customer thus enhancing customer value. According to PricewaterhouseCoopers, on average, this improves customer profitability from −3 per cent in year one to +7 per cent gross profit by the end of year three (Brown, 2000).

6.6 Uses of sales information systems (SIS)

The key uses of SIS are

1 *Sales reporting and analysis*, which offer improved speed and accuracy on previously manually operated information. In other words, the new technology helps with collecting, classifying, storing and analysing data. Such data might include

- call reports;
- sales against plan;
- sales by product, customer or segment;
- profit and cost dimensions of sales performance.

Such is the range of information which can be electronically handled that computer technology can assist in saving time spent on analysing data and improving feedback. Reporting systems can also be modified to redesign work. Remember that collecting data is not an end in itself but enables more selling time and face-to-face customer time to be achieved. The system should fit the task, not the other way. Salespeople should find the systems user-friendly and helpful and their involvement and participation are necessary. The aim is to relieve salespeople and sales managers of routine information, analysis and reporting rather than creating it. Instead, sales managers can measure variances between salespeople or against planned levels which enable quicker and more appropriate responses.

2 *Sales planning*. Information systems are increasingly being used to help in three major areas:(1) identifying leads and classifying prospects, for example by geography, industry, market segment, turnover and potential, (2) building up customer profiles across a variety of criteria such as organisation, buying criteria or spending patterns and (3) helping with alternative call patterns and territory planning. Sales managers must be careful not to look for instant success in this new information technology age.

3 *Future options and projections*. Computerised information systems help the sales manager with 'what if?' types of question, with the evaluation of different options and with the prediction of future scenarios. This does not mean they provide the right answer but they can assist in directing effort, improving productivity and assisting in decisions which can subsequently be evaluated more accurately. This enhances management ability in the control and evaluation of salespeople.

When properly developed and implemented, an information system provides timely and relevant information to decision makers. Because of problems which are inherent in the decision making and communication processes, the cost-efficient development of systems is not always possible. Although these problems cannot always be eliminated, they should be understood and accounted for. Common problems include the following:

1 *Information overload*. An efficiently designed information system should focus on the collection of information that facilitates decision making. Information that just satisfies a curiosity, confirm one's suspicions or is not utilised should not be included in the system. Research has shown that very little information solicited directly from the sales force is used in the SMIS (Donaldson and Wright, 2002). Unfortunately, many sales managers do not know what information is needed to make decisions. They simply ask for all available information and therefore waste the time of salespeople and researchers who have to collect the information and computer systems personnel who are required to design systems to process the information. In order to minimise the information overload problem, it is necessary precisely to define decisions to be made and identify information that is necessary to facilitate decision-making. Sales managers today need to be managers of information. They collect this information from sources as diverse as call reports, debriefing sessions, minutes of sales meetings, sales invoices, customer record files, cost accounting files, budgeting systems, market reports and research, production schedules and inventory and service reporting.

2 *Inaccurate input data*. Inaccurate input data not only impede decision making but can destroy employee confidence in the information system. If this happens, salespeople have little confidence in the system and become dissatisfied with management and the software system being used.

3 *Language barrier*. People who develop systems are often technical people who have little knowledge of the sales manager's requirements. Similarly, the sales manager is unaware of what can be provided by an effective computer-based information system. The result is inadequate communication between the designer and the user. The sales manager tells the systems designer what is needed and the designer then converts that request into a usable format. The request is often either not interpreted correctly or the designer develops a format that will fit into the system rather than developing a system that will accommodate the request. Even worse is the enthusiastic amateur who designs their own system incompatible with any other MIS, causing misunderstanding and confusion.

4 *Changing management requirements*. As firms grow and mature, the amount and type of information needed to manage the sales function effectively changes. Sales managers need more information on territory potential, customers' characteristics, sales force productivity, competitive activities and so on. They may also add new products, open new markets and change remuneration plans. These changes in information requirements lead to changes in data files and programs. Unless the system is flexible enough to accommodate these changes, extensive and expensive system modification may be necessary.

5 *Selling the system*. Systems frequently fail when psychological reactions and organisational factors are not considered during system development. Firms that do not train, educate and involve their employees in the development, uses and strengths of the system may find that it is unacceptable to employees and does not function as planned. In order to avoid such problems, firms should

■ identify employee needs;

■ develop a system concept;

- test acceptance of the concept among employees;
- modify the concept to accommodate employee requests;
- develop the system;
- educate employees on the uses of the system;
- promote the system to users;
- redesign the system when needs change.

6 *Assessing costs and benefits.* Although costs of developing a system can be calculated and distributed to various operating divisions, benefits are not so easily identified and measured. Each manager must subjectively assess the impact of the system on the quality of decision making:

- Are decisions made faster and more accurately?
- Are sales territories more productive?
- What effect has the system had on selling costs and gross margin?
- Has turnover been reduced?
- Has the system improved employee morale?
- What effect has the system had on the compatibility of various operating divisions?

The rising cost of a personal, face-to-face sales call has necessitated a reappraisal of the way in which companies interact with their customers. This applies, in particular, where a large number of customers account for a relatively small proportion of sales. It is no longer economic to service these accounts with intensive personal means of communication and sometimes less effective where the information customers need is computer-based and relies on the company's information system. Hence the use of marketing and SIS has been accompanied by other forms of communication, principally the telephone. These forms of communication, some of which have been around for some time, need careful evaluation and appraisal before being used by different organisations in different ways. They include the major tools of direct marketing such as catalogues, direct mail, television direct response, radio/magazine direct response, electronic shopping, kiosk shopping and telemarketing. The basis for these integrated communication systems is database marketing.

6.7 Database marketing

Any file that contains data can be referred to as a data file; however, the term is usually reserved for those files which contain structured data that are intended for future retrieval or manipulation to produce meaningful output. A database will enable a picture of historical (and future) activity of customers to be kept. It will make sure that each salesperson or member of customer contact staff knows what has been done or is scheduled, and enables sales management to monitor sales staff, thus improving customer information and giving better management control, better customer service and reduced costs – a powerful combination of benefits.

Traditionally, a salesperson's record card in a filing cabinet was the database consisting of a record containing information or headings or related elements called fields, which are variable within a record. Now held electronically the principles are the same and a sales field forming a database may contain, as a minimum, the following:

■ customer name, address, telephone and fax numbers and e-mail address/website domain;

■ the names of all contacts;

■ the customer order history and a purchasing profile by product, supplier status and share of business;

■ a customer description, products sold, sales volume, credit rating, number of employees, service requirements and standards, buying group data and standard industrial classification (SIC) code(s);

■ a customer production profile, facilities, R&D capability and transportation status;

■ a customer market profile, including their market share and promotional profile;

■ competitor activity with the customer;

■ any non-sales interaction with the customer.

To this can be added daily information regarding buying mix and customer analysis reports to analyse potential as well as current sales performance.

The accessing, retrieval and processing of such data fields is heavily influenced by data file organisation and management, that is, the way in which data elements, field and records are stored and accessed. Conventional and database files as well as more recent Internet and intranet systems require careful planning and routes of access to a number of different constituents.

6.8   Telemarketing and call centre management

Telemarketing is interactive communication with customers over the telephone which can provide the ability to target specific contacts quickly and at lower cost than can a person-to-person sales call. Telemarketing can also be used to prospect and qualify leads and for a range of service support activities other than merely order-taking. Furthermore, those customers who are small, make only a marginal contribution and are perhaps geographically remote can be handled more effectively and more efficiently through telemarketing than in person. The telephone is obviously far quicker than a face-to-face meeting and has at least four key benefits:

1   As a low-cost substitute for personal selling. As a rough guide, five or six personal calls can be replaced, in cost terms, by a number of relatively long telephone calls. On average, each telephone call is estimated to cost one-tenth that of a personal call, mainly because of the absence of travel and waiting time, and this is clearly a more profitable approach for small accounts with limited potential. The telephone can be used productively with other forms of promotion and communication, such as television and radio direct response or mail order catalogues. Catalogue selling is far from a new channel but the speed and service that can be provided using today's

technology coupled with the telephone interaction can greatly increase business done in this way.

2   To supplement personal selling calls. Salespeople themselves can increase their personal productivity by using the telephone wisely. Time and effort previously wasted by calling on accounts when not required can be replaced by a telephone call which, if the customer requires, can be followed up personally. It can generally be expected that most salespeople will increase their ratio of telephone to personal calls and, overall, fewer person-to-person calls will be required. Mobile telephony makes this both possible and often desirable as a means of communicating with regular contacts.

3   As an alternative to direct mail, especially if a 0800 freephone or reduced rate lines are used. Advertising and promotional campaigns can be targeted at encouraging customers to call for additional information and service or to place their order. In some cases, these sales leads will be followed up by personal selling. Companies such as BT, of course, use this medium extensively but other consumer goods firms such as Kellogs and Procter and Gamble encourage consumers to communicate any queries, complaints or suggestions they may have relating to products or services the company provides for customers. The efficacy of this medium can be verified by the fact that response to advertising with 0800 numbers is significantly higher than to those adverts without such a number.

4   The most significant developments in the use of the telephone has been in providing better customer support and service than other forms of communication can provide. Integrating telephone activity with computer-based technology has had a dramatic impact on many different businesses. This is most apparent in financial services, initially led by Direct Line in car insurance but now extending to almost all financial service providers. Where the customers are comfortable with this medium and with products which are fast moving and require no, or a limited, physical examination yet have a high value, telemarketing is very effective. The result is more effective communication at lower cost.

How to go about telephone selling

Like any management activity, telemarketing requires management of the process and not merely the activity itself. Six stages can be suggested:

1   *Define the objectives*. Since use of the telephone is now so widespread, so is its misuse. Most people receive many unsolicited telephone calls from companies they neither know nor care about and with whom they do not wish to do business. Despite some initial success, most companies are now wary of using the telephone for cold prospecting, although to sell new products or services to existing customers it is still a powerful and effective tool. Objectives can range from identifying leads and the qualification of prospects to order-taking and service activities. Clear objectives of which activity, response times, orders to calls and so on need to be set and measured is part of setting objectives.

2   *Planning*. To alienate existing customers with overzealous selling by telephone is to be avoided but, equally, missing opportunities to cross-sell to existing customers is to miss potentially the most lucrative sales prospects. Similarly, to have several people,

seemingly uncoordinated, contact the same customer on different issues is equally damaging to one's reputation and credibility. De-duplication and address and contact verification is essential and using a variety of call strategies and different means of customer contact requires careful planning and coordination. This avoids multiple contacts at different times and ensures effective use of the telephone in a customer-friendly way. From a sales perspective, scoring and propensity modelling are some of the techniques now being used. This has important implications for marketing strategy since what can be observed is reverse market segmentation based on a bottom-up approach using an identification of individual customers in a more sophisticated way.

3 *Customer contact staff*. While certain aspects of selling by telephone are similar to those of personal selling, other aspects are quite different. Like personal selling, good communication skills, empathy and an ability to respond in the correct manner by asking questions will be helpful but a different approach and different skills are also needed.

4 *Relationships with other salespeople and other departments*. A key to an effective and efficient telemarketing operation is to obtain the early involvement and participation of other sales staff and functions in the organisation. In particular, competition between different departments or functions must be avoided, and there should preferably be some interchange of staff to appreciate what each other does, how and why.

5 *Sell the idea to the customers*. Most important in any telemarketing operation is to ensure that the customer is better served by the operation, that the system is designed to meet their needs and that there are benefits to the customer from operating in this way.

6 *Measurement and control*. Before introducing any telesales or telephone support operation, it should be critically tested and appraised to remove and avoid any pitfalls. Targets for performance should be set, effectiveness and efficiency measured and monitored, and adjustments made as necessary. Response times, the number of complaints answered by first operator, comparative sales and service levels are some of the areas that should be measured and monitored. Management of call centres or telemarketing operations has become a subset area of sales management. It requires an effective contact management plan, careful call list preparation and development and, very often, prepared scripts for staff to respond to customers in the correct manner. Furthermore, it is a management responsibility to ensure that what is promised is delivered so that customer expectations are met and, if possible, exceeded. Efficient call centre management, again using today's technology, should be able to provide management reports and statistics far in excess of any manual operation. The net result should be improved customer service, well-motivated staff and a more efficient operation.

However, the telephone is not only a vehicle for selling but has an important role in providing service and information in pre-sales, transactions and post-sales stages in the exchange process. For many companies this is most efficiently handled through a call centre where the benefits of instant, real time information can be used to provide a range of benefits for the customer/user. Although they may convey the impression of creating unsolicited, intrusive contact on an unsuspecting audience this is not how most call centres and reputable firms operate. An example may confirm this position.

Resolution plc (www.resolutionplc.com) is the United Kingdom's largest specialist manager of in-force life funds with an estimated 7 million customers, employing 3500 staff in the United Kingdom with assets managed in excess of £60 billion. It is better known under its previous brands of Britannic and Abbey's life business. According to human resource business manager, Gary Pailing 'We don't work shifts, we don't sell via the contact centre – it's not like the typical image of a call centre where people are under pressure to meet certain selling targets . . . staff are dealing with general enquiries. When you are calling a call centre . . . most of us want a conversation rather than go through a stock question-and-answer list when you know that the person on the other end of the line is under pressure to get the call done and dusted in so many seconds and move on'. As a result, the company recruits people from different backgrounds with a range of experience not necessarily within the business, and the company aims to provide learning and development for all staff to enhance their contribution within the organisation. They claim they 'need people who are team players, who will be enthusiastic about new ideas and new ways of working, who will take ownership of a customer's problem, and act quickly and positively when a problem arises' (*Herald*, 20th October, 2006).

6.9 Internet-based selling

Just as the telephone has changed the way in which companies interact, computer technology is radically altering the methods and costs of commercial exchange. More efficient ways are emerging to search, order and progress the exchange of goods, services and ideas. The Internet is a powerful tool for providing information and is an important means of buyer–seller communication. Many traditional intermediaries, particularly those who do not stock a physical product, will find that the consumer empowers themselves to collect information and make the purchase decision. Travel agencies, car dealerships and financial intermediaries are all affected by such a process. Information itself is proving more robust. The demand for secondary sources of information is passing from a number of individual and independent sources to software programs such as Google which can browse the Internet and report the findings directly to users. Information itself is the market opportunity and the facilitation between source and consumer the new challenge.

In terms of information provision, the Internet is unrivalled. It can reach an audience cheaply with the message you want to convey and allows full interaction, the ultimate in communication – two way. However, unless the web site is properly designed and maintained, it may prove damaging. To create a web site requires that you identify the information you want to communicate and that the users will need, that it is effectively linked to other databases and that, as a communication vehicle, it conveys the image as well as the content you wish to get across.

Just as telemetry (automatic reordering) and electronic data interchange (bar coding and so on) have removed many mundane order-processing tasks, such as stock checking, inventory management and order filling and processing, so the Internet is likely to remove much of the more mundane information role that salespeople perform. The result, already identified in the changing role of salespeople, is higher-skilled, more well-informed, computer-literate salespeople who operate as customer account managers coordinating the difficult interface between customer and company. It is to some of the current *electronic tools* that we now turn.

1 *Portable computer*. It would be typical of today's salesperson to find them equipped with a laptop and other electronic equipment such as Blackberry for instant up-dates to head office and with customers. Further, most will have some form of opportunity analysis programme and other software such as salesforce.com to help them plan their activity and identify the best prospects.

2 *Virtual office* Many salespeople will be able to operate as if they were in the office. While not strictly virtual it is possible to operate in real time.

3 *SFA tools* will contain power point presentation, excel spreadsheets and customised software to provide instant customer solutions. They can be used as a stand alone presentation, interconnected and integrated depending on the hardware and software configurations.

4 *e-mail and voice mail* are now commonplace which enables the salesperson to deal with customer requests more expediously and helps stimulate more formal communication in writing. Care must be taken on the legal implications of this kind of contact.

5 *Mobile phone* is now a portable multi-media device capable of text, images and video on screen with remote Internet access.

6 *Portable tools* such as electronic scanners help salespeople do instant stock checks and facilitate customer re-ordering if required.

7 *Contact management and opportunity analysis* are some of the ways that the salesperson can keep up to date with multi-contact sales teams, and the use of lotus notes or similar software can be used to provide any time, any place data relating to a customer account.

6.10 Electronic commerce (eCommerce)

In an effort to drive down costs, improve efficiency and deliver competitive products buyers are increasingly using eCommerce systems. eProcurement is a specific form of eCommerce incorporating inter-company cooperation, supply chain management and instant data access between buyer and seller. Increasingly, these systems are using web-based tools and other forms of B2B solutions such as eRFQ, eRFI, catalogue procurement or eAuctions. These systems offer costs savings but it is as yet premature to suggest the demise of the salesperson. Indeed, what emerges is a new form of selling where integration of information from several sources and the ability to negotiate still prevail.

For example, in a study of electronic reverse auctions (eRA) in the automotive industry in Europe there are limitations to automated forms of exchange with sales managers' attitudes to the use of eRA very mixed (Donaldson and Resch, 2006). It appears that to achieve more effective B2B exchange a compromise between the softer notion of relationship building and the harder notion of blind electronic auctions where lowest price wins is required. The way value is created and delivered still holds the key to customer retention and profitability.

Did you know?

eRAs have during the last few years become a popular tool to negotiate online and reduce prices for purchased goods. The procurement community has been strongly focused on the development and implementation of electronic procurement tools in general such as electronic catalogues, electronic auction tools or electronic requests for quotation systems.

In the automotive industry, on average, the share of value added has decreased from 50 per cent in the early 1980s to currently 30 per cent or less (Hahn and Kaufmann, 2002). The rest of the total turnover is purchased goods mainly bought-in parts and systems. A company with 3 per cent profit on turnover can, by reducing the costs of purchased goods by 5 per cent, double its profit to more than 6 per cent (Bovet, Toy and Kochersperger, 2003). eRAs are seen as a tool that would help achieve these kinds of savings.

(Source: Donaldson and Resch, 2006)

However, eRAs are judged by some to be a destructive cost reduction practice. Its use is said to reduce long-term competitiveness of both buyer and seller (Emiliani and Stec, 2002). Among the studies, eRAs have been described as unserious, unethical, relationship destroying tools of the devil's design that has never ever a right to exist at all (Krizan, 2003). eRAs are widely perceived as a purchasing tool designed principally to reduce prices without giving adequate consideration to other factors like quality, relationship, experience or know how (Tulder and Mol, 2002; Jap, 2003). They damage supplier relations and create distrust among incumbent suppliers (Emiliani, 2004). It is, as yet, premature to suggest that eRAs are a suitable replacement of expensive personal interaction in B2B exchange.

Some of the concerns include the following (OICA, 2005; Jap, 2003):

- gaining market data without having ambitions to award work to the bidders;
- accepting bids from suppliers that are not qualified to do the work;
- making side-deals, where work is awarded to bidders that didn't participate in the reverse auction;
- not advising eRA participants of the outcome in a timely manner;
- not awarding the work as quoted – for example, unbundling lots of partial lot awards;
- Not disclosing if buyer's internal operations are bidding on the work.

Some large industrial buyers, namely Toyota Motor Corporation, Honda Motor Corporation or Harley-Davidson are reported to abstain from eRAs owing to the following reasons (Emiliani, 2004):

- Focus is on price not on cost.
- eRAs do not correctly account for total costs.
- eRAs damage supplier relationships and teamwork.
- Buyers and sellers do not learn how to jointly solve problems.

■ The focus is on short term, rather than long-term results.

■ Power-based bargaining blocks or corrupts information flow between buyers and sellers.

Surprisingly all this is not specific to eRAs. Focus on price not on costs is independent from auction or traditional negotiation – it's a matter of purchasing professionalism. Purchasing managers who decide to use eRAs may be indulging in bad business behaviour regardless of whether they are negotiating online or not. Emiliani raises the interesting question with respect to the role of online auctions, that eRAs may just provide a short-term solution to much deeper problems within the buying firm, such as poor cost management and the inability to adopt modern supply chain management principles and lean production methods that 'are needed by both buyers and suppliers in order to truly eliminate waste and reduce total costs'.

'Some suppliers cannot sustain sharp price reductions over the long term. While Buyers might be happy about savings these might come out of the suppliers profit. A supplier that will not be able to compete at lower price level will eventually be forced out of the industry' (Jap, 2000; Jap, 2003). Jap believes that finally the supplier will suffer since he will end up with fewer alternatives and bargaining power shifts to the supplier.

eRAs are a tool and like any tool, it can be used appropriately or inappropriately (Krizan, 2003). What has to be stated is that eRAs do shift existing markets between buyer and seller more to a kind of perfect market where knowledge is available very quickly and to many participants. During an auction, the buyer and supplier are informed almost immediately of changing conditions and prices. What took several days to negotiate before has become a matter of a few hours. eRAs have increased in popularity because they emphasise short-term price savings and can simplify and support negotiations (Jap, 2003).

One benefit out of eRAs as well as for eCommerce as a whole is speed. The use of web enables a global sales management team to participate real time in a bidding process. The quick collection of proposals speeds up the sourcing decision and enables more rapid award. Overall cycle time reduction reaches the level of more than 70 per cent (Ore, 2003).

Suppliers want to maximise sales, particularly through long-term relationships that emphasise quality and delivery. These conditions can also breed discord and suspicion (Jap, 2003). Buyers can be greatly rewarded for saving money and lowering costs but will be fired within the first months of delivery if they had focused only on price and the supplier fails (Oliva, 2003) – using eRAs or not. On the other side, it is too little nowadays for a selling agent to rely on relationship selling without being competitive in total value or total cost evaluation – this will not succeed, because price always matters (Oliva, 2003). Everyone entering one of these online dynamic bidding events needs to do their homework in advance, know their walk away point and keep emotion out of the process.

6.11 Summary

New technology and IT, coupled with the use of management information, provide the sales manager with a powerful means of obtaining and sustaining competitive advantage. The key to more effective management is to use these resources to improve customer contact, enhance service and operate more efficiently. Telemarketing is one route to consider and use of the Internet has already proved a powerful information vehicle but in most cases as a supplement to personal selling rather than its replacement. Although there are some examples of direct marketing and telephone marketing being highly effective, these have so far been confined to limited areas, mostly service businesses. Sales managers must welcome new ways of communicating effectively with customers at lower cost but ensure their sales operation meets the needs of both company and customer.

Questions

1   According to reports 60–70 per cent of CRM projects, including sales automation systems, fail as perceived by the companies that use them. By considering the principle causes of such failure what recommendations can you make to avoid this occurrence?

2   Choosing your own example explain how a close customer–supplier relationship differs from a transactional one. Focus particularly on the information that you need to develop and maintain a close long-term profitable relationship.

3   It has been argued that the corner shopkeeper has greater and better knowledge of her customers than the CRM manager with expensive software and databases at her disposal. State whether you agree or disagree with this statement, giving possible reasons and indicate the areas where information may be lacking.

4   Your sales director has asked to make a case for reducing personal face-to-face visits in favour of greater telephone contact. Submit a report outlining your views.

5   From a buyer's perspective consider the merits of eCommerce, particularly on-line auctions. What precautions would you take to ensure that they worked in your firm's interests?

Case study   ## Agere Systems

Agere Systems (www.agere.com) is a semiconductor company that was a spin-off from Lucent Technologies, itself a spin-off from AT&T/Bell Laboratories. It is therefore by tradition a product-oriented business. The semiconductor industry is a cyclical one subject to economic fluctuations and is characterised by rapid product innovation and obsolescence, evolving standards, rapid price erosion and dramatic changes in end-customer demand for products such as mobile phones, digital cameras, computer related products of all types and other electronic products. For any semiconductor company end-customers would be, for example, hard drive suppliers such as Seagate; PC suppliers such as Dell and HP; mobile phone companies like Nokia and Samsung; networking equipment such as Cisco and Huawei; telecommunications including Ericsson and Nortel.

Agere has a worldwide sales organisation with approximately 300 employees with 8 US sales offices and 14 outside the United States. Most sales, around 90 per cent of revenues, are direct sales approached in one of three ways:

1   Key account selling – two companies account for roughly 25 per cent or revenue, but no other customers account for more than 10 per cent of sales. These two companies are managed as key accounts.

2 System or team selling – Sales, marketing and technical personnel work with customers primarily to achieve a design solution. Therefore this is a classic organisational buying situation involving the purchasing manager finance, production and various technical support staff comprising the decision-making unit (DMU).

3 Industrial direct – where the end customers, typically, would conduct a competitive process of supplier and component selection. To win the design technical sales consultants need to work with the customer's product design team to demonstrate Agere's ability to solve the customer's problem. Where necessary the salesperson may require the help of a team depending on the contract being sought.

The sales approach is one where the emphasis is on a design solution, seeking to add value by working with customers in joint cost reduction, joint product development and multiple interaction between personnel of both companies. A quality focus, high levels of customer service and the need to retain customers are all vital in this business. Even with this commitment to customers and technology the industry is highly competitive. To sustain and win business Agere must change and develop their sales operations.

Consider your solution in three different areas:

1 What objectives should be set for improving information in the sales process with what purpose?

2 How can the market be segmented so that different sales approaches can be used for different customer groups?

3 What initiatives should be pursued to establish an online presence for sales in this sector?

Key terms

- customer relationship management
- database marketing
- electronic commerce
- Internet
- sales force automation
- sales information system
- telemarketing

References

AMR Research Available at: http://www.amr.com [Accessed 24 July 2006]

Bose, R. (2002) 'Customer relationship management: key components for IT success' *Journal of Industrial Management and Data Systems* **102** (2): 89–97

Bovet, D., Toy, P. and Kochersperger, G. (2003) 'Why senior executives should care about sourcing' *Mercer Management Journal* **16** (Nov): 32–41

Brown, S.A. (2000) *Customer Relationship Management* John Wiley and Sons: Ontario

Burns, T. and Stalker, G.M. (1961) *The Management of Innovation* Tavistock Publications: London

DeVincentis, J.R. and Rackham, N. (1998) 'Breadth of a Salesman' *The McKinsey Quarterly* no. 4: 32–43

Donaldson, B. and Resch, G. (2006) 'Why it is too soon to kill off the salesperson: some limitations with electronic reverse auctions' *Proceedings of the Academy of Marketing* Middlesex University: London

Donaldson, B. and Wright, G. (2002) 'Sales information systems: are they being used for more than simple mail shots?' *Journal of Database Marketing* **9** (3): 276–84

Emiliani, M.L. and Stec, D.J. (2002) 'Realizing savings from online reverse auctions' *Supply Chain Management: An International Journal* **7** (1): 12–23

Emiliani, W.L. (2004) 'Regulating B2B online reverse auctions through voluntary codes of conduct' *Industrial Marketing Management* **34** (5): 526–34

Engle, R.L. and Barnes, M.L. (2000) 'Sales force automation usage, effectiveness, and cost-benefit in Germany, England and the United States' *The Journal of Business and Industrial Marketing* **15** (4): 216–41

Erffmeyer, R.C. and Johnson, D.A. (2001) 'An exploratory study of sales force automation practices: expectations and realities' *Journal of Personal Selling and Sales Management* **21** (2): 167–75

Garbarino, E. and Johnson, M.S. (1999) 'The different roles of satisfaction, trust, and commitment in customer relationships' *Journal of Marketing* **63** (Apr): 70–87

Hahn, D. and Kaufmann, L. (2002) *Handbuch Industrielles Beschaffungsmanagement* Wiesbaden: Gabler

Handen, L. (2000) 'Putting CRM to Work' in Brown, S.A. (ed.) *Customer Relationship Management* John Wiley and Sons: Ontario, 7–18

Herald (2006) 'Changing the conceptions about call centres' 20 October: 4

Jap, S.D. (2000) 'Going going gone' *Harvard Business Review* **78**(6) Nov/Dec: 30

Jap, S.D. (2003) 'An exploratory study of the introduction of online reverse auctions' *Journal of Marketing* **67** (3): 96–107

Jones, J., Sundaram, S. and Chin, W. (2002) 'Factors leading to sales force automation use: a longitudinal analysis' *Journal of Personal Selling and Sales Management* **22** (3): 145–56

Keillor, B., Bashaw, R.E. and Pettijohn, C.E. (1997) 'Sales force automation issues prior to implementation: the relationship between attitudes towards technology, experience and productivity' *Journal of Business and Industrial Marketing* **12** (3/4): 209–19

Krizan, W. (2003) 'New guidelines may take some pain out of reverse auctions' *Engineering News Record* **251** (21): 14

Lawrence, P.R. and Lorsch, J.W. (1967) 'Differentiation and integration in complex organizations' *Administrative Science Quarterly* **12** (1): 1–47

Mintzberg, H. (1983) *Structure in fives: Designing Effective Organisations* Prentice Hall: Englewood Cliffs, NJ

OICA (2005) OICA Statistics [Online] Available at: http://www.oica.net/htdocs/Main.htm [Accessed 19 June 2005]

Oliva, R. (2003) 'Sold on reverse auctions' *Marketing Management* **12** (2): 44

Ore, N. (2003) 'The reverse auction: a strategic perspective' [Online]. s.t. s.l. Available at: http://www.ism.ws/ResourceArticles/Proceedings/2003/CoundouriotisGI.pdf

Parthasarathy, M. and Sohi, R. (1997) 'Sales force automation and the adoption of technological innovations by salespeople: theory and implications' *Journal of Business and Industrial Marketing* **12** (3/4): 196–208

Parvatiyar, A.and Sheth, J.D. (2001) 'Customer relationship management: emerging practice, process, and discipline' *Journal of Economic and Social Research* **3** (2): 1–34

Payne, K. (2000) 'Improving sales force productivity' in Reeves, J. (ed.) *Customer Relationship Management* Caspian Publishing Ltd, CBI Business Guide: London, 58–62

Peppers, D. and Rogers, M. (2004) *Managing Customer Relationships* John Wiley & Sons: Hoboken, NJ

Perrien, J. and Ricard, L. (1995) 'The meaning of a marketing relationship: a pilot study' *Industrial Marketing Management* **24** (1): 37–43

Rivers, L.M. and Dart, J. (1999) 'The acquisition and use of sales force automation by mid-size manufacturers' *Journal of Personal Selling and Sales Management* **19** (2): 53–73

Robey, D. and Boudreau, M.C. (1999) 'Accounting for the contradictory organizational consequences of information technology: theoretical directions and methodological implications' *Information Systems Research* **10** (Jun): 167–85

Speier, C. and Venkatesh, V. (2002) 'The hidden minefields in the adoption of sales force automation technologies' *Journal of Marketing* **66** (July): 98–111

Sujan, H., Weitz, B.A. and Kumar, N. (1994) 'Learning orientation, working smart, and effective selling' *Journal of Marketing* **58** (Jul): 39–52

Sviokla, J.J. (1996) 'Knowledge workers and radically new technologies' *Sloan Management Review* **37** (Summer): 25–40

Tulder, R.V. and Mol, M. (2002) 'Reversed auctions or auctions reversed: first experiments by Philips' *European Management Journal* **20** (5): 447–56

Venkatesh, N. (2000) 'Determinants of perceived ease of use: integrating control, intrinsic motivation and emotion into the technology acceptance model' *Information Systems Research* **11** (4): 342–65

Venkatesh, N. and Davis, F.D. (2000) 'A theoretical extension of the technology acceptance model: four longitudinal field studies' *Management Science* **46** (2): 186–204

Widmier, S.M. and Jackson, D.W. (2002) 'Infusing technology into personal selling' *Journal of Personal Selling and Sales Management* **23** (3): 189–98

Wright, G. and Donaldson, B. (2002) 'Sales information systems in the UK financial services industry: an analysis of sophistication of use and perceived barriers to adoption' *International Journal of Information Management* **22**: 105–119

7 Sales forecasting and setting targets

7.1 Overview

One activity that all businesses do to some degree is to anticipate future events. From the one-man business to the multinational conglomerate and regardless of whether the business is product-, production- or sales-oriented, enterprises have to operate on the basis of expectations about the future. Particular questions concerning how much capital will be required, what scale of plant, how much product to make and stock, what level of sales support and advertising and how many people to employ require an estimate of revenue from future sales. It is one of the major responsibilities of the marketing function to make sound and careful appraisal of business opportunities and is not the responsibility of the finance or sales departments. For this reason, a detailed appraisal of sales forecasting methods should be part of a marketing or specialist text on the subject. The topic is introduced in this book for four particular reasons. First, most companies use sales force input in their forecasts. This is as it should be, although the extent and method of this input needs careful evaluation. Second, although it is a marketing responsibility, salespeople and sales managers must understand the importance, the process and the methods of sales forecasting. Third, the sales forecast ought to be the major influence on sales targets at both company and individual territory level. Finally, developments in information technology make it necessary for sales management to understand and use modern marketing information systems, of which the sales forecasting process is a major component.

7.2 Learning objectives

This chapter aims to

- help you realise the importance of sales forecasts and understand their use;
- describe the process of forecasting and some of the techniques;
- explain the connection between sales forecasts, sales budgets and sales targets;
- illustrate the components in a sales budget;
- consider the different ways of setting sales targets;
- evaluate the options in sales targets both quantitative and qualitative.

7.3   Definitions

A **company sales forecast** is an estimate of the level of company sales for a future time period.

The **sales budget** is the sum allocated to convert sales effort into sales over a definite time period.

A **sales target** is the portion of total work that an individual or group should aim to achieve by their own efforts.

7.4   Sales forecasting

The outcome of forecasting activity is aimed at an accurate sales figure, but it is more appropriate to view forecasting as a process. It is important to be clear on the terminology since often there is confusion about the difference between forecasts, budgets and targets (Figure 7.1).

The sales forecast itself will normally be in three parts. Part A is a general forecast of economic and business conditions. This is an estimate of the total level of demand based on the number of consumers, their desires and their purchasing ability. Part B is an industry sales forecast including the anticipated effects of competitors' past, present and future activity. This represents the immediate market potential. Part C is the company sales forecast based on the company's share of the market but taking into account current business, marketing and sales planning activity. Beware of possible confusion over this circular process. Company plans are based on market and industry conditions and on aspects of strategic goals and environmental appraisals. Part C, the company sales forecast, must be based on the marketing effort planned and not the other way round. Sometimes if the company is large with monopoly power in the market, its plans will affect not only company sales but the industry and market forecast as well. The company sales forecast provides the input for budgets which are

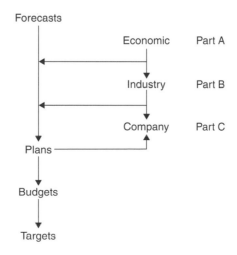

Fig 7.1   The forecasting process

financial expressions of these plans. These budgets are used by individual functions and departments to monitor and control their activities, for example, capital budget, sales budget and so on. Targets, sometimes called quotas, can be set at the same level as forecasts (best estimate) but are usually set higher for the sales force as an incentive but lower by finance for prudence and conservatism.

With sales forecasting, the first step is to set objectives related to the purpose of the forecast and the time period. The relevant time period must relate to the nature of the business since the ability to react is clearly limited for a new power station or steel plant compared to a retailer. Forecasts normally relate to a given trading period but may be classified as

- *short-run forecasts* of up to one trading period which are used to decide operating budget levels, stock levels, production schedules and cash flow.
- *medium-term forecasts*, normally covering one to three years ahead, although in some cases a five-year period; these forecasts help to decide on the number and type of machines, the raw material, manpower and other asset-building decisions.
- *long-run forecasts* of up to ten years for decisions of a more strategic nature, such as the need for new plant, premises and technological developments; forecasts for the very long run or technological forecasting will not be covered in this section.

Before addressing the techniques and methods of sales forecasting, the different uses and purposes of the sales forecast must be identified. Sales forecasts are of critical importance to the modern enterprise, yet it is surprising to see the degree of sophistication in financial appraisal techniques, such as net present value and yield, which rely primarily on an accurate sales forecast with nothing like the same degree of exactness, sophistication or objectivity. The sales forecast is likely to be used by operations, logistics, supply-chain partners both up and downstream, human resources, finance and marketing as part of their planning activities. Important to all users is accuracy as each department uses the forecast as the starting point for its own operations and budgets. It should be apparent that accuracy is relative to the purpose the forecast is being used for and in some cases, such as cash flow, accuracy is crucial. In all uses, a trade-off between cost and accuracy has to be made, as shown in Figure 7.2. Again, better

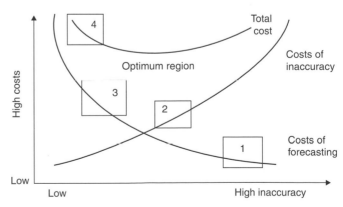

1 Guesswork, consensus methods   3 Statistical models and regressions
2 More sophisticated research methods 4 Causal, econometric models

Fig 7.2   Cost versus accuracy in forecasting (*Chambers et al., 1971*)

management will require more explicit, quantifiable benefits of the accuracy versus costs of forecasting. The need is to attempt to minimise the total cost, which is a summation of the cost of forecasting and the costs of inaccuracy. On this graph can be superimposed the different methods of forecasting, from simple estimates to complex econometric causal models (shown as 1 to 4 in Figure 7.2).

Did you know?

Forecasting accuracy

In a 1998 study consisting 75 per cent consumer and 25 per cent industrial organisations, it was found that the degree of forecast error could be attributed to three main areas (competition intensity, degree of technological change and degree of promotional activity). Surprisingly, the study found that 15 per cent of companies did not measure forecast error or forecasting accuracy. The companies most satisfied with the forecasting process had the common elements of a dedicated sales forecasting function (which was both accountable and had high credibility) and also measured accuracy to some extent.

(Source: Kahn, 1998)

Sales forecasting methods can be classified into three groupings: first, forecasts based on the use of market research and customer knowledge, second, using a consensus approach by the sales force or top management, and third, using statistical methods. These three approaches are not mutually exclusive and all three methods, and various techniques within each method, can be used together. There are some basic rules which need to be considered before choosing the most appropriate sales forecasting technique.

7.5　Basic rules of sales forecasting

Rule 1:　Distinguish between hard and soft data. Hard data are facts which can be objectively assessed such as past sales or verifiable information. Soft data are subjectively assessed, such as measures of opinion or attitude. When using soft data, questions need to be asked about how the data were collected, who collected the information, for what reason and by what method.

Rule 2:　Use as few variables as possible and distinguish between dependent and independent variables. The dependent variable, normally sales, is related to changes in many independent variables such as sales activity, price, advertising and so on. If too many variables are included, the forecast model becomes complex and expensive but not necessarily cost-effective in terms of accuracy. Past sales, trend and seasonal and cyclical factors are usually sufficient to explain most variations.

Rule 3:　Use general economic and industry indicators that have proved most reliable, such as housing starts or brick production in construction indices and disposable income for consumer markets.

Rule 4:　Identify appropriate time relationships, particularly lag effects.

Rule 5:　Do not use variables which cannot themselves be forecasted, such as the persuasiveness of salespeople.

Objective forecasts are those which use hard rather than soft data and incorporate quantitative and mathematical technique rather than guesswork. Subjective techniques are guesses about the future based on knowledge and experience. The advantage of objective or explicit techniques is that the assumptions and relationships on which forecasting is based can subsequently be evaluated for relevance and accuracy. This does not, however, mean that accuracy is more assured. As we know all forecasts are wrong but they differ in the extent of their wrongness. There are problems which beset any forecast and which must be at least anticipated if not always measured. Such problems include

- the multivariate nature of marketing problems – many factors impinge on the sales response function and, while models can reach high levels of complexity, every eventuality in a dynamic situation cannot be incorporated;
- related to the first problem is the difficulty in detecting and isolating the interaction effects between different elements in the marketing mix;
- competitors' actions, which are difficult to predict yet crucial to the outcome;
- short-run fluctuations, such as increased stocking prior to a price increase, which affect sales stability and possibly long-run trends;
- some variables such as selling effort and advertising, which have a significant effect yet are very difficult to measure; this leads to quantifying subjectivity and often spurious accuracy;
- new products, which are always likely to be a special case.

A *model-building*, more explicit approach to forecasting should be preferred to the use of hunch, guesswork or consensus methods. Models may at some point lose realism by becoming over-sophisticated and unrealistic in their assumptions and common sense is required in the application of any technique.

What do you think?

Factors important in the evaluation of a sales forecasting system

Mentzer and Khan (1995) reviewed a number of studies to assess the factors that were considered to be important in evaluating forecasting effectiveness:

Criteria	Sample size	% important
Accuracy	205	92
Credibility	206	92
Customer service performance	199	77
Ease of use	206	75
Inventory turns	198	55
Amount of data required	205	46
Cost	205	41
Return on investment	199	35

(Source: Mentzer and Khan, 1995, p. 474)

Since cost and return on investment are viewed as less important, it is concluded that forecasting techniques are often not evaluated on financial measures. The findings from their forecasting technique familiarity study suggested that forecasting techniques alone will not necessarily improve accuracy.

7.6 Methods of forecasting

Using market research and customer knowledge

To implement the marketing concept, the most appropriate approach is to understand and assess the needs of customers and potential customers. As a method of forecasting, this is not always possible, seldom easy and not always accurate. It can be done by senior executives and salespeople in industrial goods where there are a few large customers with readily identifiable needs. Generally, customers themselves do not know their own requirements and, in the case of consumer goods, there is a lack of hard data on large numbers of customers. 'Will you buy product X?' could provide answers of 'yes', 'no', 'don't know', 'maybe' and 'maybe not', which is quite different from what consumers actually do. More sophisticated market research techniques and questioning can minimise the error and improve accuracy, but it is costly for individual products and a weak means of continuous forecasting for purposes such as stock levels, production scheduling or cash flow. The main difficulties are overoptimism by customers and a lack of commitment. Important, too, is the representativeness of the sample and the quality of respondent, since many markets are typified by a few large buyers. For example, in 2005, four supermarket groups accounted for 56 per cent of UK food retail sales (Mintel, 2006). The uncertainty of competitive actions and reactions compound the problem. The use of these assessment methods of forecasting should be restricted to where there are only a few users who are likely to know their future requirements, where competition is known and where inertia between buyer and seller is strong. This means that a consistency and predictability will exist. The use of continuous survey material, retail audits and omnibus surveys can contribute to build up in forecasting methods, especially where distribution channels are long and complex. If suppliers become separated and remote from buyers or end users, such information is vital. Even in these circumstances, surveys are best used in conjunction with other forecasting methods.

Since salespeople are an expensive resource the amount of time they should spend on information gathering is a hotly debated issue among practising sales managers. This issue also relates to the sophistication and use of sales automation systems discussed in Chapter 6.

Using a consensus approach

This is normally conducted by a jury of executive or expert opinion or by the sales force. The advantages of sales force consensus methods are primarily that each person within the organisation who is closest to their customers provides the input. Other advantages could be that it provides a necessary discipline for the salesperson to identify opportunities and understand market trends. As noted earlier, the modern salesperson has had to be more strategic so that they know, understand and help their customers own marketing and sales plans. Also, participation and involvement in future planning is important for salespeople's morale and motivation.

Consider also some of the disadvantages:

■ Forecasting can be time consuming when there are many customers and product groups;

■ Accuracy on individual customers and products is likely to be variable;

- Value forecasts are subject to inflationary distortion and future price changes that salespeople will have limited understanding of and even less control;
- It is difficult to set individual sales targets, which may conflict with the salesperson's own forecast;
- Salespeople want to beat their forecast rather than achieve accuracy;
- Salespeople are generally optimistic – too optimistic over the longer term – and the future always shows unjustified increases, making long-run predictions overstated;
- The usefulness of salespeople as providers of market information has to be used carefully, objectively and in a cost-efficient manner. If salespeople have a few large customers on single or limited products and have regular contact with informed buyers, their input will be invaluable.

The other consensus methods, such as the jury of executive opinion, vary from the board agreeing that next year's forecast will be this year's sales plus 10 per cent, to using a range of experts such as investment analysts or using internal personnel, such as the sales manager's estimate. Various procedures can be recommended to conduct such a consensus, but the danger of this is that it implies some scientific method to what is, after all, guesswork. The main advantage of expert or executive opinion is that people making such a forecast are also the people who have it within their power to achieve it.

Using objective techniques

The objective techniques fall into two categories: time series and causal methods. Time series refers to a family of techniques where time is used as a proxy to replace all other independent variables and thus permits the application of straightforward arithmetic to what is a complex problem. The evidence for this approach can be summed up as a combination of cost and pragmatism. Sales do not depend on time, and the longer the time lapse, the less appropriate the method becomes, but the inertia between buyers and sellers referred to earlier does permit the use of this notion in sales forecasting. Dramatic changes do not normally occur overnight and the use of ceteris paribus (other things being equal) assumptions can be used.

With causal methods an attempt is made to predict the dependent variable (sales) from one or more identified independent variables (price, promotional effort, economic and industry trends, etc.), the value of which is known or can be predicted with reasonable accuracy. If the independent variable cannot be estimated, there is no point guessing it or using this method since this is tantamount to guessing the forecast. Certain indicators, for example, economic growth, industrial production and housing starts, are well predicted and hence good indicators which can be used for the particular product or market in question. The sales manager should not worry about their quantitative skills with these techniques as modern computer software provides the calculation. However, it is important to understand the basic concept and appropriateness of each technique.

Remember

- that forecasting is a process;
- to identify the uses of the sales forecast and the time periods covered; new products will create special forecasting problems;

- to clarify the purpose of the forecast, follow the basic rules and be clear on problems and assumptions; particular attention must be given to matching the sales forecasting technique to the decision task;
- to set up and use a forecast procedure;
- to use a combination of techniques and approaches to verify the result.

7.7   Sales budgets

The sales forecast is the base prediction of future sales, given certain assumptions which form the basis for the company's operations in the next trading period, usually one year ahead. From this, budgets can be set within different departments and operating areas of the business. For example,

Forecast sales revenue for the period	£20 million
Material Costs	£6 million
Operational costs/ gross margin	£4 million
Contribution (50%)	£10 million
Selling, administration and distribution (SAD)	£5 million
Profit (25%)	£5 million

In formulating budgets, account has to be taken of strategic and marketing objectives such as the planned increase in market share, the means to achieve this and the degree of realism in these plans. A 10 per cent increase in sales does not materialise from being written or stated. They come from successful implementation of the sales plan. At this stage of planning the inputs from marketing research can be added to existing policies on product, price, promotion and distribution in the marketing operations plan. An essential ingredient is the financial expression of these plans in the form of a series of budgets which turn intentions into assignments at a cost, capital budgets, expense budgets, cash flow appraisals and schedules, of which the sales budget is a part.

The sales budget therefore is the sum allocated to convert sales effort into sales over a definite time period. Since resources are scarce, growth in profits is achieved by greater efficiency in returns over expenditure. The management decides where to allocate each pound of expense to best effect – a new machine, a market survey, an advertising campaign or an extra salesperson? The sales manager is primarily concerned with the sales budget. Decisions have to be made to achieve £x sales revenue with £Y expenditure on people and £Z on expenses. Should the sales manager offer greater incentives to existing staff, offer better car and expenses or recruit extra salespeople?

The sales manager's problem is to decide on the required amount of money and the best means of allocation. Improvement comes from increasing sales, reducing costs or changing the product mix to produce a more profitable result. If the manager tries to economise on the budget (reducing costs), the risk increases of sales volume not being achieved. Conversely, if sales volume is achieved or increased but at a higher cost, the overspending reduces profitability. This is a basic dilemma for management or as the Americans might say, 'You put your budget money where you get the most bang for your buck'.

Sales budgets set out in financial terms the responsibilities of the sales manager in achieving sales objectives. A budget is a financial or quantitative statement prepared and approved prior to a defined period of time for the sales policy to achieve a given objective. The sales budget has three benefits:

1 *Planning*. The cost of different options can be assessed revealing whether the selected approach is satisfactory.

2 *Coordination*. It helps management to link the different cost centres to coordinate responsibilities and objectives within marketing as well as between sales and production.

3 *Control*. Since budgets serve as a quantitative expression of measuring performance, they indicate if going off course and warn to take remedial action.

There are several methods used for setting sales budgets, each with many variations:

■ *Percentage of sales*. The most convenient for administrative reasons this method, for example, sales costs at 10 per cent of revenue, has little to commend it with the exception of simplicity and clarity.

■ *Executive judgement*, which is often vague in justification but does have the advantage of top management involvement, implying also commitment.

■ *Unit build-up method*, which attempts to allocate on the basis of specific objectives for a salesperson or area. Funds can be increased or reduced between weak and strong areas to improve effectiveness. The advantage should be greater flexibility since cost centres will otherwise tend to repeat the previous period's allocation, regardless of need. Experience may encourage managers to request more than is needed and to spend all they can get. A variation of this method is the so-called zero-base budget which expects each manager to identify the tasks, costs and benefits of each area of responsibility and assign a priority to its execution. This clearly requires time and effort to complete but avoids the year-on-year ritual of spending without real objectives or justification.

■ Rate of return on investment. The sales force can be viewed as both investment and expense. For most sales forces, variations at the margin are not easily achieved. The case can be put forward for treating sales revenue and expense as an investment decision on which the rate of return can be calculated. By increasing sales, reducing costs or influencing the deployment of assets the rate of return can be improved. Figure 7.3 shows the elements of the sales budget and Figure 7.4 a control document to assess individual performance:

7.8 Sales targets

A sales target (or quota) can be defined as the portion of the total work that an individual or group should aim to achieve by their own efforts. The normal methods by which targets are set are sales volume or value, costs of sales or selling activities and, in some cases, profit contribution.

Almost all firms use sales volume or value for an individual salesperson as a basic sales target, that is, to achieve £X,000 sales in Y weeks for A, B or C product groups.

		Approx. 60% of total
Salaries and wages Employers contribution Pension scheme		
Motor expenses Travel Entertainment Telephone		Approx. 20%
Sales incentives Sales conference Direct sales support Miscellaneous		Approx. 20%

Fig 7.3   Sales budget – selling expenses

	Salesperson A			B	C
	Mean	Actual	Variance		
Salaries Employers' contribution Other costs (pension, BUPA)					
Motor and transport Lodging and meals Telephone Entertainment					
Sales incentive Direct sales support Samples/literture Miscellaneous					

Fig 7.4   Budget

They can be set by area, product line, customer or a combination of these. Alternatively, targets can be set against operating costs or expenses and measured on net profit or some contribution rate of return. Another way in which targets can be set is against some activity measure such as call rates, new business or specific tasks set by management. Many companies use a combination of targets, the appropriateness depending on both their objectives and the ability of salespeople to achieve them.

Purpose of sales targets

1   *To evaluate sales performance.* Some managers of 'the hire and fire school' set targets to be achieved, or else, in this school, if a salesperson fails to make their quota, they are dismissed. Little more needs to be said about this approach. To be workable as a means of evaluation, targets set should be realistic and accurate for each territory

if they are to be used as a measure of productivity for salespeople. Since many factors affect performance, such targets should incorporate sales, budget costs and activity measures. Indeed, in many service selling jobs, 'activities' may be more important to success than a purely quantitative sales objective. If sales alone are used to measure performance, other tasks, identified as crucial to the selling job, may be neglected. This is yet another reason for specifying in writing what needs to be done, for having a job description and a fair evaluation procedure.

2   *As an incentive for salespeople.* If self-motivation and drive are characteristics which salespeople ought to have, targets promote a 'go for it' type attitude. Salespeople, more than those in most categories of job, will have an in-built desire to achieve and beat target. Targets, to work as motivators, must be set neither too high nor too low or they may become counterproductive in subsequent trading periods. While the old school of leading-from-the-front motivation can and does work, there is a danger of setting targets too high or 'moving the goalposts', which may discourage good performers (Chowdhury, J.1993).

3   *As a means of remuneration.* Combination methods of payment, such as salary and commission or salary and bonus, are common in payment structures. This is because incentive payments are powerful motivators for salespeople to achieve results. Sales above the target level are a bonus for the company, yet highly desirable and, as such, deserve a reward. Careful evaluation of these schemes is required to balance good and bad trading periods.

4   *To control activities.* Targets permit specific objectives to be set which direct selling activity, such as the type of account or specific product targets. Again, these type of targets will be more effective if rewards and appraisals are built into the scheme.

Well-designed targets may achieve all of these purposes, but it must be borne in mind that sales do not operate independently of marketing policies, product acceptance, competitive factors and the overall promotional spend. It follows that the onus is on management to set and control targets on a realistic and fair basis. Between the extremes of paying salespeople a basic rate like everyone else or paying on the basis of individual greed lies a target level which can both motivate and control individuals to achieve sales objectives. The most common methods used to determine sales targets are as follows:

1   *Based on economic or leading indicators in the market.* Economic growth, disposable income, new car sales, population trends and housing starts are a few of the indicators which could be used to set targets for salespeople. This is similar to the breakdown method used in forecasting and may be appropriate where specific territory information is not available and sales do closely follow lead indicators.

2   *Historical perspective.* This is usually no more than last year's sales plus a desired percentage increase. This is a very quick and convenient method but has little else to commend it. It would assume that there is no variation between areas, individuals or growth rates in products. Any previous inadequacies or errors would be perpetuated ad infinitum. Past sales are one factor in setting sales targets but not the only one. Some account must be taken of changing conditions resulting in varying growth rates between products and territories.

3   *Managerial judgement.* In the absence of any other information, this way may be as good as any but will often result in targets which are arbitrary, unfair and ill informed. There is, however, some merit in leading from the front, although the target will too often be morale-defeating rather than effort-stimulating.

4 *Salespeople set their own.* Since it is desirable to enhance the managerial responsibilities and status of salespeople, one way of achieving this would be to allow sales staff to set their own objectives. Their ability, expertise and motivation can all be questioned in this approach, and the outcome is likely to be over- or understating the estimate. It may also be an abdication of management responsibility rather than a delegation of authority. Salespeople must be involved, but loss of control by management cannot be allowed.

5 *Targets based on territory potential.* The response models previously outlined are a powerful way in which to set sales targets. Salespeople are allocated on the basis of sales potential, and this should also be the sales target. Targets are, however, likely to be somewhat less than the optimum to take account of variations in ability, market standing and regional conditions. With better information, forecasting and computing capability, sales managers have the facility to be more accurate in setting targets.

The means of setting targets is important but so too is the accuracy and speed of information exchange between head office and the sales force. Accuracy in reporting sales against target, expense levels against budget and customer-specific data can have an effect on salesperson motivation. Great time and effort are often spent on setting standards and measuring the performance of production operatives, for example, through work–study methods. With sales representatives, it is more difficult, for a variety of reasons. For example, activities in selling are mostly performed without direct observation by management. Furthermore, each territory has differences, some of which are unique to that area – its geography, level of competition and customer prosperity. The result is that direct comparisons between one salesperson and another are difficult, even where territory potential, age and experience may be similar.

Part of the sales management task is to get salespeople to do the job in a cost-efficient manner, to optimise the return on investment for the sales budget. Otherwise, salespeople will seek their own objectives, which may be inefficient and wasteful. It is necessary to set achievable targets which encourage improved performance but take into account many other factors, particularly the ability and experience of salespeople themselves.

7.9   Quantitative sales targets

Sales by volume or value

Almost all firms who set targets will use some sales volume basis. This is simple to understand and easy to calculate. Each salesperson must generate sufficient volume to cover the costs of operating – salary, expenses, supervision, administration and contribution to profit. There are potential problems in such a direct approach. For example, on what basis is the target set, orders received or sales invoiced? Is it based on a geographical area, number of customers, time period, multi-products or total sales? The danger may be that, in answering these questions, achievement of the target may be well below the optimum.

Most salespeople, like most firms, find the easiest option is existing sales in existing products with current customers. Orders from existing accounts – service-selling – may be at the expense of potential new business. While some business may be lost and new accounts won, the amount of effort in one time period may not show until future time periods – development selling. Similarly, there is no incentive to improve performance by modifying the product mix, a very difficult job to achieve at any time. However, greater profits can be achieved by selling less at better margins than maximum output at low margins. Again, the tasks that salespeople are expected to accomplish vary. To do a balanced job as information-provider, technical adviser, complaint-handler or whatever requires emphasis on the service elements of the salesperson's task and not only on achieving sales volume target in one period. Volume targets discourage a balanced selling effort since they stress sales volume to the detriment of non-selling activities.

Product targets

These are similar to sales volume targets except that the salesperson is expected to achieve sales according to a specified product mix, thus overcoming one of the disadvantages of the sales volume target, that is, achieving a more profitable mix. It does not cure the other disadvantages mentioned above. Furthermore, in many industrial-type markets, information on customers and competitors may change, as could the added value of different product groups. The main criticism of product targets is that they are seldom market-related. Salespeople are asked to sell more of what the customer does not want at higher prices to meet company production or financial objectives. This seldom works as intended since it is a sales rather than a marketing-oriented approach. It is also against all the principles of consultative/solution selling.

Both sales and product quotas can suffer other practical drawbacks. For example, head-office contracts affect sales to individual retail outlets and trading between intermediaries overlaps company sales territories. That is, sales by one person to an account may actually be delivered to another person's area. Most companies have major accounts with widespread geographical areas where the salesperson's role may be service- or merchandise-, rather than volume-, related. Computer allocation to fictitious areas could overcome this problem, but the effect on individuals can be demotivating if they are servicing an account yet not being credited with achieving the sales.

Expenses to sales ratio

In improving sales performance, the combination of sales increases and cost reductions is the most potent, yet these are clearly conflicting objectives. Expense to sales ratios attempt to motivate salespeople to compromise on these objectives by permitting higher costs or expenses, if higher sales are achieved. Strangely enough, most higher management squeal when higher sales equate with higher levels of payment to salespeople, especially if sales staff earn more than the managing director!

Gross margin on orders

This type of target assesses performance on profitability, usually by a balance being achieved between product groups and customers. It requires adequate, often confidential, information to salespeople on the profitability of sales – contribution, trade discounts, customer rebates – and creates a security problem with a larger sales force. Performance in one time period may be detrimental to performance in the longer term where new products and new account business is in the growth/development stage.

Market share

One important measure of competitiveness and profitability is market share. For many products, especially consumer goods, market estimates by region or sales area are available. If this is so, it is possible to set targets on the achievement of a desired market share level. Definition of what constitutes the market will be important. For example, market may be by volume, value or number of outlets, the share of each being quite different. Most companies operate multi-product lines in diverse markets, making definition more spurious. Selling costs, profitability and potential new accounts are neglected with this target method. Furthermore, the main effects on market share may be the ability accurately to segment the market, to identify target customers and to provide the most suitable mix to maintain a competitive advantage which the salesperson can then promote. The sales force cannot do an effective job with poor tools.

Sales versus potential

In territory design, it was found that potential is the most important discriminating factor in performance. If sources of market and customer information are accurate, it would be desirable to measure sales performance against potential. This would be particularly appropriate where there are a fixed number of contracts, and a strike rate of 1 in 3 or 1 in 5 may be expected to be achieved. This takes account of new business and specific sales objectives. The practical difficulties in the realistic measurement of potential will be a problem.

Calls made

Most salespeople operate on the basis of a system of daily and weekly calls. Management can establish an average call rate for their company and compare with averages for the industry or type of selling. Salespeople below average can be asked to increase their call rate; those above may be asked how productive each call made is in achieving sales objectives. Remember, areas and customers vary considerably as do specific call objectives and the type of selling, so coverage may be a measure apropos of nothing. Calls do not equal sales.

Call frequency ratio

Territory models, particularly salespeople's own input, are helpful in selecting between calls and improving journey planning. Pre-set call targets can be established against which sales performance can be assessed. Likewise, specific development calls on specifiers can be built into an individual's sales programme. Alternatively an order-to-call ratio could be used. This is favoured in direct selling to assess the sales leads converted and attempts to score representatives on some form of 'batting average'. These measures usually fail to take into account territory differences, customer quality and competitive influences in an area. This may reflect better on some than on others. Profit is again neglected.

Average order size

The aim is to improve average order size (that is, total sales divided by the number of orders) and presumably reduce small orders or uneconomic accounts. One problem is that particular situations may result in a relatively low figure as a result of intermediaries own sales and stocking policy, not necessarily a reliable measure of sales performance.

Return on investment

As described in the sales budget section, return on investment (ROI) can be used at the individual level. For example, for every £X000 sales, there will be a company cost (A) plus expenses (B) plus profit (C), which can be calculated to estimate the rate of return:

(X) Sales revenue	£1000
(C) Profit (6%)	£60
(A) Company cost (2%)	£40
(B) Selling expenses (7%)	£30

Therefore ROI = 85% (100 − 6 − 2 − 7)

One difficulty with this sort of calculation is to ignore the impact of the carry-over effect of sales effort into subsequent trading periods.

The above list is by no means exhaustive of the quantitative targets which can be used. The level of sophistication in their use can also vary depending on managerial judgement, economic or regional assessments, historical factors and anticipated growth rates. Whatever measures are selected, purely quantitative methods have many potential weaknesses relative to a complete selling job. In all cases, speedy, accurate information from management or head office to salespeople will be important.

7.10   Qualitative sales targets

The weaknesses of certain aspects of quantitative targets, together with a desire by management to achieve wider tasks by sales staff, suggest that various qualitative sales targets can be used as part of the target-setting procedure. Evidence in the United States suggests that top companies are more flexible in their choice and use of targets than averagely performing companies, relating them not only to the individual but in a team selling context (Brown *et al.*, 2005). In other words, targets are adapted and varied according to corporate, marketing and sales objectives. Qualitative targets could include the ability to

- do the entire selling job;
- service existing accounts;
- locate and secure new customers;
- help intermediaries to sell on to users;
- provide technical advice;

- train retailer salespeople;
- provide information to customers and users on product changes and promotional support;
- secure display space and adequate stock with intermediaries;
- collect market and competitive information;
- be ambassadors for the company.

The relevance of these qualitative factors will vary between firms, and neither are they, by any means, a comprehensive list. Other factors considered by sales managers to be important include

- attitude;
- product knowledge;
- selling skills;
- appearance;
- customer knowledge;
- competitor and market knowledge;
- report writing and administration;
- company image and goodwill.

Good sales targets require selecting the most appropriate quantitative and qualitative objectives relevant to the job and tasks. The best targets are not only the most appropriate but also those which involve the sales force. Performance will be influenced by the degree of personal involvement in target-setting, itself another determinant of role clarity and job satisfaction. As far as management control is concerned, targets can have an important influence on job satisfaction. Good targets

- are clear and concise;
- are measurable and attainable;
- fit organisational goals;
- cover short-, medium- and long-term objectives;
- are both qualitative and quantitative;
- are rewarded for achievement;
- contribute to job satisfaction and improved performance by involving salespeople;
- do not encourage the salesperson to utilise behaviours that will damage the organisation's purpose/brand

7.11   Summary

An understanding of the process of sales forecasting and the techniques which are available is necessary if the modern sales manager is to function effectively. The calculation and the detail can be done using current software packages, but the sales manager must realise the importance of accurate sales forecasting throughout the organisation. Sales budgets also must be set and controlled. Salespeople are frequently used as sources of information which can improve management decision-making processes, but such information gathering is time consuming, expensive and may be biased. Sales managers need to understand how to use salespeople effectively in this role. Almost all salespeople are set some form of target to achieve in their job. Most common of these is a sales volume or value target, but many other forms of quantitative and qualitative measures can be used. These measures are useful as a means of evaluation, as a motivator, as a means of control and sometimes for remuneration. Management must be careful that targets set reflect the whole selling job and the key dimensions which discriminate between success and failure.

Questions

1 The sales force composite method is a widely used means of sales forecasting. What are the advantages and disadvantages of this method and in what circumstances do you feel it is appropriate to use this method?

2 'In our rapidly growing markets opportunities are lost because of the restrictions on sales budgets imposed by the finance department.' How would you react to this statement?

3 What are the possible dangers in using salespeople as market researchers?

4 Purely quantitative methods of setting sales targets can be limiting and unfair. Do you agree?

5 In deciding suitable sales targets, some firms prefer to set sales targets low, expecting higher levels to be achieved. Others may set targets artificially high while yet others set targets as accurately as possible. Evaluate the appropriateness of these methods.

6 'Evaluating salespeople is easy. They either make target or they don't!' Critically assess this statement by identifying the criteria that you would use to assess an individual's sales performance.

7 Why is flexibility important in setting sales targets?

Case study

Scottish Paper Products

Scottish Paper Products (name disguised) is a manufacturer and supplier of business communication and speciality papers, with 270 employees. In Britain, they are the market leader in recycled paper with their product 'Repeat'. They also hold the number two position with contract stationery, supplying envelopes to technical and industrial users. The majority of sales are to major distributors who are wholesalers and their customers, although not the final consumer. Some direct accounts are Hewlett Packard, Xerox and Strathclyde University. In total, there are only five salespeople and the sales manager.

The company's sales targets are set by using a bottom-up approach with top-down control. The sales forces are encouraged to be involved in setting their targets but they must be realistic and justified to satisfy management. According to the sales manager, 'if sales performance is considered poor, then this will be discussed with the individual'. Each year, targets are set on a mutual basis, taking into account age and experience, but the only reward for achievement is a salary increase. Historical data are considered along with changes in the competitive environment, but the sales manager admits that the target should also increase each year by a 'few per cent'. The targets used are sales by volume, gross margin on orders and product targets. Some qualitative targets, including filling in market information and locating new customers, are used but these are sacrificed to the more important quantitative profit targets.

1 Critically assess the approach taken to sales targets in this company.

2 A form of management by objectives is operating. Make recommendations on how to improve the effectiveness of the scheme.

3 Bearing in mind that profit is linked to the high cost of raw materials in this business, what other sales targets would you consider appropriate in this firm?

Key terms

- budgets
- call-frequency ratio
- causal methods
- consensus methods
- expense to sales ratio
- forecasting process
- management by objectives
- market potential
- order to call ratio

- qualitative sales targets
- quantitative sales targets
- return on investment
- target
- time series
- trend
- unit build-up method

References

Brown, S.P., Evans, K.R., Mantrala, M.K. and Challagalla, G. (2005) 'Adapting motivation, control, and compensation research to a new environment' *Journal of Personal Selling & Sales Management* **25** (2): 156–67

Chambers, J.C., Satinder, K.M. and Smith, D.D. (1971) 'How to choose the right forecasting technique' *Harvard Business Review* **Jul–Aug**: 45–74

Chowdhury, J. (1993) 'The motivational impact of sales quotas on effort' *Journal of Marketing Research* **XXX** (Feb): 28–41

Kahn, K.B. (1998) 'Benchmarking sales forecasting performance measures' *The Journal of Business Forecasting, methods and system* **17** (4) Winter: 19–23

Mentzer, J.T. and Bienstock, C.C. (1998) *Sales Forecasting Management* Sage: Thousand Oaks, CA

Mentzer, J.T. and Kahn, K.B. (1995) 'Forecasting techniques, familiarity, satisfaction, usage and application' *Journal of Forecasting* **14** (5): 465–76

Mintel (2006) Food retailing November, Mintel Group: London

8 Selling in international markets

8.1 Overview

Meeting the needs of any market or market segment can be daunting but as a firm moves into international markets it faces additional challenges. In today's complex world, it may be that a firm has international customers from day one although for pedagogical simplicity we will assume a firm already in existence is intending to operate in or sell to new overseas markets. Marketing in another country means the business has to cope with many different issues, such as culture, legal systems, currencies and documentation requirements. It will have to decide whether to use agents and distributors as their method of selling in foreign markets. Agents and distributors already have a sales organisation, understand the local culture and can be a more cost-effective means of market development than is establishing a sales subsidiary.

International marketing is littered with examples of firms that made expensive mistakes simply because they did not take the time to understand the market they were dealing with. In this chapter, we argue that taking time to assess the market and plan market entry and development will improve the chances of success.

8.2 Learning objectives

In this chapter, the aim is to

- understand why selling in international markets is more complex than selling in the domestic market;
- discuss the different forms of selling used in international markets;
- identify the main factors influencing the choice of selling mode;
- explain why a long-term view of market development is preferable;
- discuss how to manage agents and distributors in foreign markets.

8.3 Definitions

Culture is the sum of the knowledge, values, beliefs and attitudes that are shared by a particular group of people or society.

Global firm is a firm that gains by operating in more than one country in areas of marketing, R&D or production thus enhancing its reputation and reducing costs not available to domestic competitors.

Terms of trade refers to the specification of the duties and obligations of both exporter and importer when dealing in international trade.

8.4 The international marketing environment

The international marketing environment is undergoing profound and rapid change. In most industries today, competition is becoming fiercer as more firms enter international markets and access to markets becomes easier. Even if a firm does not sell abroad, it is likely that it faces more competition from foreign firms in the home market and its domestic competitors may, by selling abroad, become more competitive in the home market.

Did you know?

Changes in international trade: The percentage of UK trade as a share of world trade has continued to decline. Where the UK once led the world it is now ranked seventh behind Germany, US, China, Japan, France and the Netherlands. UK share of world trade fell to 3.6 per cent in 2004.

(Source: World Trade Organisation, 2006)

To be able to sell successfully, an understanding of the international marketing environment is vital, one of the key elements of the environment being the multiplicity of cultures that firms sell in.

The cultural environment

Culture underlies all our relationships in international marketing. It shapes the beliefs or standards of groups and helps individuals to decide what are appropriate behaviours and actions. One aspect of this is the existence of national or regional styles of doing business and conducting negotiations. For example, it is commonly held that there are typically Middle Eastern, Japanese, American and British ways of doing business. To demonstrate how radically different two negotiation styles can be, there follows a description of Middle Eastern and American negotiation styles. In describing the basic characteristics of a Middle Eastern style, it must be borne in mind that almost all countries in this category are Arab–Islamic yet other religious groups, notably Christian minorities, are found throughout the region. Thus the assumption that this region is entirely Arab–Islamic is not the case. Usunier (1996) describes the characteristics of Arab–Islamic culture in the following way:

■ Knowledge of the subgroup to which the negotiator belongs is essential; the relationships between the parties must be explored with great care, to find out who is who and what relationship each negotiator has with the different groups.

■ The role of intermediaries ('sponsors' in Saudi Arabia) is very important. As a result of European colonisation over the past two centuries, the majority of 'middle Eastern' business people speak French or English and understand European

151

civilisation; whereas the reverse is rarely true. Intermediaries must be employed for a simple reason: we (the Europeans and Americans) systematically underestimate the cultural divide.

- It must always be borne in mind that Middle Eastern civilisations were largely the founders of those in Europe. They have left many traces behind, and as far as art and culture are concerned, their influences were dominant for many centuries during the Middle Ages. The pride of the person with whom you are dealing must be – truly – respected.

- One must expect a great deal of emotion, theatricality and demonstrativeness, interspersed with true pragmatism. The mixture is often bewildering. Friendship is sought, relationships are personalised, and the idea of a cold 'business-like' relationship is difficult to envisage. Once a true friend has been made (which is far from straightforward), the sense of loyalty can be very strong.

- When loans and interest are discussed, it is best to be very cautious as interest or riba is forbidden by the Koran. There are acceptable forms of finance for business but the subject should be handled sensitively.

In contrast, the American style of negotiations is characterised by the following:

- A recognition that in conducting business negotiations the selection of negotiators and the preparation for talks is methodical.

- There is a tendency not to take sufficient account of the culture of other parties; a belief that the American way of doing business is the best way and other nationalities would benefit by adopting this way of doing business.

- Emphasis is placed on issues, facts and evidence in negotiation and the need to reach agreement by certain deadlines. Others groups, like the French, have a generally less timely sense of negotiations and debate more general principals relating to the negotiation which could be interpreted as delaying tactics by Americans and may lead to resentment.

- Americans value frankness and sincerity, although being overly frank could in the extreme be construed as arrogance in cultures which have a more restricted view of self-assertion.

- A 'win' mentality where there is little sympathy for a loser, and business negotiations which may be conducted on the basis of may the 'best man win'.

- A recognition that contracts should be drawn up carefully and precisely in law and that these can be the basis of legal action if disputes arise in the future; Americans are a litigious nation.

- A tendency to be short-term oriented with an emphasis on getting results quickly; this can be a disadvantage in negotiations.

There are clearly major differences in the negotiating style of the Arab–Islamic and American cultures which can lead to misunderstandings and failed negotiations. It is not the case that every member of the Arab–Islamic or American cultures exhibits all of the characteristics attributed to the cultures above, but as a group the negotiating styles are recognisable and are characteristics of the business groups. The key issue in discussing culture is to understand that culture is an important part of international business and has tangible effects on negotiations.

What do you think?

When doing business in international markets, it is important to take the time to find out about the culture and styles of negotiation before going into a market, so that the likelihood of mistakes and misunderstandings is reduced. Government export promotion agencies publish information on doing business in foreign markets, and talks with export promotion officials, chambers of commerce and businessmen, who have knowledge of particular markets, is a good starting point for understanding and working in a different culture.

What other sources might be used to understand overseas markets?

Political, legal, economic and technological environments

Globalisation has become a key issue as a number of factors change the way in which companies, not only multinational corporations but also smaller firms, organise and carry out their business activities. Firms can now identify and sell to similar market segments around the world and have developed global marketing strategies to exploit these markets. Multinational corporations have gradually changed from conducting business on a country-by-country basis to conducting business on a regional or global basis. This is done to achieve cost savings arising from increased economies of scale and from reducing the duplication of activities in markets. This is now possible because the information technology revolution enables firms to coordinate and control operations on a global basis. Communication within organisations and externally with customers and suppliers is now quicker and more informative with the advent of improved international telecommunications and the Internet.

The Internet offers new capabilities for selling in international markets, and firms are developing strategies for the use of the Internet to support their international marketing. The ease of communication between the exporter, customers and intermediaries will improve levels of customer service, with response to customer queries being faster. There are new tools for selling too. The provision of a web site is feasible for any company and the Internet can be used to search for customer prospects.

As a tool for international research, there is vast array of sales-related information on the Web. For a director's briefing on research into export markets, go to www.hie.cu.uk; for preparing to trade abroad go to www.uktradeinvest.gov.uk; for help with exporting go to www.export.org.uk; for trade associations use www.taforum.org and for help through your chamber of commerce go to www.chamberofcommerce. org.uk. Examples of purchase guides can also be found, such as Europages at www.europages.com, while others offer help in gaining access to trade-lead systems, such as www.imex.com. For help with export credit, the government site at www.ecgd.gov.uk is essential. Many other sites offer different services and information for would-be exporters and, like most business decisions, it pays to do your homework.

From a political and economic standpoint, access to many markets is becoming easier with the increasing integration of markets. The European Union is dismantling barriers between member states and there has been a general reduction in barriers to trade, partly owing to the work of the World Trade Organisation (WTO), formerly General Agreement on Tariffs and Trade (GATT). For example, under the auspices of the WTO, many countries have signed an agreement to eliminate almost all tariffs currently levied on information technology products, and other categories of products are being introduced into trade-free areas.

8.5 Agency law in the European Union

Legal and regulatory systems also have a direct bearing on selling in international markets. For example, European Union agency law in the form of the Commercial Agents Directive has widespread implications for firms selling in the European Union. The main points of the Commercial Agents Directive are summarised as follows:

- The Directive applies only to agents who operate in connection with the sale of goods and only within European Union countries. Distributors who buy goods and then resell them on their own account are not covered.
- Where there is no agreement between parties, the agent will be entitled to remuneration that commercial agents 'are customarily allowed in the place where he carries on his activities'.
- Agents are entitled to commission on transactions completed, not only during the course of the agency contract but also afterwards if the transactions have been mainly attributable to their efforts.
- Agents must be supplied with a statement of commission due and the agent has the right to ask to see an extract from the principal's books.
- Where an agency contract is entered into for an indefinite period, each party is given a right to terminate it on notice. This provision may not be varied. The period of notice is one month during the first year of the contract, two months during the second year and three months thereafter.
- Agents are entitled to compensation for the damage they suffer when a contract is terminated.
- Compensation is not paid where the agent is in substantial breach of contract, if the agent terminates the contract, except where that termination is due to age or illness of the agent or due to facts attributable to the principal. There is no entitlement to compensation where the agent assigns the contract with the agreement of the principal to a third party (Croner, 1993).

When this legislation was introduced, many firms had to consider whether or not to change their sales and distribution network in the European Union because the new legislation gave much greater protection to agencies. As a result, some exporters replaced agencies with distributors, and firms that continued with their agencies had to make sure that their agency agreements complied with the legislation.

Exporters considering appointing agents in the European Union should consult a lawyer about the details of the Commercial Agents Directive. If the agency agreements are not carefully drafted and agreed, exporters may not realise the extent of their liability in the event of termination of an agency agreement. In some cases, companies may consider setting up a distributorship rather than an agency.

Countries also differ in the extent to which businesses and consumers will resort to legal action. One of the consequences of the propensity to sue in the United States is that firms are advised to insure against the crippling damages and legal costs that can be awarded. This is never truer than when a company is selling products that have a high consequential risk. For example, manufacturers of crash helmets have been sued for large amounts of money by customers and relatives claiming that defects in the design and manufacture of helmets contributed to personal injury and deaths.

There is also the question of the single currency in the European Union. Some member states have adopted the single currency and this has facilitated more trade between these states thus putting countries outside the single currency agreement at a disadvantage. At the time of writing, it is not clear whether the single currency will be adopted by all EC states making it a reality. Firms trading with countries outside the single currency still have to deal with the risks arising from fluctuating foreign exchange rates.

8.6 The choice and forms of selling organisation

There are many ways in which firms sell goods in international markets. Some means of selling do not require the exporter to have a direct presence in the foreign market. Other selling modes require the exporter to play an active role in setting up the sales and distribution channels in the foreign market. When firms sell to international markets with little or no presence in the markets, this is referred to as indirect exporting, where the products are sold in foreign markets without any special activity for this purpose being undertaken within the company. The export operations, including all the documentation, physical movement of goods and selling of the goods, are carried on by others. In contrast, direct exporting occurs where the firm undertakes the export task itself, builds up contacts, undertakes market research, handles documentation and transportation and develops marketing plans for the markets, either in conjunction with agents and distributors or through its own direct salespeople or sales subsidiary (Young *et al.*, 1989).

As Figure 8.1 illustrates, direct exporting gives a firm more control of the market and more market information compared with indirect exporting, but more resources

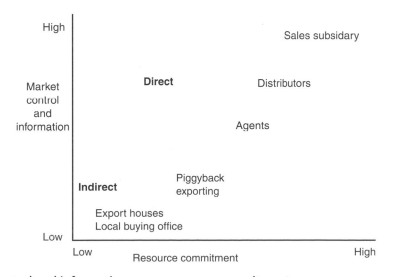

Fig 8.1 Market control and information versus resource commitment

are committed. Export houses and buying houses are a low-risk method of selling but do not have the potential of agents, distributors and sales subsidiaries to develop sales in a market.

Indirect selling to international markets

Export houses

The functions performed by export houses vary but the most comprehensive role is where the export house buys from a firm and sells abroad on its own behalf. This has the following advantages for the firm (Young *et al.*, 1989):

■ It does not have to sell in the international market.

■ It is paid in the currency of the home market.

■ It is not responsible for any of the export operation or for collecting payment from the buyers in the foreign market.

There are, however, disadvantages:

■ These are primarily the lack of control over sales abroad, as export sales volume is entirely dependent on the performance of the export house.

■ The image and reputation of the products is not within the control of the domestic firm.

■ If the company sells on its own behalf at a later date, its efforts may be hindered by a product image and reputation not consistent with its marketing strategy at the time.

Confirming house

When a foreign buyer places an order with a manufacturer, the manufacturer may want to protect himself from the possibility of non-payment by the foreign buyer. One way of doing this is for the exporter to agree terms with a confirming house, which will then guarantee payment to the UK manufacturer.

Local buying offices

Local buying offices are set up by organisations such as department store chains to buy goods from suppliers outside their home country. The buying office handles the export transaction with the exporter supplying the goods to the specification and price agreed. The manufacturer does not have any representation abroad and does not have any direct contact with the end user. The advantage for the exporter is that sales to the consumer or the end user are handled by the buying office and its parent company.

Piggyback exporting

As the term implies, this is an arrangement where a firm, the carrier, agrees to sell the products of another, the rider, through a sales network already built up by the carrier. The rider is often the smaller of the two parties. The agreement between the parties is usually that the carrier either sells the goods on a commission basis or acts as a distributor and buys the goods from the rider. Compared with export houses and buying offices, the rider may have more knowledge of the market depending on the relationship established with the carrier. Where this is the case, piggyback exporting has similarities with methods of direct exporting. For the rider, there are a number of advantages:

- The firm can use an existing sales network straight away, saving the time and costs of developing its own network.

- It is a comparatively low-risk method of selling because the investment in the international market is low.

- Being a low-risk, low-cost method of selling means that it is suitable for sales in markets where demand is small and would otherwise not be worthwhile. Agents, distributors and a firm's own sales force all require more time and money to develop than piggybacking.

- If the rider is not committed to exporting, piggybacking offers a way of developing international sales yet still leaves the rider free to concentrate on the domestic market.

The disadvantages are

- finding a suitable carrier;

- that the rider's products may take second place to the carrier's product line, something which the rider may not find satisfactory;

- that the rider does not have direct access to the market and does not build up a knowledge of customers in the market.

Piggyback exporting, like export houses and other indirect means of selling in foreign markets, has the advantages of low risk and low cost for the new exporter, but knowledge of the market is restricted and sales growth is governed by the activities of the carrier.

Direct selling to international markets

Agents

Agents represent an exporter directly in the market. Effectively, they are the company abroad and if the relationship between the exporter and agents develops well, the exporter will have much greater knowledge of the market compared with other means of selling already discussed. In most situations, the exporter can actively manage the agency, developing market segments in a planned and progressive way. The exporter should be able to work closely with the agency to formulate marketing plans for the foreign market. To do this, the exporter has to

- be much more committed to exporting;

- be prepared to invest the time and resources to find a good agent;

- develop the relationship over a period of years.

Export agents have many roles in international markets. Some agencies undertake all the selling activities on behalf of the exporter while, at the other extreme, agencies are used simply as 'enquiry-finders' or 'lead generators' for their principals. Such agents are often a small organisation, perhaps run by one man with some administrative or secretarial assistance. The agency's role is to pass on or generate enquires for the exporter, who will then visit the customer prospects, usually with the agent as well. This restrictive service is relatively cheap to provide and the commission paid to the agent will be as low as perhaps 3 or 5 per cent of the selling price.

Distributors

Whereas agencies operate on a commission basis and do not take title to the goods, distributors buy the goods from the exporter and make their money from their mark-up, that is, the difference between the prices at which they buy and sell. Generally speaking, distributors are larger organisations than agencies and are able to offer a wider range of functions.

Company sales representatives

Using a company representative in a foreign market has several advantages:

- They have specialised knowledge of the company's products.

- They are familiar with the company's marketing strategy and are able to give feedback on customers and markets directly.

- Being a company employee, the sales representative is much more easily controlled and evaluated.

The disadvantages of using a sales representative are as follows:

- Although international travel is nowadays much easier and arguably less expensive, there are limits to the time that a representative operating from the home market can spend abroad.

- If foreign languages are required, it may be difficult to recruit representatives who have the necessary language ability.

- They cannot be in the foreign market all the time, and consequently the use of an agent or distributor may be preferred by foreign buyers and be seen as a sign of greater commitment to the market.

Local sales subsidiary

This is generally interpreted by foreign customers as a sign of greater commitment to the market. The decision facing the exporter is how to staff the sales office. Should the exporter use salespeople from the home market or should local salespeople be recruited? Locally recruited representatives have the advantage that they know the local culture, can speak the local language, if required, and may have previous experience in the industry. On the other hand, they lack knowledge of the exporter.

One of the advantages of the sales office is flexibility. The number of people employed can be expanded or reduced as sales rise or fall. Nevertheless, starting a sales subsidiary takes a considerable amount of time and resources and would usually not be the first mode of selling considered by an exporter.

Furthermore, where an exporter sets up sales subsidiaries in several countries staffed by local sales representatives, the exporter will have to consider how best to manage sales forces of different nationalities and cultures. The management of a sales force in the domestic market is not likely to be an appropriate model for managing in other cultures, as a study of the management of sales forces in Japan and America by Graham *et al.* (1987) reveals:

■ Firms in Japan provided more training and organisational culture-building activities than in America.

■ The preferred way of motivating a Japanese sales force was by fostering their commitment to the firm.

■ Because Japanese sales representatives are more closely supervised, a sales manager would be responsible for fewer representatives than in the United States.

■ In the United States, it is much easier to set up a sales force and financial rewards are a much more effective way of controlling the sales force.

In the context of the discussion of culture earlier, these findings are not surprising but rather confirm the role of culture in shaping the beliefs and actions of individuals within a cultural grouping.

A summary of the characteristics, advantages and disadvantages of selling modes is given in Table 8.1.

Table 8.1 Export modes

Export mode	Characteristics	Advantages	Disadvantages
Indirect			
Export houses	There are a number of types of export but the most commonly understood is the organisation that buys from a firm and sells abroad on its own account	May handle all aspects of the export operation	Little market control or information. Limited sales
Confirming houses	Act on behalf of foreign buyers who pay them on a commission basis. The confirming house guarantees payment to the exporter on shipment of the goods	As above, but also guarantees payment	As above
Buying houses	Acting on behalf of clients such as foreign department stores, buying houses purchase from domestic manufacturers	As above, but the domestic manufacturer is approached by the buying house and need have no involvement in exporting other than supplying the order	Finding a suitable partner. The domestic company's product may take second priority. Growth may be impeded by existing arrangements
Direct			
Agents	There are several types of agent: some will sell only one company's products; other agents will sell products from a number of companies,	More market control and information than with the channels mentioned above. Permanent presence in the market. Costs of agency are related	May sell more than one company's products. Agency agreements can be difficult and expensive to terminate

Table 8.1	Continued		
Export mode	Characteristics	Advantages	Disadvantages
	some of which may be competing. An agent does not take title to the goods, is usually a national of the country concerned and is paid on a commission basis	to sales	
Distributors	The distributor takes title to the goods and therefore earns revenue from the mark-up on the product rather than the commission	Like the agent knows the local market. Able to provide after sales service. More control of the market	Costs of termination are high should exporter's market development plans require new channels
Direct selling	Sales representatives operating from the home country may be used in foreign sales territories	Detailed knowledge of the company and its products. High level of market control and information	Suffers from a lack of market knowledge, increased travelling time and, depending on the country, language problems
Local sales offices	These may be staffed by representatives either from the home market or from the foreign market	Perceived as a commitment to the market. Easier for local companies to deal with the exporter. Flexible and can accommodate growth	Problem of choosing appropriate personnel for the sales force. Domestic reps may be reluctant to move overseas: Local reps have less company knowledge but more country/market know-how

Exporter–importer relationships are dynamic. Some relationships endure while others flourish, decline and die. This is partly because the exporter wants to develop markets and discards the first intermediary used, often indirect intermediaries, as the market develops. Agents particularly were used so that closer contact could be established and maintained with customers abroad.

A study by Rosson (1987) of Canadian firms exporting to the UK revealed other reasons for change. These changes were identified as

■ changes in the level of sales;

■ changes in the state of the exporter;

■ changes in the environment.

These are outlined in Table 8.2.

The patterns of relationships built up during foreign market entry and development are complex. In Table 8.3, the main forms of representation used by firms are shown. On average, each exporter used four types of sales organisation for exporting, ranging from buyers based in the home market through to sales subsidiaries.

Not only are companies prepared to use several forms of selling in foreign markets but they will also use more than one means of selling in a market where necessary. A study by Turnbull (1987) of marine diesel, motor vehicle components and

Table 8.2 Responses to change in exporter–distributor relationships

Source of change		Response to change
1. Changes in sales	Poor sales	The distributor was split
	Good sales	Changed role for the distributor
		Distribtor agreement was terminated and other arrangements were made
2. Changes in the status of the exporter	Exporter closed	Relationship ended
	Ownership of the exporter changed	Country becomes a lower market priority
		Rationalisation of international marketing
		Exporter and foreign distributor come under common ownership
3. Changes in the environment	Exchange rate became unfavourable	Exports to country stop
	Market dies	Exports to country stop
		New products sold through corporate sales network in country

Table 8.3 Types of channel structure

Types of channel structure	% of firms using
Domestic-based buyers/buying agents	67
Domestic-based distributors	49
Domestic-based agents	63
Foreign-based agents	46
Foreign-based distributors	48
Firm's foreign sales offices/subsidiaries	61

telecommunications equipment manufacturers selling to France, Germany and Sweden found that two-thirds of the firms in the study used more than one form of representation in all three countries.

If it is the case that exporters may work with several sales intermediaries, it is also true that agents and distributors frequently work for more than one exporter. Moore (1992) studied German agents and distributors working with UK exporters and found that four out of five agents/distributors worked with more than one exporter and there were instances of agents and distributors working with six or more exporters. Given the fact that the majority of intermediaries work for more than one exporter, the management of the exporter–intermediary relationship is especially important because if the exporter does not work effectively with the intermediary, the intermediary will put more effort into working with the other exporters it has links with.

Finally, it should be noted that sales subsidiaries set up by exporters also take on agents. In a study by Wheeler *et al.* (1996), the reason that sales subsidiaries gave for holding a number of agencies on behalf of other manufacturers was that this spread the costs of operating the subsidiary over a wider product range and careful selection of agencies could improve the attractiveness of the subsidiary's main product.

8.7 The management of exporter–intermediary relationships

Evidence and experience show that more than half of export marketing ventures fail because the wrong distributor was selected. Usually the reasons for this is that the distributor company had not the technical experience claimed, had exaggerated its influence with buyers, was poorly located, and wasn't prepared to commit itself to the exporters' products. Getting it right at the beginning is essential. This confirms the importance of agency/distributor relationships and underlines the fact that many firms do not manage these relationships well. This is supported by many studies that have found that firms cited establishing sales and distribution networks in foreign markets as a problem. How then do exporters manage these relationships effectively?

Selecting agents/distributors

The sources most frequently used to identify potential distributors are personal visits to search the territory but government sources through the British Overseas Trade Board are also used, as are colleagues, customer recommendations and trade fairs. Also, a number of firms find that their source for identifying overseas distributors is often an unsolicited contact by distributors.

Most exporters use similar criteria when selecting their agents/distributors. The criteria can be split into three categories:

1 sales and market factors;
2 product and service factors;
3 risk and uncertainty factors.

The most frequently used criteria are market and customer knowledge and customer contacts, not carrying competitors products, enthusiasm for the contract and hunger to succeed. These factors emphasise the basic reason for choosing foreign distributors, which is to obtain effective market representation. It is essential for the success of the exporter that the distributor has these characteristics. Exporters clearly prefer to have a distributor concentrate on their own products rather than divide their time between competing products. It would seem, at least for some of the firms, that it is more important to have distributors who are enthusiastic and have good knowledge of the market than to have generally good track records and good financial standing. The majority of firms draw up a short list of potential distributors and interview them in their own country which underlines the importance in the selection process of personal contact in market surroundings.

Motivation

An exporter needs to understand what will motivate their intermediaries abroad. With the caveat that different motivations may apply across different countries (Hofstede, 1981), exporters need to look carefully at each market. Perhaps most important is the need to maintain effective exporter–distributor communication. These include keeping the distributor up to date and maintaining regular personal contact.

Generally, the most important criteria in managing the exporter–agency relationship are

- high/consistent product quality;
- competitive prices;
- suppliers' fairness and trustworthiness;
- an ability to keep his/her promises.

Clearly, fairness, trust and keeping promises are important issues in working with and motivating an agent/distributor.

Evaluation

Nearly all the firms evaluate their distributors, most on an annual basis. Criteria and standards vary but most exporters employ a wide range of criteria and, not surprisingly, achieving sales is the most frequently used evaluation measure. Sales volume, sales value and new business are commonly applied. In some situations, criteria include the quality of the distributor's market feedback, customer services and selling/marketing inputs. Comparison against past performance is an often-used approach.

The conclusions to be drawn about the management of exporter–agent/distributor relationships is that good personal contact and joint decision-making with the channel members have a positive bearing on export performance. The rational for this must be sought in the fact that increasing personal contact will lead the firm to a better understanding of customers and channel members' needs and behaviours. Improved target market selection, adaptation of marketing policy and better relations with channel members – including qualified joint decision-making – are the natural consequences which affect performance positively. The reason for better performance may be attributed to better decision quality and larger commitment from both parties. Good personal contact with the market and a close relationship with channel members further enhance the exporter's capability for careful planning and the control of sales in export markets.

There is a great deal of debate in the academic literature about exactly how firms increase their international activities, of which increasing the capacity to sell is one dimension. The competing explanations of internationalisation emphasise different aspects of firm behaviour and the environment. Internationalisation is not necessarily a formal rational process, although, as already identified, there is much support for the view that firms who assess international markets and plan their market entry and development improve their chances of success.

The discussion of the forms of organisation in this chapter has emphasised that, when firms are choosing sales intermediaries, there is a trade-off between the control of marketing activities and access to market information required versus the resources committed to that market. The decision to use a particular type of sales intermediary is partly based on the firm's assessment of these factors. Apart from this, the choice of sales intermediary is influenced by

- the firm's own international marketing strategy;
- the structure of the exporter's industry, which may place constraints on the types of selling organisation used; for example, if competitors providing after-sales service is important, direct forms of export are more likely to be used;
- the operating environment of the firm abroad; for example, selling in Japan usually means working with an intermediary in the first instance (Turnbull, 1987).

8.8 Pricing

Compared with selling in the home market, selling in foreign markets entails a number of additional activities and costs that increase prices. This is sometimes referred to as price escalation and the effect on the final price of some of these factors is shown in Table 8.4. In the example, there are additional shipping costs and tariffs in the foreign market but otherwise both channels are similar. Nevertheless, the final price is 68 per cent higher in the foreign market. If more intermediaries are used, the price will increase even more.

Exporters, however, do have a choice of how they calculate the costs of manufacture of the goods exported. They may take a view that the fixed costs of manufacturing will not be spread evenly across all production, regardless of its destination, but attributed only to production for the home market. The decision could be to attribute only the variable costs of production to the product destined for export markets. This means a lower price abroad.

Selling at low prices in a market may, however, lead to charges of dumping and governments may put an additional tariff on the goods to raise the price, but anti-dumping charges are fraught with problems because it is difficult to establish exactly what costs should be attributed to exported products. It is precisely this problem of determining costs that allows some governments to use anti-dumping charges as a barrier to trade. They unfairly protect local industry by imposing a levy when it is not warranted, in effect protecting inefficient home market manufacturers from genuinely competitive foreign competition.

Table 8.4 Price escalation

	Domestic market £	Foreign market £
Manufacturer's price	10.00	10.00
Shipping costs		4.00
Landed cost		14.00
Tariff (20%)		2.80
Distributor's cost	10.00	16.80
Distributor's margin (33.33% on cost)	3.33	5.60
Retailer's cost	13.33	22.40
Retailer's margin (40% on cost)	5.33	8.96
Retail price	18.66	31.36
% Price escalation		+ 68%

An important aspect of pricing in international markets is how the price is quoted. Should it be a fully delivered price, that is, delivery duty paid, where the exporter quotes for delivery to the customers premises and agrees to do all that is necessary, such as preparing the documentation, arranging insurance, shipping the goods, paying any tariffs and clearing customs? Alternatively, the exporter might make the goods available at their own premises and quote an ex-works price which only includes the cost of manufacture. The customer bears all the costs and takes responsibility for transporting the consignment.

In international trade, there is an internationally agreed set of terms of trade called Incoterms which specify the duties and obligations of the exporter and importer when using an Incoterm such as ex-works (EXW) or delivery duty paid (DDP). Incoterms drafted by the International Chamber of Commerce (ICC) were last revised in 1990. Hence they are currently known as Incoterms (1990) and are a reference point in a court of law in the event of a dispute.

Another aspect of pricing is the cost and provision of credit. Exporters can arrange for their credit arrangements to be handled by other organisations, but many firms make their own arrangements for credit assessment and provision. It is important that credit references are taken out on customers initially and on a continuing basis. References can be taken out through credit-checking agencies based in the exporter's home country, such as Dun & Bradstreet or Infocheck, or it may be cheaper to go direct to foreign-based agencies which provide services across a number of countries. Example of these are

■ Sereco, based in Egypt, covering most of the Middle East;

■ Harlow, based in the USA, covering all of North America and Canada;

■ the Maypole, based in Bangladesh, which covers a very large area including the Far East and Africa.

In offering credit, the exporter has to balance the provisions of attractive, cheap, long-term credit to gain more orders against short-term and expensive credit which may lead to a loss of orders. To find the ideal balance, a firm should develop its own credit policy by deciding on such questions as

■ What percentage of total assets should be represented by debtors?

■ What will be the range of credit terms on offer?

■ How will the credit-worthiness of new customers be assessed?

■ How will the company deal with slow payment and default?

Putting together tailor-made credit packages depends upon knowledge of the customer. The kinds of information sought should include the taking of credit references, credit terms desired and detailed information about the customer, possibly given through the use of a formal credit application. Clearly, the firm should have a clear idea of the cost of credit, which is determined by

■ the quantity of credit sales;

■ the average credit period;

■ the opportunity cost of capital.

A firm's credit policy should have a monitoring system to help to identify problems with customers and with the functioning of the policy within the firm's financial structure. For example, monitoring the ratio of credit sales to total sales enables the firm to see and assess changes in its risk exposure. The ratio of bad debts to total credit sales provides a view of how well the firm is managing the approval of credit applications and the collection of credit.

8.9 Summary

Selling in international markets presents new challenges for the firm selling abroad for the first time. The various facets of the international marketing environment directly affect the selling activities of firms. Sales managers need to understand, for example, the role of culture in shaping diverse negotiating styles and the impact of legislation on the selection and management of agents and distributors.

Much of the research on successful exporting supports the view that planning pays. If the firm assesses a market it is interested in and plans how it is going to enter and develop that market, it will increase its chances of success.

The research on the management of agents and distributors underlines the unstable nature of some relationships and the necessity to carefully select agents and distributors. Export sales managers who consciously build close relationships with their agents and distributors will usually have more success in foreign markets.

Besides the above, there are many additional issues which the new exporter has to master. These include dealing with export documentation, selecting appropriate Incoterms and setting prices. Some firms may see these issues as a barrier to success but, given the commitment of management, there is no reason why a firm should not sell successfully in international markets.

Questions

1 In what ways can the overseas sales operations support the segmentation, targeting and positioning strategy of the firm?

2 Do you consider that relationship selling is more or less important in overseas markets than in the home country?

3 What are some of the difficulties with geographic distance that hinder effective international sales operations?

4 As trade barriers generally reduce, it becomes harder to control price across borders. What advice would you give to companies who sell at different prices in different geographical regions (for example, this is a common problem between western and eastern Europe).

5 Find at least three products where sales have grown substantially through online exchange. What does this imply for selling in international markets?

Case study

AB chemicals

AB Chemicals (name disguised) supplies fine chemicals in pre-pack and semi-bulk quantities for research and industry. As part of a larger group, AB Chemicals is well positioned to reap substantial economies of size. It can develop stable, long-term strategies required for product and market development and for broadening its product differentiation capabilities. This gives AB a strong starting position for winning new customers and improving its service to existing ones.

However, the market can be described as saturated and starting to decline. Many existing customers are moving their chemical production facilities to Asia because of less strict government regulations. Currently, 80 per cent of the market is in the hands of one monopoly player, 15 per cent is held by AB and the remainder divided over a number of smaller players.

The market is mature and the products are commodities. Price and delivery are the two main differentiators. There is very little opportunity to add value for the customer. Most users are experts or researchers which offers limited opportunities for any add-on service support. Because it is a commodity product, ease of purchase is probably the single-most important purchasing criterion. This can be translated in the ease to find the right reference to order the product and placing the actual order. In many cases, the customer requires several products to conduct an experiment. These customers in pharmaceuticals, chemicals, healthcare and education will then try to order all these products from the same supplier if possible.

AB has been able to win market share thus far based on lower prices than the main competitor, a more user-friendly catalogue and 24-hour delivery. The field sales force visit the companies and users who received their catalogue. Because the main competitor no longer had a field sales force, this enabled AB to develop personal relationships between users and the company. Apparently, other things being equal, people still prefer to buy product from other people who they know personally.

Thus several channels to market were established – a field sales force; independent distributors for regions where no field sales force was available or where they were servicing a group of customer which were not well represented by the sales force; a call centre; an eCommerce web site. The channels were not chosen in terms of the costs involved to serve a customer but so that the maximum number of new orders could be obtained.

However, after early success, growth in market share has started to level off in several regions. This raises the following questions:

1 Is expecting further growth in those market realistically possible or have they achieved their fair share of the market?

2 How can the company bring its costs of sales in line with current sales revenue and growth?

3 If we reduce our sales force, how will our customers react?

As one manager explained it to us, we have to shift our sales approach from hard selling and calling on as many customers as possible to a smart selling approach where new opportunities will be looked for within specific accounts.

Called in as a consultant to AB, what solutions would you recommend and why?

Key terms

- agency law
- confirming house
- cultural environment
- export house
- globalisation

- multinational corporation
- piggyback exporting
- price escalation
- terms of trade

References

Croner, C. (1993) 'EC Agency Law' *Exporter's Briefing* 50: 1

Graham, J.L., Ichikawa, S. and Apasu, Y. (1987) 'Managing your sales force in Japan and the U.S.' *Euro-Asia Business Review* January in Meloan, T.W. and Graham, J.L. (1995) (eds) *International and Global Marketing* Irwin: Chicago, IL

Hofstede, G. (1981) *Cultural Consequences: International Differences in Work-Related Values* Sage, Beverly Hills: CA

Moore, R.A. (1992) 'A profile of UK manufacturers and West German agents and distributors' *European Journal of Marketing* 26 (1): 41–51

Rosson, P.J. (1987) 'The overseas distribution method: performance and change in a harsh environment' in Rosson, P.J. and Reid, S.J. (eds) *Managing Export Entry and Expansion* Praeger: New York

Turnbull, P.W. (1987) 'A challenge to the stages theory of the internationalisation process' in Rosson, P.J. and Reid, S.J. (eds) *Managing Export Entry and Expansion* Praeger: New York

Usunier, J.-C. (1996) *Marketing Across Cultures* 2nd edition Prentice-Hall: Hemel Hempstead

Wheeler, C., Jones, M. and Young, S. (1996) 'Market entry modes and channels of distribution in the machine tool industry in the UK' *European Journal of Marketing* 30 (4): 40–57

WTO (2006) 'World Trade in 2004 overview' Available at: http://www.wto.org/english/res_e/statis_e/statis_e.htm [Accessed 13 June 2006]

Young, S., Hamill, J., Wheeler, C. and Davies, J.R. (1989) *International Market Entry* Harvester Wheatsheaf/Prentice-Hall: Hemel Hempstead

Part III

Selling in practice (the management of sales operations)

The selling process in practice

9.1 Overview

Throughout this book effort has been made to incorporate many of the changes taking place in the sales profession. As an introduction to part three, this chapter attempts to synthesise current thinking in selling and sales management theory reflecting on how this might translate into practice for the salesperson in their job. Four theoretical perspectives are outlined:

- selling from a sales activity perspective;
- selling from a value added perspective;
- selling from a relationship perspective;
- selling from a customer-based perspective.

These perspectives are followed by a consideration of the need to translate marketing strategy into customer account management (CRM) and integrated multi-channel routes to market. There is then an exposition of the sales process and selling activities that reflect these changes in practice. Finally, the chapter concludes with some legal issues in sales.

Thus the nature of the selling function is changing to the extent that it renders obsolete many of the currently available sales management practices and the existing sales philosophies and cultures. Subsequently it also questions sales performance measures, which have been focussed on training, reward and sales volumes rather than relationship and account performance. Before examining sales management practices these changes need to be more formally documented.

9.2 Learning objectives

This chapter aims to

- review the four popular perspectives of selling;
- understand the link between marketing strategy, segmentation and account management;
- assess the importance of an integrated channel strategy;
- show how the sales strategy can be implemented by studying the steps in the selling process reflecting current market changes;
- be aware of legal restrictions impinging on the sales job.

9.3 Definitions

Multi-channel routes to market define the combination of channels that a firm uses to achieve its sales objectives. These channels include, amongst others, a direct sales organisation, telesales, agents, licensing, joint distribution agreements, the Internet and other means of connecting to customers.

Data Protection Act was first introduced in the United Kingdom in 1984 and amended in 1998 to protect individual personal information. Businesses must comply with the law and follow set practices for information handling.

Enterprise selling is the ability to mobilise resources so that the solutions offered contribute to the customer's strategic success.

Consultative selling is a sales process based on the ability to understand the extrinsic value needs of the customer and provide appropriate solutions.

Transaction selling is where the salesperson's role is to make it as easy and efficient as possible for the customer to do business with you.

9.4 Current theoretical perspectives in selling

Being market oriented requires companies to have close relationships with their customers in order to discover what their customers' needs are. The development of such relationships increases the cost of acquiring new customers and emphasises the need to retain the existing customer base. In this context selling cannot be viewed as a stand-alone function but is an integrated part of the overall marketing mix, which defines the value proposition. Changes are taking place that require the salesperson to communicate value and to listen to the customer thus adding value to the exchange process. This focus on customers' needs and wants requires the organisation to identify those customer segments whose needs and wants it can satisfy better than competitors. For salespeople it means that sales territories are no longer based solely on geographical areas but on specific customer segments (Rackham and DeVincentis, 1999). This notion of building an infrastructure that operates on the intelligence of the system rather than simply on the talent of the sales force requires a combination of skills, knowledge and professional intellect conceptualised by Quinn *et al.* (1996) as a hierarchy of knowledge, including

- cognitive knowledge (knowing what);
- procedural knowledge (knowing how);
- causal knowledge (knowing why);
- self-motivated creativity (care why).

9.5 The change from transactional to relationship selling

There are many different views in today's sales literature about the difference between the old and the new selling. The differences between these views are mainly based on each author's perspective.

From a sales activity perspective

The most obvious way to compare traditional and new sales processes is to consider the activities that the salesperson or sales team need to undertake. The evolution towards relationship selling through the addition of some new activities such as; building relationships with customers, networking inside customer operations, managing team interactions with customers has already been noted (Marshall *et al.*, 1999). However, most new activities were the result of technology (Moncrief, 1986; Marshall *et al.*, 1999; see insert).

Did you know?

Changes in sales activities 1981–1999

In 1981 Moncrief identified 121 sales activities across a range of different selling jobs. Some 18 years later he and others found that few of these activities could be deleted but that 49 new activities could be added. Most of these concerned technology such as using e-mail, the web and Internet, lap tops, mobile phones and video conferencing. However, new non-technology activities also featured such as litigation awareness, adaptive and consultative selling and relationship and team selling (Moncrief, 1986; Marshall, Moncrief and Lassk, 1999).

From a value added perspective

Another way to examine the difference between the old and new sales approach is based on the amount of added value the salesperson brings to the transaction. Rackham and De Vincentis (1999) argue that there are three types of selling, transaction, consultative and enterprise selling. In a transactional selling approach the added value a salesperson can bring is limited to communicating the existence of the product and demonstrating its features. These functions are disappearing as customers become more aware of the existence of products and their features through other means of communication. Transaction selling is a sales process that matches the needs of intrinsic value buyers who treat suppliers as a commodity and are exclusively interested in price and convenience. Consultative selling is a sales process that matches the needs of extrinsic value buyers who are willing to pay for a selling effort that adds value by providing additional benefits to their product or service. Enterprise selling is a sales process that most effectively works with strategically important customers who demand an extraordinary level of value creation from a single supplier (Rackham and De Vincentis, 1999).

Rackham and De Vincentis (1999) argue that it is the added value you can bring to the sales transaction that will determine the appropriate sales approach and the relationship potential. Determining the level of added value a salesperson can bring is performed by looking at the different stages of the customer buying cycle and determining at which stage you can help the customer.

From a relationship perspective

According to Millman and Willson (1996) the process of key account management (KAM) consists of several stages; Pre-KAM, Early KAM, Mid KAM, Strategic KAM and Synergetic KAM. In their view, relationship selling requires the existence of

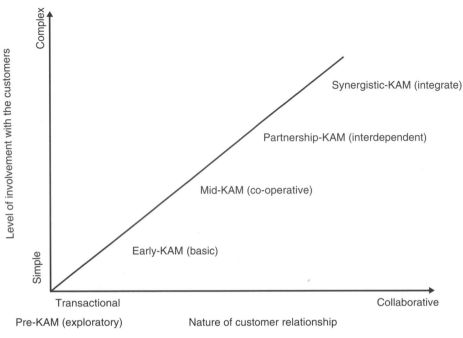

Fig 9.1 Key Account Management

a relationship between the customer and the vendor. Therefore they argue that transactional selling is the first step in the process towards relationship selling. The KAM stages represent the transition from transaction to collaboration (see Figure 9.1). The main measure, that indicates the stage of the relationship, is the customer's share of wallet (McDonald and Rogers 1998). Over time the KAM model has evolved and alternative labels are now being used by the "KAM best practice club" at Cranfield. Their terminology is shown in brackets in Figure 9.1.

From a customer-based perspective

The sales approach in transactional selling is based on a fixed or canned presentation that is aimed at moving a customer through a series of stages that will eventually lead to them buying the product (Futrell, 1999; Ingram *et al.* 2001). The approach is based on either the stimulus response or the mental state sales method. The sales approach in relationship selling is based on the needs of the customers (Ingram *et al.* 2001). The terms customer-oriented selling and adaptive selling are often used to describe relationship selling stressing the fact that the salesperson must focus on the customer situation and adapt his or her presentation to this situation (Saxe and Weitz, 1982; Spiro and Weitz, 1990). According to Ingram *et al.* (2001) the sales method used in relationship selling varies according to the stage the customer is at in his or her purchasing process. If a customer is looking for help on how to achieve their strategy the consultative selling method is appropriate. If a customer knows how to achieve their strategy and is looking to solve some of their problems then the problem solving method is best showing how different solutions may be appropriate. If a customer knows what

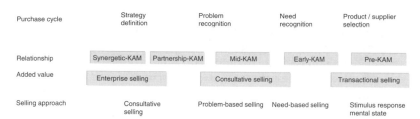

Fig 9.2 Different perspectives in the sales process

solution he or she needs then the need satisfaction method is appropriate showing how the vendor's product or services meet those needs.

The similarities and differences in these selling approaches is shown in Figure 9.2.

9.6 From marketing strategy to customer account management

Ingram *et al.* (2001) argue that a marketing strategy provides basic guidance but that the battle is won on an account-by-account basis. They suggest a framework that consists of four elements; account targeting strategy, relationship strategy, selling strategy and a channel strategy.

Account targeting strategy

Account targeting strategy is the grouping of accounts into segments with the purpose of making strategic selling approaches to each of these segments (Ingram *et al.*, 2001). Typical segmentation for a go-to market strategy as described by Zoltners *et al.* (2004) is usually based on the following factors; industry, customer size, customer behaviour, geography, application, benefits, usage situation and/or contribution to profitability. No matter what basis is used realistic segmentation should have the following characteristics:

■ Segments should be of an adequate size to provide the company with the desired return for its efforts.

■ Members of each segment should have a high degree of similarity, yet be distinct from the rest of the market.

■ Criteria for describing segments must be relevant to the purchase situation.

■ Segments must be reachable.

This being so an organisation has to choose which segments it will pursue by taking into consideration the market attractiveness of that segment and the organisation's strength in addressing the needs of that segment (McDonald and Rogers, 1998).

Relationship strategy

Relationship strategy is a determinant of the type of relationship that will be developed with different accounts and account groups (Ingram *et al.*, 2001). Millman and

Wilson's five stage model of key account management (see Figure 9.1) delineates the transition from transaction to collaboration which ultimately will determine the share of wallet obtained from an account.

The nature of the relationship is determined not only by how an organisation will develop a relationship but also on account potential. Thus, for each of the target segments in the marketing strategy an account plan by customer or customer group is needed to estimate account relationship potential and objective. The attractiveness of an account in terms of sales volume will be the main factor in an organisation wanting to develop close and strong customer relationships. This must be a two-way process taking into account the relationship needs of the customer as well as sales objectives of the supply firm. Customer needs are determined by the amount of risk involved in the purchase and the availability of substitutes. Some organisations may purchase large volumes of products or services but may see no added value in developing a relationship with the vendor because they regard the product as a commodity. All relationship development attempts of the vendor will therefore be wasted on that account (Donaldson and O'Toole. 2002).

Selling strategy

Selling strategy is the planned selling approach for each of the defined customers or customer groups (Ingram *et al.*, 2001). Figure 9.3 indicates how this might operate. In transactional mode the stimulus response and mental states approaches are most likely to yield the desired results. As a move to more relationship-based and collaborative strategies is required then the selling approach must also change to problem-solving and consultative selling.

Channel strategy

Channel strategies ensure that accounts receive selling effort coverage in an efficient and effective manner (Ingram *et al.*, 2001). The components of a channel strategy are, Internet, Industrial Distributor, Independent Representative, Team selling, Telemarketing, and Trade Shows.

According to Zoltners *et al.* (2004), based on the nature of the activities that are required, the selling organisation has to decide who is going to perform which type of selling activity. Costs are usually the key driver when choosing the go-to-market strategy. The other driver is quality. Some activities when performed by a direct sales force can

RELATIONSHIP STRATEGIES

Transaction	Solutions	Partnership	Collaborative
Stimulus response Mental states			
	Need satisfaction Problem solving		
		Consultative	
			Consultative Customised

Fig 9.3   Relationship strategies

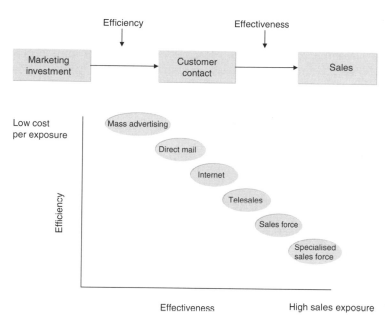

Efficiency

Effectiveness

Marketing investment → Customer contact → Sales

Low cost per exposure

Efficiency

Mass advertising

Direct mail

Internet

Telesales

Sales force

Specialised sales force

Effectiveness   High sales exposure

Fig 9.4 **Channel strategy**

generate response where other methods would generate no response at all. Efficiency and effectiveness provide a natural framework for examining the costs and benefits of alternative go-to-market strategies. Efficiency is measured by the amount of customer response based on the sales investment. Effectiveness is measured by the results of the customer contacts (see Figure 9.4). In many industries hybrid go-to market strategies are being developed whereby the role of the traditional sales force may be fairly limited.

9.7 Implementing the sales strategy

The process of establishing sales objectives consists of selecting the type of customers and establishing sales potential per account based on sales volume, financial and activity objectives (Johnston *et al.*, 2003). These four steps; account targeting; relationship strategy; sales strategy; and channel strategy suggest how sales objectives might be achieved. In practice the sales process can be understood if the individual elements are understood first at the personal or individual level then at the customer or account management level. It is to selling in practice that we now turn.

Activities that make up the sales process at the individual level

Prospecting

External sources: Use a referral approach by asking each prospect/customer for the name of another prospect; use community contacts such as relatives and friends for the name of potential prospects; obtain introduction by one customer or prospect to another via letter, email or phone; contact organisations, service clubs or chamber of commerce to seek sales leads; seek leads from non-competing salespeople; cultivate visible and influential accounts that will influence other buyers.

Internal Sources: Examine company records, directories, membership lists and other documents to obtain names of prospects; respond to customer inquiries from company advertising and promotional campaigns; respond to phone, mail or email inquiries from potential prospects.

Personal Contact: Use personal observation to look and listen for evidence of good prospects; make cold calls to canvass for potential prospects; organise and attend trade shows directed at potential prospects.

Pre-approach

Interview Approach: Use various contacts including friends, call centre, existing customers, intermediaries to arrange the sales interview with the prospect; send the prospect a personal letter/email to present yourself and request an interview; alternatively, have a present customer send a letter to a prospect introducing the salesperson and requesting an interview; phone for an appointment; call the prospect in order to set up an appointment for a sales interview.

Information sources: Gather intelligence about the prospect's business before the appointment; ask current customers specific information about a particular prospect; use other company salespeople for information about a particular prospect; read local newspaper or search the Internet to obtain information about the prospect.

Planning activities: Determine the sales objective and intended outcome of the meeting; plan the subject areas that need to be addressed during the meeting; establish a valid business reason why the prospect should meet with you; plan the questions that will be asked.

Approaching the customer

Problem/Need Information: Do a situation analysis; request information about the prospect's business situation; identify potential problem areas the prospect might have, asses their needs and how to satisfy/solve them; enquire about the costs of the problem and the benefits it will bring if solved.

Purchase information: Assess the decision-making unit (DMU); enquire about the people and their role involvement in the purchasing decision; enquire about the budget and the decision date; assess competitors and inquire about which other vendors the prospect is seeing; identify the steps in the prospect's buying process and which step they are now; identify the criteria that will be used to make the purchase; assess how the individual influencers will personally benefit from this purchase.

Give information to obtain credibility: Establish credibility by presenting an overview of the company, experience, products and references; use company brochures to provide the prospect with documentation about the company and the product.

Planning the next activity: Understand the DMU and request the contact person at the prospect firm facilitate a meeting with other members of the DMU; schedule meetings with other members of the DMU; obtain commitment by requesting some form of action from the prospect in order to move the sales process forward.

Presentation

Sales Presentation Types: Tailor the sales presentation specifically for the prospect; but, where possible, standardise the presentation so that it is the same for everyone, reflecting the organisation's key messages to its market; develop an initial business proposal for the customer; make the sales presentation yourself; cover the DMU, if necessary, make the presentation to other members of the DMU.

Visual Display Techniques: Make a product demonstration for the prospect; provide proof and guarantees about the product / service performance; provide detailed product documentation; provide a copy of the presentation material.

Provide proof: Provide proof and guarantees about the product / service performance.

Closing

Clarification close: Make a comparison close by comparing the product features with those of a competitor.

Tailored proposal: Develop a tailored formal proposal; organise a reference visit or contact; demonstrate the product to counter objections; make an implementation plan for the product or service; consider a price discount to counter objections; reduce prospect risk by offering a smaller solution to start with.

Follow up

Customer Service Activities: Serve as a consultant by giving special advice to the customer; ensure proper billing procedures and policies; interpret the firm's policies and procedures to the client; provide customer training and also to their employees in the use of the product; if appropriate, install the product for the customer and service it when necessary.

Customer Satisfaction Activities: Handling complaints; address any customer complaints expeditiously after the order has been signed; follow-up by ensuring that preparation for the acceptance of the product is in order and that initial use is satisfactory; periodically check with the customer to ensure that the customer continues to be satisfied; reassure the customer by seeking to rebuild or maintain the customer's confidence in his or her purchase; send thank you notes to the customer; send a letter of appreciation to the customer.

Customer Referral Activities: Continue to seek customer referrals by asking the customer for new sales leads; develop account penetration through contact with other employees within the company to sell the products.

Concomitant with individual activities, the sales manager needs to manage *the account*, particularly in terms of information and customer contact flows.

Activities that make up the sales process at the account level

Account management

Identification of potential account: Assess account attractiveness by identifying account size, purchasing volume, current suppliers, purchase criteria; identify the requirements and chances to win over the account based on price/promotion/place/product/service/information mix; estimate the amount of effort that will be needed to sell to this account.

Account analysis: Assess industry position and identify how the account is doing in its industry; identify the account's strategy and how they are planning to implement it; analyse the account's current financial situation; identify all the key activities within the client's business and which areas are likely to have problems; understand how these problems can be solved to benefit the customer; identify the employees and their role as part of the DMU; identify the main competitors and the products they are selling; identify what the main selection criteria are for a supplier; identify the typical buying steps and the buying process in the company; conduct a SWOT (strength, weaknesses, opportunities and threats) analysis for the account; analyse the value of the product service for the account.

Account strategy development: Set targets by estimating yearly volumes; define account objectives; determine the relationship wanted with the account; quantify investments needed to implement the plan.

Account action plan: Identify which account objectives are the most important ones; plan the objectives that can be accomplished during the coming year; identify all the activities needed to accomplish the objectives; review the selling proposition; identify how the objective / activities will help the customer achieve better results.

Sales and support programme: Identify how customer service problems can be solved; identify how the customer product problems can be solved; identify how you could be perceived as a higher added value provider than today by the account; identify how we can help the account to increase their sales revenue; identify how we can help the account to decrease their costs; communicate by making the account objectives and plan formally known to other colleagues within the organisation.

Account review: Review the account situation and see if the objectives and plan are still valid; review and communicate what has been accomplished so far on the account; review sales opportunities that have been lost and identify the reasons why.

9.8   Legal and other issues affecting sales in practice

An important area and one in which the sales job has changed over the last two decades concerns the legal conditions under which a business, and salespeople in particular, have to operate. In some cases these conditions will be particular to the industry. Therefore, different and more stringent controls apply in the financial sector whilst the most regulated is perhaps that of pharmaceutical sales. Similarly, in the area of building and construction contract and tendering procedures are different from

Prospecting			Pre-Approach			Approaching the customer			
External sources	Internal sources	Personal contact	Interview approach	Information sources	Planning activities	Problems and needs	Puchasing information	Obtain credibility	Planning next activities
Community contact: ask relatives and friends for the name of potential prospects	Examining records: examine company records, directories, membership lists and other documents to obtain names of prospects	Personal observation: look and listen for evidence of good prospects	Other intermediaries: use prospects, friend, call centre, customer to arrange the sales interview with the prospect	Prospect's business: gather intelligence over the prospect's business before the appointment	Planning: plan the subject areas that need to be addressed during the meeting	Situation analysis: request information about the prospect business situation	Decision making unit: inquire about the people and their role involved in the purchasing decision	Establish credibility: present overview of the company, experience, products and references	Commitment: request some form of action from the prospect to show some commitment in order to move the sales process forward
Noncompeting salespeople: seek leads from noncompeting salespeople		Cold canvassing: make cold calls to potential prospects	Personal letter to prospect: send the prospect a personal letter/email to present yourself and request an interview	Current customers: ask current customer specific information about a particular prospect	Valid business reason: establish a valid business reason why the prospect should meet with you	Problem analysis: Identify potential problem areas of the prospect and asses the needs they have to solve it	Competitors: inquire about which other vendors the prospect is seeing	Company brochures: provide the prospect with brochures and documentation about the company and the product	
			Customer letter referral: have a present customer send a letter to a prospect intriducing the salesperson and requesting an interview	Other company salespeople: ask company salespeople for some necessary information abou a particular prospect	Questioning: plan the questions that will be asked	Costs and benefits: inquire about the costs of the problem and the benefits it will bring if solved	Decision criteria: Identify which criteria's will be used to make the purchase		

Fig 9.5   Summary of sales activities

those operating elsewhere. These matters are not covered in detail but five areas are highlighted which salespeople ought to be aware of; trade descriptions; credit rules and consumer protection; terms and conditions of sale; contract and tenders; data protection.

Trade descriptions

As it was put to me by an IBM senior sales executive 'We consider it a sacking offence to promise something we cannot deliver'. While such openness and honesty is to be admired most salespeople have at some time or in some situations exaggerated, 'over egged the pudding' or, dare one say it, lied to clinch a deal or make the sale. When a buyer asks '. . . and what else is good about your offer?' it is hard not to cross the line. However, there are those who often break the rules to make a sale in search of anything for a 'quick buck'.

What do you think?

John Patterson is selling a customised software CRM package to a major client. In all the business will be worth £1.5 million. Most aspects of the deal look to be in place but the client wants the solution with four months. John knows this is impossible and expects, with pilot testing and the like, at least six months to be his best estimate. There are others pitching for the business and John knows, if he is totally honest, the deal is likely to fall through and go to a competitor. Both he and the client are about to sign the agreement for completion within the four-month time frame.

What would you do if you were John?

In most countries, there are legal constraints on how business is conducted in order to avoid exploitation and unethical practices. Some of the restrictions affecting salespeople and sales managers are considered here but companies who are innovative, progressive and enlightened will be operating at standards well above those required as a minimum in law. The Trades Description Act 1968 seeks to control the accuracy of statements made by businesses about goods and services. Most factual statements about goods are covered, except their price – for which see Consumer Protection Act 1987 Part III. It is an offence to apply a false trade description to goods, or to supply goods to which a false trade description is applied. Powers under this Act are extensive and greater than most people, especially consumers, realise. For example, a personal advertisement for a second-hand car in a local paper is covered by this Act. A statement such as 'excellent condition' can only be used if the car is in such a state. Untruthful claims, such as one owner when there have been several, would enable the buyer successfully to prosecute the vendor under the terms of this Act. Furthermore, the Act relates to oral as well as written claims and this will affect the salesperson who oversells, misrepresents or deceives the customer with unsubstantiated claims. However, verbal promises are much harder for the buyer to prove.

One particular area of concern is that of country of origin. The Trade Descriptions Act was modified in 1988 making it compulsory for the country of origin to be specified on the product. Consumers have a tendency to be positively influenced to pay a higher price for Japanese or German goods because of their reputation for quality and reliability. However, many companies have used low-cost economies such as China, India and Korea in an attempt to sell their goods as being Japanese in origin. In the European Community, this is illegal. One way of overcoming this, used by a number of retailers, is to brand their range of electrical goods with Japanese sounding names when in fact the country of origin may be anywhere.

Credit and consumer protection

Another area impinging on sales in practice is pricing, covered in the UK by the Consumer Protection Act 1987. This Act, covering and preceded by the Sale of Goods Act 1979, the Supply of Goods (implied terms) Act 1973 and the Abolition of Resale Price Maintenance Act 1956, influences what can and what cannot be claimed regarding product quality and price. This means that goods must be "fit for purpose" and that it is an offence to supply known faulty or defective products. Any guarantees must be honoured and prices clearly marked with restrictions on displayed prices, sale prices, credit prices and so on. Despite these legal controls many firms find ways to circumvent the law. Apparently, the rewards are just too great for many firms and their salespeople to resist the temptation to deceive. Although many sales are special purchases and others are reductions in a future proposed price or a price deliberately high to allow 50 per cent off, customers are still attracted to these claims but it is questionable ethics. In the long run, with important consumer protection groups now being more visible and active, it is likely to be detrimental for companies to pursue these dubious pricing policies.

The Financial Services Act 1986, revised in 2000 as the Financial Services and Markets Act, imposed a number of rules on how firms and individuals must conduct their business. Most of the powers of this Act are regulated by the Securities Investment Board (SIB), which has agreed new training and competence standards for those selling financial services. The life assurance industry is also self-regulated and is controlled by the Personal Investment Authority (PIA), which imposes specific requirements on those selling investment, pension and life policies. Overselling and misrepresentation by some in the industry, estimated by the SIB to have affected 1.5 million people with a potential compensation of £ 2 billion (*Economist*, 1994), has led to the need for regulation and control to ensure that financial advisors act in the best interests of their clients and have the necessary training and proof of competence to advise their customers accurately. Furthermore, advisors must disclose their commission, the management charges and expenses and the salesperson must clearly state whether they are a company representative or an independent financial advisor.

The Consumer Credit Acts of 1974, revised 2006, forced suppliers to state the real cost of credit to consumers by stating the annual percentage rate (APR) on all credit agreements in order to discourage unfair or misleading price claims. While many dubious and unethical sales practices still exist, most companies do not sacrifice a customer for a sale. The idea of salespeople being held in relatively low esteem dates back to Arthur Miller's Willy Lomas image of salespeople riding on a 'smile and a shoe shine' and selling goods and services directly to customers. In this mode, selling operated on the *caveat emptor* principle – let the buyer beware – the idea being to sell something to customers who do not come back. Selling today is all about getting customers to come back again and again.

Control over distribution is another area of legal concern. Restricted access to products and services can frustrate suppliers who feel they can offer potential customers a better deal and government in most developed economies see wider consumer choice and minimum restrictions as being a good thing per se. However, not everyone views this is the same way. For example, Levi Strauss, as part of their marketing strategy, would like to operate selective distribution to exclude supermarkets from selling their denims since it conveys the wrong image of exclusivity which is supported by their £ 50 plus price tag. Defending the brand is everything but the right of a manufacturer to pick and choose distribution outlets is a complex legal and ethical dilemma. Levi Strauss help to clarify their position by treating company values as absolutes, insisting that suppliers and customers adhere to their own rules (Donaldson, 1996). Their detailed code of conduct provides a clear direction – take-it-or-leave-it.

At the reverse end of the price scale, charging too low a price, called dumping, is another dubious practice. Here the supplier is getting rid of merchandise but it may only be temporary. Existing stocks may be sold but suppliers are then faced with price increases in the future as competition recedes. These cases are difficult to prove but companies and sales management should be aware of these situations and the rules in the United Kingdom and European Community (EC).

Terms and conditions of sale

For legal reasons companies will have standard terms and conditions of sales. Normally the back of an order form will specify these and it is now customary on any web-based transaction to tick the box to ensure that the customer has read these conditions. Terms basically state issues such as conditions of supply, delivery, payment and other aspects relating to the supply of goods and service.

What do you think?

Check any order that you have placed for goods or services or a quotation you have received. On the reverse will be the supplier's terms and conditions. Are there any surprises you didn't expect? Check with a small sample whether most people read these before, during or after placing on order?

In today's more litigation prone world, careful attention to many aspects of the legality of a contract is necessary. Such legal issues have been in force for centuries but salespeople must be aware of the extent and nature of the way business is done. For example, in the construction industry disputes over final specifications, costs and alterations to projects are commonplace and often require much legal bargaining to resolve, sometimes not always amicably.

Contracts and tenders

In industrial and business-to-business (B2B) markets, open-to-tender contracts are often the norm. Here again, difficult legal conditions may arise of which the salesperson must be cognisant. First, it is sometimes the case that a bribe (posing as commission) may be a prerequisite to get on the tender list. In America, the Foreign Corrupt Practices Act forbids such payments. Second, does everyone have a level playing field on which to compete? An African mining equipment contract out to tender received eight worldwide bids. These were opened and the lowest presented back to one favoured company. They then matched the lowest bid and got the contract. Real life or unethical business or both, and what is to be done about it? Play the game, cry foul or withdraw?

Did you know?

The original contract for the new Scottish Parliament built at Holyrood in Edinburgh was orignally budgeted at £ 45 million and was due to be completed within two years. In reality the project was almost ten times over budget, completed at a cost of £430 million and was four years late. Several inquiries were held during and after the project was completed to account for these discrepancies but no-one was held personally responsible and the Scottish taxpayer has had to foot the bill. Most sales/project managers have spent their time haggling over blame and trying to ensure their own interests are served. Hardly a recipe for relationship-based selling. Such occurrences are comon in building and construction although seldom on this scale. Submitting tenders and honouring contracts is a high risk business.

Another B2B problem concerns reciprocal trading. Large companies with different operating divisions may buy from other divisions within the same group but should they invite competitive bids if the orders are subsequently not going to be placed? Should IBM only buy Ford cars if Ford buy IBM computers and so on? Again, there are no easy, and sometimes no right, answers but such arrangement distort the sales process in practice.

Data protection

Today consumers are more assertive of their rights and they are also protected in law. The Data Protection Act of 1984 was given more teeth in 1998 so that an individual's privacy can be respected. Such data covers manual and electronic information of a personally sensitive nature including characteristics of race, religion, criminal records and the like which can only be accessed and held by legitimate bodies. It is against the law to hold or use data in certain ways. Any information that is held can be subject to time limitations and individuals have the right to know what type of information of a personal nature about them is being held by an organisation. Therefore, while salespeople and marketing information specialists would perhaps wish to know more about their customers they are restricted by law in doing so. This may explain why so many expensive CRM systems and sales databases are used for little more than mail shots (Donaldson and Wright, 2002). However, the act covers individuals not organisations so this is, at best, only a partial excuse for the ineffectiveness of many sales automation systems.

9.9 Summary

This chapter introduced Part III of the book by attempting to link sales theory and practice. Four popular approaches to the study of the subject were considered: sales activity, added value, relationship and customer-based selling. Consideration of account management was seen as prominent and the importance of an integrated multi-channel strategy was emphasised. To add realism, the sales process and activities of a salesperson were highlighted to understand what is done in practice. Finally, some legal restrictions on selling activities were considered.

Questions

1 Choosing your own relevant examples, analyse some of the different sales activities that a salesperson pursuing consultative selling might undertake that someone is unlikely to use in transactional selling.

2 Discuss the view that selling has always been customer-based and new approaches are merely a case of 'the emperor's new clothes'.

3 Unilever traditionally organised their marketing and sales around brands. Now their organisation is based on customer account management teams. What environmental factors have precipitated this type of organisational change?

4 Sales managers are under pressure to make the sales effort more effective and more efficient. Explain how integration of multi-channel routes to market with the sales operation might achieve this objective.

5 What are some of the legal restrictions faced by salespeople and how might they be overcome?

JohnsonDiversey

JohnsonDiversey (www.johnsondiversey.com) is an international company of cleaning products. Its parent company is S C Johnson whose headquarters are in the USA. Originally a British company JohnsonDiversey was sold to an American conglomerate in 1985 who in turn sold it to Unilever in 1996 before it was acquired by S C Johnson in 2001.

The company have a sales force in excess of 300 calling on all sorts of private and public organisations. The sales organisation use 'FrontDesk', a sales reporting tool developed internally using software based on Lotus notes. The aim is to hold full details on all customers at the head office. Specially filtered information is held by individual salespeople on laptops and up-dated by them on a daily basis. The system is intended to allow the company to more accurately tailor its products and services to the needs of the customer. The system is also used to monitor and measure sales force efficiency. FrontDesk has been designed to work with SAP which is used to optimise the company's financial performance and the two systems interface three times a day to provide as near as possible real time measurement of sales and customer activities.

The success of FrontDesk relies on the salesperson updating customer information in full every day but less than 30 per cent of the sales force actually does so. This is despite full training and one-to-one training sessions with every member of the sales team. Changes have been made to work patterns and activities to ensure time and resources are available. Although some downsizing of the sales force has resulted in recent redundancies, changes were made to the pay structure with field salespeople receiving pay increases on the understanding that FrontDesk was rolled out and utilised. To date, no improvement in the usage of FrontDesk has materialised.

Questions

1 Why do you think there has been reluctance to use the FrontDesk system?

2 What else can the company/management do to increase usage of the system?

3 IT failures in Western Europe have been estimated at $40 billion (Dalcher and Genus, 2003). What proposals would you make to assess the financial worth of the system?

Key terms

- account management
- consultative selling
- consumer protection
- contracts and tenders
- data protection

- enterprise selling
- multi-channel routes to market
- trade descriptions
- transaction selling

References

Dalcher, D. and Genus, A. (2003) 'Avoiding IS/IT implementation failure' *Technological Analysis and Strategic Management* **15** (4): 403–7

DeVincentis, J.R. and Rackham, N. (1998) 'Breadth of a salesman' *The McKinsey Quarterly* **4**: 33–43

Donaldson, B. and O'Toole, T. (2002) *Strategic Market Relationships: from strategy to implementation* John Wiley and Sons: Chichester

Donaldson, B. and Wright, G. (2002) 'Sales information systems: are they being used for more than simple mail shots?' *The Journal of Database Marketing* **9** (3) March: 276–284

Donaldson, T (1996) 'Values in tension-ethics away from home' *Harvard Business Review* Sep–Oct: 48–56

Economist (1994) 'But not as we know it' 29 October: 135

Futrell, C.M. (1998) *Sales Management: teamwork, leadership and technology* 5th edition Dryden Press: Orlando, FL

Ingram, T., Laforge, R., Avila, R., Schwepker, C. and Williams, M. (2001) *Sales Management: analysis and decision making* 4th edition Hartcourt: Orlando, FL

Johnston, M. and Marshall, G. (2003) *Churchill/Ford/Walker's Sales Force Management* 7th edition McGraw-Hill: New York

Marshall, G.W., Moncrief, W.C. and Lassk, F.G. (1999) 'The current state of sales force activities' *Industrial Marketing Management* **28** (1): 87–98

McDonald, M. and Rogers, B. (1998) *Key Account Management* Butterworth-Heinemann: London

McMurry, R.N. (1961) 'The mystique of super-salesmanship' *Harvard Business Review* **39**: 113–22

Millman, T. and Wilson, K. (1996) 'Developing key account management competencies' *Journal of Marketing Practice* **2** (2): 7–22

Moncrief, W.C. (1986) 'Selling activity and sales position taxonomies for industrial sales forces' *Journal of Marketing Research* **XXIII** (Aug): 261–70

Newton, D.A. (1961) 'Get the most out of your sales force' *Harvard Business Review* Sep–Oct: 16–29

Quinn, J.B., Anderson, P. and Finkelstein, S. (1996) 'Managing professional intellect: making the most of the best' *Harvard Business Review* **74** (2) Mar–Apr: 71–80

Rackham, N. and DeVincentis, J.R. (1999) *Rethinking the Sales Force: redefining selling to create and capture customer value* McGraw-Hill: New York

Saxe, R. and Weitz, B.A. (1982) 'The SOCO scale: a measure of the customer orientation of salespeople' *Journal of Marketing Research* **XIX** (Aug): 343–51

Spiro, R.L. and Weitz, B.A. (1990) 'Adaptive selling: conceptualisation, measurement and nomological validity' *Journal of Marketing Research* **XXVIII** (Feb): 61–9

Zoltners, A.A., Sinha, P. and Lorimer, S.E. (2004) *Sales Force Design for Strategic Advantage* Palgrave MacMillan: Basingstoke

10 Recruitment and selection

10.1 Overview

Despite the fact that good sales management practices have an important effect on individual and company sales performance, it cannot be disguised that a major determinant of sales performance is the quality of those recruited to the job. Training, leadership, remuneration and motivation are important but require quality raw material which can be developed. It follows, then, that careful attention and a professional approach are required to recruit and select the most appropriate candidates for the job. The physical and personality characteristics which appear to be important in sales jobs were evaluated in Chapter 4. The range of these attributes makes it difficult to find the perfect recruit. Also, a good transactional seller or order-getter does not necessarily make a good technical sales specialist or key account manager and vice versa. The problems of status and role conflict increase this difficulty, not only with securing the right candidates but also with keeping them. These key issues of recruitment and selection are the subjects of this chapter.

10.2 Learning objectives

This chapter aims to

- provide understanding of the importance of a planned approach to staffing the sales force;
- help you compile a job specification and a job description for sales positions;
- provide the means to evaluate the different sources of new recruits;
- explore the problems in selection and with selection techniques;
- assess current best practices in recruitment and selection.

10.3 Definitions

Job description refers to the role and duties that are attached to a particular position in the organisation.

Psychometric testing is the use of a group of techniques to assess an individual's attitudes and behaviour to different situations and circumstances.

10.4   The recruitment process

Recruitment is important not least because of the costs associated with hiring new salespeople, the costs of employing the wrong people and the effect of mistakes on future business prosperity (Darmon, 1993). The effect on the individual's well-being should also be a major consideration. Salespeople are recruited for their effect on sales. The starting point for recruitment is to assess the responsiveness of sales to selling effort, and to determine the job to be done and the size of the sales force. An appraisal of manpower required, including estimates of those who might leave, be promoted or be dismissed, can help to complete this jigsaw. The recruitment process which is considered in this chapter is outlined in Figure 10.1.

Sales managers complain about a shortage of suitable applicants for many types of sales position. It appears that people with the knowledge, skills and experience required, or perceived by sales managers to be required, are difficult to find. Formally addressing the recruitment process will help in defining the job, attracting the most suitable applicants and avoiding unnecessary problems and costs. The time and expense in recruiting, including advertising, selection procedures and first and second interviews, are not insignificant. Added to this may be other costs, including induction training, the potential cost of lost sales, the costs of dismissal if the wrong applicant is selected and the cost of repeating the process. Recruitment costs can be a major headache for sales managers.

Another problem is that managers find it easier to select applicants who are similar to themselves. First-line sales managers are particularly susceptible to forming selection decisions on this basis. Anti-discrimination laws must be considered and

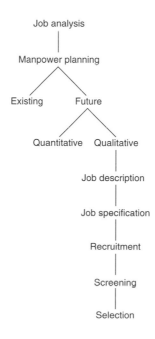

Fig 10.1   The recruitment process

professional guidance sought as appropriate. In the United Kingdom, it is illegal to discriminate on the basis of gender, race or ethnic background and, from October 2006, age. This confirms the need to view recruitment as a process, and it is to the individual stages in the recruitment process we now turn.

What do you think?

The following is a list of personal traits:

Appearance	Enthusiasm	Handshake	Numeracy	Courtesy	Flexibility
Friendliness	Non-smoker	Poise	Knowledge	Speech	Originality
Self-control	Persuasiveness	Handwriting	Mental alertness		
Ambition	Interest in the job	Curiosity	Healthy	Self-starter	

Evaluate each one (perhaps into categories of essential, desirable, not relevant) as to why it may or may not be important in a selling job?

Select three types of sales jobs and discuss with others what you feel to be desirable characteristics or traits.

Would you suggest companies should choose from such a list?

Job analysis

Prior to the job description and independent of the job specification, the starting point in recruitment is job analysis. Job analysis specifies the tasks involved in a particular job and the factors which affect job performance. These factors might include

- the type of selling job;
- the objectives of the job;
- the reporting relationship;
- the role and tasks necessary to perform effectively;
- the environment in which the job operates, including policies on sales, distribution and competitors;
- company rules and regulations.

Did you know?

Type of person suited to sales jobs

Adult playfulness has two primary factors: fun-loving and frivolous. Researchers (Maxwell *et al.*, 2005) recently found that fun-loving had a positive effect on adaptive selling by creating a learning orientation, and that it also had a positive effect on job satisfaction by lowering stress. Frivolous, however, had a negative effect on sales performance.

It should come as no surprise to learn people who enjoy their job generally perform better.

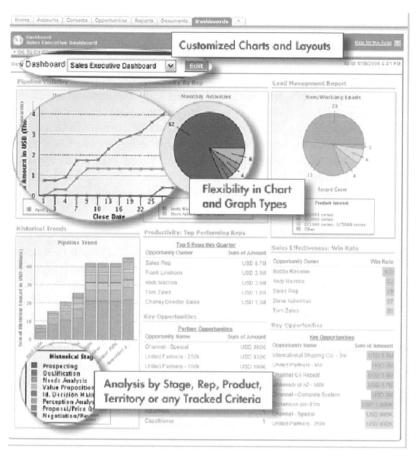

Fig 10.2   Sales activity analytics (used with permission from Salesforce.com)

Sales managers should be careful not to be too intuitive in their job analysis. The job should, of course, reflect corporate ethos, marketing strategy and the specific reporting relationships but job analysis also requires assessment of what existing salespeople do. Surveys using questionnaires, observation and data returns can be used to confirm duties, tasks and time spent on the selling job. This information should be held as part of the sales automation system, an excerpt from which is shown in Figure 10.2.

Manpower planning

The job description will be written for an individual in a sales position. Prior to this it is necessary, if organisational objectives are to be achieved, to integrate the individual positions into a team or business unit. To achieve this, care should be taken in manpower planning, the aim of which is to determine existing and future staffing levels. Manpower planning has both a quantitative dimension (how many?) and a qualitative requirement (what type?). The first of these problems has already been considered in determining sales force size and deployment. The quality aspects now need greater consideration.

Two factors affect decisions on manpower. First is the current sales force, its organisation and quality of personnel. The starting point is to assess how adequate and effective the current sales force are in meeting sales objectives and the characteristics considered necessary to do the particular selling job – the knowledge, skills and motivation an individual should possess. The second factor is the turnover in personnel. That is, people may be recruited to add to the sales force while others will be recruited to replace those who are promoted, leave, retire or are dismissed. A measure of turnover is the number of people who leave per annum divided by the total number in the sales force. Again, in today's information-led environment, management has a wealth of data from which to assess both quantitatively and qualitatively how well each salesperson is performing.

Job description

The job analysis is the cornerstone on which the job description for the salesperson is based. Therefore the job description should begin with repeating the main duties, tasks and responsibilities of the job. Before sales managers embark on such a task, they should ensure that they themselves have an adequate job description. Figures 10.3 and 10.4 are exhibits of job descriptions for a copier salesperson and an area sales manager in building materials. The key areas can vary but a job title, the main purpose of the job, key and secondary activities and performance measures should be included. It is preferable to be specific in the job description about job functions and duties. For example, indications can be given on time allocated to prospecting, travelling, merchandising, servicing and reporting as well as selling time. Controls can be incorporated to report on travelling time, call rates and assessment criteria.

A job description can be defined as a written statement of the tasks to be performed and the relative importance of each. It should provide assistance and clarification on what functions and activities have to be performed and how best (priority) to use time available. A good job description will be

- *written* to permit a greater degree of understanding, cooperation and motivation. A verbal job description is a waste of breath.
- *accepted* by salespeople, first-line managers and senior management. This is getting agreement on the priority tasks and evaluation criteria.
- *specific* in terms of activities. The example in Figure 10.3 above is rather vague. A set number of new accounts, an average call rate or other specific measures would add clarity.
- *comprehensive*, in that all key areas of the job, together with measures used to evaluate performance, should be included. Managers should not evaluate salespeople on dimensions not specified. If an adequate job analysis has been conducted, the measures listed in the job description should be appropriate.
- *short but detailed*. If too short, it may be too general to be of use. If too long, it becomes difficult to use and evaluate.

To facilitate writing a job description, a checklist of duties and responsibilities may help. Figure 10.5 is an example of such a checklist.

JOB TITLE   Area sales representative

JOB PURPOSE   To achieve product sales and strategic objectives, in line with company policies.

NATURE OF THE POSITION

The area representative reports to the regional manager. Sales will be achieved by:

- prospecting for new accounts
- developing and maintaining customer rapport
- identifying customer needs
- preparing written proposals
- providing product demonstrations
- advising and training customers and users
- ensuring satisfactory customer care, resulting in high levels of customer satisfaction
- negotiating sales closing and any necessary follow-up, including all relevant paperwork.

The company will provide the sales representative with data information on customer turnover and performance and sales and contribution in their territory against target. Assistance will be given by the regional manager in the analysis of the economic and commercial potential for the company's products. This information assists in maintaining contact within the short-term sales situation and in taking remedial action as required.

The representative is expected to visit an agreed number of customers each month in consultation with the regional manager, thereby ensuring that call rates are in line with company requirements.
The representative will cooperate with and advise the regional manager in recommending effective support and promotional activities suitable to meet area needs.

Any special reports required by the regional manager will be submitted in addition to the weekly and monthly reports.

PRINCIPAL ACCOUNTABILITIES

1 To accomplish product sales targets.
2 Through direct selling, to develop and maintain contacts that improve product turnover.
3 To ensure that all sales opportunities are fully exploited.
4 To inform the regional manager of any problems and all competitors' activities within an area.
5 To effectively utilise the company's support services, for example technical advice service, advertising and PR.
6 To continually keep up to date on product developments and market trends allied to the business.
7 To be involved in the appropriate levels of customer product training.
8 To absorb training as necessary and attend all courses, seminars and training meetings as arranged.
9 To follow company procedure regarding cars and ensure that their vehicle is constantly in a satisfactory condition.

KEY PERFORMANCE INDICATORS

Target achievement
Customer records
Customer satisfaction
Opportunity identification
Personal profile

Fig 10.3   Job description – copier salesperson

JOB TITLE   Regional sales manager

JOB PURPOSE   To secure acceptance of and implement company sales policies at a regional level, which will enable the region to achieve its product sales and other strategic objectives.

PRIME JOB OBJECTIVE

To achieve regional product sales targets in line with company targets, maximise sales and ensure that satisfactory customer relations are maintained at all times.

NATURE AND SCOPE OF POSITION

The regional sales manager is one of seven sales managers reporting to the sales director. The regional sales manager has a team of area representatives reporting to them.

They will allocate product targets across the range with a view to securing maximum product awareness in the marketplace. This will be achieved by recognising it from intelligence information, customer forecasts and trends for products from users, specifiers and stockists.

By means of the monthly report, the regional sales manager will interpret information provided from area representatives' reports to enable the sales director to be fully aware of the commercial outlook, application and competitiveness of the company's products.

The regional sales manager receives appropriate data on order intake, sales by customer and performance against target information. These returns enable close surveillance with the short-term sales situation and can direct remedial action if required.

They are also responsible for maintaining the appropriate level of control documents to monitor sales area and regional achievements.

In the field of price changes and sales policy procedures, they will be responsible for the total understanding and acceptance of details communicated to sales staff and customers.

The manager will be given flexibility to negotiate trading terms or rebates with stockists and major contractors. Judgement in this field shall be used prudently to ensure that there is no adverse effect on product volume, product mix and profitability.

They will be responsible for maintaining close personal contact with key account customers and contractors in their region. They are also responsible for effective journey plans and customer call frequency for representatives and will ensure that the level of calls made and customer category mix are appropriate to meet regional requirements as defined at appraisal sessions.

The manager will recommend the appropriate levels of expenditure in the field of support for trade days/evenings, sales promotion and local advertising and will be requested to quantify the effectiveness of such expenditure.

The manager is responsible, with the sales director, for the selection and appointment of representatives up to the regional establishment to enable effective manning of sales territories. Also, to be responsible for the continual training and appraisal of staff and to recommend to the sales director any corrective action as deemed necessary, including such recommendations that could result in termination of employment.

The regional manager has the authority to monitor representatives' monthly personal expenditure in line with company policy.

PRINCIPLE ACCOUNTABILITIES

1   To provide representatives with stimulating leadership, maintaining an atmosphere in the team conducive to the accomplishment of regional sales objectives by guiding and motivating staff so that a purposeful approach is maintained and the most effective results achieved.
2   To continually review the performance of representatives against sales targets and to guide, direct and assist the team to identify remedial courses of action and ensure these actions are taken.
3   To ensure that all activities are undertaken in the region in line with the overall requirements of the company sales plan and sales objectives.
4   To ensure that, at all times, the prudent and effective use of expenditure is maintained with a view to securing long-term business opportunities; in particular, the company's promotional material will be utilised to its maximum potential.

5 Representatives will be trained and developed to their optimum potential and the sales director will be informed of any sales activities, problems and prospects that exist in the region.

6 To ensure that all the company's support services, that is, technical design, publicity and promotional material, are fully utilised.

7 To conduct staff appraisals and formulate personal objectives for sales staff.

8 To keep up to date on market and product developments allied to our industry and to keep representatives fully informed.

9 To follow company procedure and requirements regarding cars and attend all courses, seminars and training sessions as deemed necessary.

10 To hold regular sales meetings to ensure that staff are fully aware of the requirements and progress of their activities and will use them as training opportunities.

PERFORMANCE EVALUATION

(a) Target achievement
(b) Motivation of sales team
(c) Field accompaniment
(d) Activity reports
(e) Regular staff appraisal
(f) Customer promotions and product awareness

Fig 10.4 Job description – building materials sales

Sales tasks	— make regular calls, explain company policies, sell product lines, handle objections, obtain specifications, close sales, enter orders.
Service tasks	— check stock, maintain display, distribute literature, train distributor staff, arrange factory visits, deal with quotations, handle complaints.
Management tasks	— plan territory , arrange call pattern, plan routes, minimise travel time, submit reports on market trends, competitive activity, lost orders, plan to develop new business.
Other tasks	— represent the company, attend sales meetings, demonstrate products, man exhibition stands, maintatin sales presentation kits, look after company property.
Authority	— approve customer credit, control agreed budget, plan call schedule, liaise with company personnel, report to area manager.

Fig 10.5 Checklist of possible factors to include in a sales job description

Did you know?

Personality profiles of salespeople

The 'big five' factors of personality are thought to be: emotional stability(neuroticism); extraversion; openness to experience; agreeableness; and conscientiousness. Four of these five (emotional stability excepted) were found to be related to the attractiveness of one or more sales activities with extraversion appearing to have the broadest influence (Stevens and Macintosh, 2003).

Job specification

The purpose of the job specification is to fit the most appropriate person to the required job description. This is difficult. It is the purpose of the job specification to list the desirable qualities and attributes that a person should have to do the job. What are these?

Not only is there a lack of consensus on these dimensions but also many of them are difficult to measure and assess. Inadequacies with new recruits in some areas can be overcome by suitable induction training, but a key problem for sales managers is whether to reduce the size of the pool of potential recruits by stipulating many qualifications, thus reducing training costs, or to reduce the entry qualifications and increase training costs. Remember also that there are legal restrictions on the extent to which employers can discriminate between applicants, for example, on the grounds of race, gender and, from 2006 in the United Kingdom, age. Nevertheless, some guidance is better than none in this case. Again, do the following:

- Decide on the most important aspects of the job.
- Identify essential criteria.
- Identify preferable criteria.
- Translate these into education, qualifications, experience and other attributes.
- Assess validity and reliability (reliability is measuring accuracy, validity is whether the factor is a good indicator of future performance).

For example, certain tests may be reliable as measures of a person's personality, for example, extrovertness. It does not follow in a particular sales job that this is valid as a predictor of job performance. Job specifications offer some help but the evidence of the high turnover of salespeople and poor performance suggests that many companies are inefficient in recruitment and much greater attention must be paid by sales managers to sourcing, selecting and screening potential applicants.

What do you think?

As a measure of the difficulty in compiling a job specification, imagine that you are recruiting a salesperson for office equipment sales. Candidate 1 is 40, well educated and from a stable family and has sales experience. Candidate 2 is 23, a graduate with no family ties and no experience. Candidate 3 is 29, ex-Army of average education and married with no children. Which is the most suitable?

Does it make a difference if candidate 3 is female or black?

10.5 Sources of sales recruits

A variety of potential sources can be used to recruit new salespeople. These sources can vary with respect to their adequacy and consistency in obtaining the best possible candidates for sales positions. Good recruitment policies will take a planned approach to this problem. For example, turnover rates will indicate how many and how often replacements are likely to be required. Furthermore, an analysis of previous recruits can indicate more and less productive sources. This analysis can be extended to discriminate between high, average and low performers. One study (Avlonitis *et al.*, 1986) suggested that sources of recruits can be linked to selling styles. For example, recruitment for missionary selling jobs favours employment agencies. For trade selling, sources are primarily from advertisements and educational institutions, while for technical selling recruiters rely more on personal contacts. The use of different sources is, and should be, related to job- and company-specific criteria as well as the matching characteristics between buyer and seller. Effective recruiting is an organisational priority as many sales positions attain strategic importance for the supplying firm (Wiles and Spiro, 2004). The most important sources are as follows:

1 *Internal applicants*. People within the organisation may be ambitious to progress in their career. Selling may be seen as a more remunerative and satisfying job, especially from inside salespeople, designers, buyers or perhaps technical personnel. Careers in sales may be considered to be internal promotion and part of a management career. Such people are likely to be company-loyal and well versed in company policies, in particular in product knowledge. The uncertainty is likely to be with their selling skills.

2 *Recommended by existing employees, managers and salespeople*. Existing personnel offer a low-cost way of obtaining candidates through personal contact, friendship or third-party contacts. Such recruits are likely to have positive attitudes to the company and the job, but the recommendations are unlikely to be objective and representative. In some cases, the refusal to recruit could offend, putting unnecessary pressure on both manager and candidate. An even more delicate situation can arise when candidates are sourced through suppliers or major customers. Again, these situations must be handled carefully but in a positive manner.

3 *Unsolicited applications*. Intelligent, motivated individuals will attempt to find employment with companies they choose and take the initiative by writing to selected companies for a job. Unfortunately, in times of high unemployment, candidates tend to flood companies with such applications; at other times, far fewer are received. These applications should be assessed on their merits on the same basis as applicants from any other source.

4 *Employment agencies*. Professional recruitment agencies are an expensive source of recruits but so is the management time and effort if the entire process is handled internally. If using an agency, do the following:

■ Select a good one with a proven reputation and experience of your business.

■ Visit the agency personally, talk to the recruiters and examine their screening procedures.

■ Aim to continue relationships with the agency rather than using them as a one-off exercise during an emergency.

5 *Educational institutions*. Colleges and universities are a rich source of intelligent applicants. Such recruits lack business experience and perhaps have a low appreciation of what the selling job entails. The attraction may be the company car, the salary or simply a job. Such people do not necessarily stay with their first employer for very long, although this may be a mutual benefit rather than a disadvantage. In a survey of

graduates' perceptions of a job and a career in sales (Donaldson and Thomson, 1991), the following were found:

- Most companies need to enhance the status of selling jobs if they are to appeal to graduates.
- Recruitment advertising and brochures should emphasise future training, opportunities for travel, earning potential and managerial prospects, providing these can be delivered.
- Alternative titles will have more appeal, providing the job reflects the title.
- Graduate students are keen to learn what selling involves, both as part of their course and particularly first hand from informal conversations with existing salespeople. This is the recruiter's most potent and under-used recruitment tool.

More recent research in the United States suggests that sales recruiters still have inaccurate perceptions of students' views on selling as a career. Generally they underestimate the importance of job satisfaction and career aspirations which rate higher to students than salary alone (Wiles and Spiro, 2004).

Motorola is one company that applies good practice in its graduate recruitment process. Based in a modern office in Aylesbury, Buckinghamshire, its sales force is currently 90 strong and serves primarily the UK market. Field sales engineers take responsibility for specific accounts and assume the role of account managers, overseeing and implementing the strategic and tactical plans necessary to broaden the accounts base. In addition to commercial awareness and technical competence, they are looking for people with good communication skills. From a very early stage, graduates are called upon to meet with senior management customers and liaise very closely with various manufacturing sites in Europe to coordinate Motorola's internal expertise in such areas as applications engineering, product marketing, customer service, production control and quality and operational management. Their sales support is comprehensive and covers field applications, customer training and customer support activity. Motorola's customers are some of the largest and most successful in the country, in a variety of industries including computing, communications and automotive technologies. They aim to strive for excellence and growth and see their sales force at the sharp end of this exciting challenge.

6 *Organisations such as the Rotary Club and others*. These are often used, initially informally, to source applicants. This is not recommended.

7 *Advertisements*. Recruitment advertising, if well conducted, can be particularly effective in obtaining a large number of applicants. The size, message and choice of media affect the response. A reputable company recruiting new or replacement staff should aim for 40–50 suitable applicants. Such advertising can also have a dual effect on company image and customers but the appropriateness of advertising varies. For example, the insertion of a general type in the *Sunday Times* or *Daily Telegraph* can generate 500 applications, although this varies with the company and job-specific circumstances. This is too many for most companies to handle and such sources are best used where a range of generally qualified salespeople are required, most of whom would have appropriate related experience. This keeps the applications to a manageable level. Remember that advertising in this case is not aimed at volume but at quality of response.

The sources of recruits can vary, as can the costs. The problems to avoid are a lack of planning in the approach, a failure to measure feedback on performance and a lack of commitment and involvement by senior management. A common failing in recruitment is that decisions and actions are influenced by immediate needs or narrowly focused opportunity. Remember that recruitment is a process and is crucially linked to the next issue that of selection.

10.6 Problems in screening applicants

When the number and type of salespeople have been determined and the various sources have been selected to obtain the necessary applicants, it is then essential to evaluate these applicants in order to recruit the best, that is, those most suitable to the job and the firm. This is not an easy task for professional recruiters and is an extremely difficult one for most sales managers.

Consider some of the problems. First, the sales manager is in unfamiliar surroundings, that is, being objective, buying instead of selling. Second, the risk of selecting the wrong candidate is high, with consequences for the company and the individual. Third, there is no valid set of criteria for assessing a person's suitability for a particular job. Pre-planning and a systematic process help to reduce error but do not provide a guarantee. Recruitment is only one of the sales manager's tasks and the individual level of expertise is likely to be low. Pressures on the manager's time and the infrequency (each area manager is on average likely to recruit one person every three years) with which this function is practised exacerbate the problem. Senior management may exert pressure on the area manager to fill the position quickly. A degree of bias often means that sales managers attempt to recruit people who are similar or inferior versions of how the sales manager sees him or her self! Selection techniques are an area of specialisation in themselves. For this reason, agencies may be used, but the decision ultimately lies with the manager, so understanding of sound selection procedure is important.

Selecting applicants

One possible cause of high turnover in sales personnel is that badly suited applicants are recruited in the first place. Turnover rates, that is, the number who leave per annum over the number in the sales force, which are above industry averages or seem to be increasing over previous periods indicate a problem and an unnecessary cost. These turnover rates vary, being higher in sales forces where the average age is younger, higher in consumer goods than industrial goods companies and significantly higher in the first three years of service. For example, higher turnover rates are found in new, young, consumer goods salespeople. Related to the turnover level are the costs of recruiting, selecting, training and supervising new recruits who are poor performers. These costs are likely to be in excess of £12,000 per person. For a company with a 200-strong sales force and a 10 per cent turnover rate, this will mean £240,000 per annum (20 × £12,000 per person). The true cost of each retained person is inflated accordingly, that is, cost of recruitment (£12,000) divided by turnover rate (0.9) = £13,333. If turnover is reduced to 5 per cent, the figure is £12,000/0.95 = £12,631.

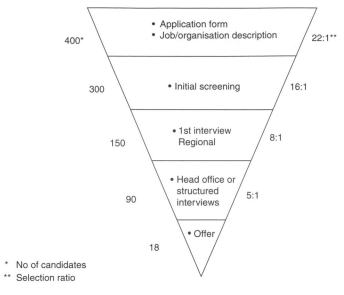

Fig 10.6   Large-scale recruitment and selection

Table 10.1   Selection tools

	Ranking	
	Effectiveness	Cost
Application forms	2	5
References	5	4
Interviews	1	1
Physical/medical	4	2
Psychometric and other tests	3	3

In addition to these costs, a salesperson leaving the company may well have a negative effect on sales in their territory and, if joining a competitor, business may be lost. The average lost sales multiplied by the number who leave will represent the total cost of lost business. Commensurate with cost is the time factor. From a decision to recruit or replace through sourcing, interviewing, screening, second or third interviews, checking references and the medical to placing and accepting an offer may take several months. Figure 10.6 demonstrates the work involved and the attrition rate for a global company recruiting an 18-strong sales force for a major UK expansion.

Despite the time and costs involved in this process, there is by no means universal agreement on the most effective selection tools. Table 10.1 shows the most commonly used selection tools and their relative cost as rated by sales recruiters.

1 *Application forms*. Rated lowest on cost and second highest on effectiveness, the application form is a very cost-efficient selection device. It provides essential information on a person's personal history, educational qualifications and previous job

experience. Forms are therefore a very useful first step in selection. The content of such forms is not always straightforward since legal restrictions apply to avoid unfair discrimination. The usefulness of such forms is as a first measure of suitability or conversely as a measure of unsuitability. Certain knock-out factors can be applied, such as

■ too many jobs in too short a time;

■ recently being separated;

■ own business folded;

■ employment gaps.

These are particularly useful topics for clarification at the first interview.

2 *References*. These are rated low in effectiveness since people will tend to select those who will give a positive reference. A good candidate will often have previous commendations or letters of satisfaction from employers. References also have a use in verifying what is on the application form. It is often a useful technique to speak on the telephone to a referee to glean what is not written by asking pertinent questions.

3 *Interviews*. Interviews are rated highest in effectiveness but are also the highest cost selection tool. It is almost unthinkable to recruit a person for a sales position without some form of interview; indeed, it is used for virtually every job. Two interviews are likely for sales positions. The first may be a screening process whereas the second may be the final selection between equally qualified applicants:

(a) *Screening interviews* will tend to be more formal in structure to verify and clarify the application form details. Such an interview should not exceed 1 hour and must aim to assess the skills, experience and knowledge possessed by the applicant. One purpose is to save senior management time. First-line managers or personnel will conduct such interviews.

(b) *Selection interviews* attempt to measure aptitude, personality and suitability factors that the candidate possesses relative to the requirements of the job. First-line managers need to assess if this person can and will work with their customers, the sales team and the manager. Again, many sales managers are not particularly effective in this role. Common failings include doing too much talking rather than listening, making frequent interruptions or overcorrecting. Inexperienced interviewers may prosecute the applicant in courtroom fashion or may alternatively be too nice. Asking the wrong or irrelevant questions and being self-opinionated are common weaknesses. The 'I'm a great judge of character' type or the 'I can spot a winner as soon as they enter the room' ones are exhibiting their own bias and prejudice.

Interviewing is a skill which requires understanding and practice. Positive guidelines for those who *conduct interviews* include the following:

■ Enlist professional help.

■ Be well prepared. Some list of prepared questions and rating charts can be used. It is also useful to rate key criteria separately using some form of (5- or 10-point) rating scale.

■ Select a suitable interview environment. Sitting behind a large desk looking down on an applicant is to be avoided. Avoid all interruptions, calls and distractions.

- Establish a rapport such as a salesperson would with a prospective customer. Be at ease, be informal and start gently with easy questions. Maintain the candidate's self-esteem.

- Listen and observe. At least two-thirds of the time, the applicant should be talking.

- Use a pre-planned rating chart, which avoids writing copious notes but weights the competencies and rates candidates on these competencies.

- If possible, two interviewers should be used to compare findings and avoid bias. Variations of the interview situation can be suggested, including drinks, dinner and meet-the-spouse sessions. Remember that it is a salesperson suited to the job who is required rather than a future son- or daughter-in-law. Select the right candidate, not the best one.

4 *Physical/medical.* This is quite important for salespeople. Physical and mental strain are a part of the job. People who have a nervous disposition or have had a serious illness are unlikely to be suitable where heavy travelling is involved.

5 *Psychometric and other tests.* Most sales managers love to point out one of their most successful salespeople who came lowest on all the tests and was recommended to work on clerical tasks. Such tests are extensively used because they are reliable, that is, they measure a particular trait accurately. What is also true is that these tests are often not valid. Possessing the trait does not necessarily equate with sales performance. Using tests requires

- job analysis and a job specification;

- reliability in results – if duplicated, would the results be similar?

- validity – does it measure what it is intended to measure?

- standardisation – is it uniform and fair?

Intelligence tests are reasonably objective, aptitude tests perhaps more relevant but they can be faked. Personality tests require extensive training and specialist skills if they are to be conducted effectively. One danger is that exact measures are being taken of inexact variables. Managers have been known to swear by such tests, others swear at them. In an effort to be more professional, more scientific and objective, new ways are needed to improve the selection process. The approach is therefore as follows:

- Determine what factors make for better performance. What evidence supports this? Does it apply to our industry?

- How can these factors be assessed? By interview, application form, reference, medical or test?

- If using psychological tests, the aim is to assess individual strengths and weaknesses relative to the job.

- Tests should be a complement to rather than a replacement for other methods. They can help.

- The test is only as good as its ability to identify those factors important in performance.

10.7 The assessment centre

Assessment centres are locations used by recruiters to test candidates for their suitability using a range of techniques including interviews, tests, problem-solving skills, group discussions and oral presentations. Originally used by the armed forces and government, they have proved worthwhile to assess managerial potential among graduates and the concept is increasingly being used to recruit salespeople. Large firms have both the resources and number of recruits to make this viable, although, increasingly, smaller firms are also recruiting in this way through specialist consultants. An assessment centre will normally appraise six to eight candidates over 1–3 days using two or three trained specialists. It is therefore a high-cost selection approach. The advantages claimed are as follows:

■ A wide variety of situations and pressures will reveal the individual's abilities and reactions in different circumstances.

■ A combination of selection techniques is superior to any one technique.

■ The results cover a period of time rather than a one-off interview.

■ The candidates have the opportunity to reveal particular strengths and not only weaknesses.

■ The information can be quantified for subsequent use and validity.

The disadvantages are clearly the time, cost and need for experts. To be effective, good candidates are required but the process requires much speculative time for little reward from applicants. For this reason, it is more likely to be used for identifying managerial potential than for salespeople.

10.8 Summary

Recruiting and selecting suitable applicants is one of the most important and difficult jobs the sales manager can undertake. The process of job analysis, manpower planning, job description, job specification, recruitment, screening and selection should be systematic and thorough. Problems of frequency, bias, time and training plague the screening process. Even professional recruiters cannot claim reliability and validity in their selection criteria for salespeople. To reduce costs, improve selectivity and be more effective, sales managers should follow a planned recruitment procedure, enlisting professional help as appropriate. A planned approach will increase your success rate in selection, build a reputation as a desirable, progressive employer and sharpen your competitive edge, thus improving effectiveness and efficiency in your sales operations. As the sales job becomes more complex and strategic the demand for more professional recruitment and selection in sales management will become obligatory.

Questions

1 Explain what steps might be taken to reduce the failure rate in selecting candidates for sales positions.

2 Discuss the benefits and drawbacks of recruiting graduates for selling jobs in fast-moving consumer goods companies.

3 Relatively new to recruiting salespeople, suggest how you would minimise your own personal bias and prejudices.

4 Put up an argument for or against the use of psychometric testing in recruiting salespeople.

5 Forecast in what ways the recruitment process might change over the next decade.

Case study

The Car Phone Warehouse

The Car Phone Warehouse (www.carphone.com) has been in business since 1989 and has grown in size and now has over 1400 stores in 10 countries with the aim of achieving FTSE 100 status by 2007. In the United Kingdom alone there are now some 600 branches. The founder of the company, Charles Dunson, originally worked for NEC and set up his business when he realised how difficult it was to buy a mobile phone. At that time, you could not go in to a shop and select but had to call a supplier who would send a salesperson to visit. The first retail outlet was set up in London and within weeks became highly successful.

Today, branches sell mobile phones, pagers, accessories, personal organisers, MP3 players, car satellite navigation systems and services for the telecommunications sector. In effect, they sell almost anything involved with mobile telecommunications. They mostly sell from their premises, although personal visits to companies are also part of their customer portfolio and their B2B interests continue to expand. They do not favour cold calling or prospecting, relying on prospects to contact them through telephone, Internet or using their retail outlets. The company regard the personal selling of their products as requiring direct contact with the customer, in-depth product knowledge and personal adaptability and flexibility to respond to customers' needs in order to provide 'the right phone for the right person'. When recruiting, the company is looking for self-confident people who are able to make decisions and think for themselves. They must be able to show that they are capable of expressing technical knowledge in a language the customer will understand. Their policy is to promote retail and sales managers from within.

In the 'early days', the company recruited through word-of-mouth, basically recruiting friends of the original staff. As they expanded and moved away from London, this was no longer possible. They now recruit from a variety of sources, including recent graduates, although they prefer someone with a track record in sales and then to train them in mobile phone products. They are currently using advertisements, personal contacts, recruitment agencies and educational institutions but rely more and more today on their website as a source of recruits.

1 Called in as a sales recruitment consultant, what sources you would recommend the company should use to recruit new salespeople?

2 Go to www.careersatcarphone.com and critically evaluate their approach.

3 What advice would you give to the company about assessing potential applicants? Explain the selection procedure you would employ.

Key terms

- aptitude tests
- assessment centres
- employment agencies
- intelligence tests
- job analysis
- job description
- job specification
- manpower planning
- psychometric tests

- recruitment
- reliability
- sales activity
- analysis
- screening
- selection tools
- staff turnover
- validity

References

Avlonitis, C.J., Boyle, K.A. and Kouremenos, A.G. (1986) 'Matching salesmen to the selling job' *Industrial Marketing Management* **15** (1): 45–54

Darmon, R. (1993) 'Sales force recruiting and training policies for minimising turnover costs' *Marketing for the New Europe: dealing with complexity. Proceedings of the 22nd EMAC Conference* Barcelona pp. 27–44

Donaldson, B. and Thomson, C. (1991) 'Recruiting graduates into sales. Preparing marketing for the new millennium' *Proceedings of the 1991 Marketing Education Group* Cardiff pp. 340–53

Futrell, C. (2001) *Fundamentals of Selling: customer for life* McGraw-Hill: New York

Maxwell, S., Reed, G., Sakar, J. and Story, V. (2005) 'The two faces of playfulness: a new tool to select potentially successful sales reps' *Journal of Personal Selling and Sales Management* **25** (3): 215–29

Stevens, C.D. and Macintosh, G. (2003) 'Personality and attractiveness of activities within sales jobs' *Journal of Personal Selling and Sales Management* **23** (1): 23–37

Taylor, S. (2005) *People Resourcing* 3rd edition CIPD/McGraw-Hill: Maidenhead

Wiles, M.A. and Spiro, R.L. (2004) 'Attracting graduates to sales positions and the role of recruiter knowledge: a reexamination' *Journal of Personal Selling and Sales Management* **24** (1): 39–48

Answers

Answer: More knowledgeable 3:1
Answer: Unanimously, businesslike.
Answer: 40 out of 43, the latter.

11 Training, coaching and leading the sales team

11.1 Overview

It is incumbent upon every sales manager to try to improve the performance of the salespeople under their control. One way this can be achieved is by training, another by coaching and of course through superior leadership and motivation. Salespeople may not know certain things which could enable them to be more effective, they may not know enough of the right things or their knowledge may be incorrect or inappropriate for the changing demands of their selling job. In these circumstances, the sales manager can help the salesperson in their job to be more effective and efficient.

11.2 Learning objectives

In this chapter, the objectives are

- to understand why and when training is required;
- to appreciate the basics of good training programmes and how they might be delivered;
- to be able to evaluate the worth of sales training;
- to identify what is meant by leadership and to consider the different theories of leadership;
- to assess the relevance of different leadership styles in a sales management context;
- to assess how sales managers can coach salespeople and thus improve sales force job satisfaction and performance.

11.3 Definitions

Leadership is about people who are able to think and act creatively in non-routine situations – and who set out to influence the actions, beliefs and feelings of others. In this sense, being a 'leader' is personal. It flows from an individual's qualities and actions.

Coaching is the means by which a manager can enable people through feedback and encouragement to achieve their objectives by using the knowledge, skills and abilities of the individual to best effect.

11.4 Training

Most training should relate to the individual in their specific job if it is to be effective. The fact that there are so many standardised training courses in personal selling is therefore something of a mystery. To be effective, training requires specialisation with the individual and the product/company/job circumstances in which they operate. Good training is to be found in company-specific programmes or individual on-the-job training.

Fundamental to training is consideration of the educational process by which learning can take place. The principles underlying this process are as follows:

■ There is a clear purpose of what the training aims to do for the individual, how it can apply to their job and what benefits can be expected.

■ The presentation is clear so that the individual can learn and appreciate what is being taught.

■ There is a planned repetition to enable the individual time and opportunity to absorb and practise new skills.

■ There is a systematic review and follow-up to assess whether the learning process is effective.

■ The development of material is orderly. This is the basic difference between learning by training and learning by experience. Experience is random and uncontrolled. Experience usually directs the individual to know what not to do rather than how to do it correctly – 'a great man never makes the same mistake twice'. In training, the emphasis is on learning from other people's experience rather than one's own mistakes.

■ The process proceeds at a suitable pace which is adaptable for slow or fast learners to absorb the material.

■ The process involves participation by the individual in the learning process.

The reason for training is to improve performance by increasing sales, reducing costs and adopting better work practices. Not all training can achieve these desirable objectives directly, but they can potentially contribute in one or more of the following ways:

■ improving the salesperson's relationship with their customers by showing salespeople better ways to do business;

■ motivating the salesperson to develop their skills and raises morale;

■ reducing staff turnover, which in turn reduces recruitment costs and the opportunity cost of lost sales;

■ making salespeople more flexible and innovative in meeting changing market conditions;

■ reducing the costs of inefficiency by weak territory coverage or ignorance of company policy or operating procedures;

■ increasing sales volume, reducing supervision costs and requiring less management control.

KNOWLEDGE, SKILLS AND ATTITUDES THE SALESPERSON REQUIRES	MINUS	THOSE THEY ALREADY HAVE	EQUALS	WHAT THEY MUST BE TRAINED IN

Fig 11.1 Training needs

Training should cover the gap between what a salesperson needs to know and what is known at present. Individuals will have varying requirements depending on the difference in this equation (Figure 11.1).

This gap will vary when

■ new people are recruited;

■ a salesperson takes on a new territory;

■ new products are introduced;

■ new business or new market segments are to be won;

■ new company policies or procedures are introduced;

■ selling habits are poor or inappropriate;

■ an individual is being considered for promotion.

Because of the variety in these circumstances and in individuals themselves, the content of training programmes is seldom standard. For example, new people will have to acquire product knowledge particularly in use applications, competitors' strengths and weaknesses and product benefits. They will also have to appreciate and understand company policy and procedures including rules, reports, expenses, credit policies and so on. Depending on their previous education, training and experience, they may also have to be trained in selling skills and in the sales process. Finally, they have to appreciate the company ethos, attitudes and behaviour as representatives of their company.

Did you know?

Content of sales training programmes

The percentage of north European firms providing sales training in specific areas was found to be as follows:

sales techniques (69% of firms providing this); market/customer knowledge (42%); computer knowledge (42%); product education (38%); company policy (35%); team work (30%).

(Source: Roman and Ruiz, 2003)

Existing salespeople sometimes need to be retrained in the same areas as new recruits. In other cases, training may relate to one or more aspects of doing their job. For example, existing salespeople tend to favour existing calls with known customers and may have to be encouraged to win new business with new customers. Training can help them to do their job better. This might include the more efficient allocation of time, how to locate new potential customers, how to identify key decision-makers, how to arrange appointments, how to open a call, how to develop relationships, how to follow up and other aspects of what constitutes the complete selling job.

Training needs vary, with more emphasis on market and customer knowledge for consumer than industrial goods companies. In business to business (B2B), there is a greater need for training on new product information, product application and service support. In larger companies with a sizeable sales force there will be a greater need for selling skills and on company policy than on product knowledge. Companies who sell to intermediaries, wholesalers or retailers will put more emphasis on customer, market and competitor knowledge. This reinforces the position of consumer goods companies, emphasising selling skills rather than having the product knowledge emphasis of industrial goods companies.

These issues relate to recruitment policies discussed in the last chapter. Should you recruit people trained in selling skills and teach them company and product knowledge or recruit those with product knowledge/technical skills and train them to sell? Companies who sell direct to customers/users often train new recruits in all aspects of the job using conditioned response techniques – trained in advance on creating business, dealing with problems, overcoming objections and closing techniques. Selling to organisations and larger-value orders require a different, insight response which is more customer-oriented.

What do you think?

Exploding the myths about selling
Stanton *et al.* (1991) suggest that many managers and salespeople themselves are not receptive to training because of their attitude and philosophies about selling. These authors identified six myths which characterise this problem. What do you think?

Myth 1: Salespeople are born not made. Since there is great difficulty in identifying characteristics of successful salespeople, it is hard to explain why this myth is so popular. It is true that some people can never be trained to sell, and it is also true that others may be easier to train. Most people will be more effective through training. Successful companies invest heavily in training.

Myth 2: Salespeople must be good talkers. Evidence suggests that successful selling is about listening rather than talking. Probing and questioning which reveals the customer's real needs is more effective than talking.

Myth 3: Selling is a matter of knowing the right techniques or tricks. In some one-off, direct sales situations, and possibly some of the time in other situations, a canned approach may work if it is relevant. Selling based on insight and a combination of skills is far more effective.

Myth 4: A good salesperson call sell anything. Most successful salespeople started by failures with the wrong approach, wrong product or wrong customer. Success cannot be achieved where product, price, service and quality are inferior, and not for long. Matching products to customers is the basis for success.

Myth 5: A good salesperson can sell ice to the Eskimos. A good salesperson wouldn't even try – the customer doesn't need it.

Myth 6: People do not want to buy and have to be conned. Most people enjoy buying and organisations have to buy for survival. Salespeople can help in this process.

11.5   Forms of training

Having identified that training is both necessary and desirable, decisions have to be taken on who should do it, where and using what methods?

Who should do the training?

The skills in teaching are quite different from those of actually doing a job. Good performers do not necessarily make good teachers, nor do bad performers make good teachers. These are not comparable. Sales trainers can be inside specialists, outside (the company) specialists or inside sales managers or experienced salespeople. In firms with large sales forces, training is more likely to be provided by company specialists who can assess individual needs and tailor programmes to suit both internal and on-the-job requirements. Where companies employ younger salespeople with little or no sales experience, outside experts on packaged sales training courses are likely to be more acceptable. Industrial goods companies are more likely to rely on internal trainers/ experienced salespeople who have high levels of customer, company and product knowledge. Whoever undertakes the task, the skilled trainer/developer/coach needs to be aware of, understand and utilise the principles of accelerated learning – now a well-accepted concept whereby individuals can customise their learning at a suitable pace to achieve their objectives.

Where should training be done?

The location can vary between an internal single location, a centralised external location or a decentralised (on-the-job) location. This provides at least nine options to consider, as shown in Figure 11.2.

The three most likely options are as follows:

1 Company specialist in central location. The advantage of this approach is the specialised knowledge and experience which can be passed on to new or younger recruits. It enables company-specific and work-oriented training to be carried out. The purpose is clearly training, not selling, and this makes for a less pressurised learning environment. Against this, the danger of unreality and a lack of customer-specific dimensions to training may reduce its effectiveness. Costs are relatively high. In larger

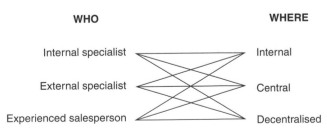

Fig 11.2   Training options

firms, sales trainers often fail to involve field sales managers in the process, with the result that training is not always relevant to the realities of the job (Honeycutt *et al.*, 1993).

2   Outside expert in central, off-company location. Again, the experience and expertise of the trainer is important but specific customer, product and company knowledge may be lacking. Older, more experienced salespeople tend to be hostile to so-called outside experts. There may also be a lack of uniqueness and a possible lack of security with such programmes.

3   Field salespeople in on-the-job location. Selling is a doing job and training can only be effective if knowledge and skills are put into practice. John Lidstone (1986) suggests the following five-step formula:

1   Tell salespeople what to do.

2   Show them how to do it.

3   Get them to practise what they have been told and shown.

4   Assess what they do and correct/coach where necessary.

5   Get salespeople to practise again and again and again.

On-the-job training occurs in real-life situations under actual market conditions. A possible weakness may be the lack of expertise in the trainer. Another weakness is that good and bad habits can be learned. There is also a problem in being sales rather than customer focused such as using sales technique as a solution to all sales tasks instead of building the ongoing relationship. In smaller companies, it is almost always the case that the trainer is the sales manager but such people tend to be weak on evaluation and follow up, which are crucial to training effectiveness (Honeycutt *et al.*, 1994). No one approach is perfect and the method used in training should be considered and evaluated, as should who is going to do it.

What methods of training should be used?

The possible options are as follows:

1   *Discussion groups*. These can take a variety of forms and potentially offer the most frequent training opportunity at regional or national sales meetings or specially convened training sessions. The use of discussion topics, case studies or idea-generating sessions helps individuals to learn from others, peers and colleagues and to seek individual improvement. While such groups are difficult to lead, control and evaluate, they also create team spirit and purpose.

2   *Lectures*. Lectures are a traditional way of teaching large numbers at low cost. They are useful to convey factual type information but suffer from a poor retention of information by participants and the inability to adapt to dynamic and dissimilar situations which characterise the selling job. Most sales training by lectures incorporates other back-up methods such as slides, flip charts, films and audio and video communications. In-car CDs are a time-efficient way of assisting in training salespeople.

3   *Programmed learning*. Developing on the previous approach, many sales trainers and companies are finding programmed learning to be a cost-effective training

approach. This enables a substantial quantity of material to be given to new and existing salespeople at their own pace. The format uses a sales manual divided into relevant sections, for example, product knowledge and sales skills. Using a loose-leaf folder, general information can be supplemented with company- and product-specific data. Video and audio communication can be used together with assignments, exercises and possibly case examples to provide a comprehensive learning package. So-called high-tech training methods, including computer-assisted learning, computer-managed instruction, teletraining and interactive video, are likely to be increasingly used in the digital age.

4 *Role-playing.* With this technique, artificial sales situations are constructed to educate salespeople in what to do and what not to do in a given situation. Different options are possible, such as using drama at sales meetings to create interest, provide entertainment and make important training points. Play-acting of this type can be a problem for some people but is useful to highlight common weaknesses in sales presentations. Role-playing, using video recording and playback, is now widely used as a learning technique. The use of actors to increase realism is increasingly common but skill, and some care, is required to avoid demotivating individuals and undermining self-confidence. The aim is exactly the reverse. Role-playing works by

- defining the sales situation, for example, to get a new product accepted by an existing customer;
- establishing the situation, for example, time of call, the individual you are addressing and relevant circumstances;
- casting a buyer and a seller – roles will be later reversed;
- briefing the participant (separately) on what their objectives should be – buyers can be told to raise specific obstacles or objections;
- playing out the sales situation;
- discussing and analysing the situation. Reshow the interaction, ask for comments for and against, develop learning points, for example, be more businesslike, identify opportunities to close, be specific on objectives and so on.

A good role-playing exercise is to create one or two salespeople acting as potential suppliers and three or four others acting in buying roles as might form the decision-making unit (DMU) to be found in organisational purchasing. This situation might be supplying a CRM system to a major bank, supplying process equipment to a major food manufacturer, environmental services to a major oil company or similar scenarios. By briefing the participants with alternative positions before or during the exercise participants can practice different approaches both strategically and in the sales/ negotiation situation. Play-back of events provides strong learning and realisation of strengths and weaknesses in individual, team and organisational sales approaches.

5 *Observed sales calls.* Most managers and trainers use some form of 'kerbside conference', but very few are trained or skilled in the technique. The problem is often too much emphasis on specific strengths or weaknesses, mostly weaknesses. To be effective as a training method, it requires some skill in preparation, purpose, observation,

analysis and coaching by the trainer. There is some merit in its participative approach and its realism, and this topic is revisited under coaching later in the chapter.

The reason for training is that the benefits to be derived from training outweigh the costs. Sales training is not an end in itself. Managers must take cognisance of the fact that not all skills and attitudes can be learned and that individuals react to training in different ways. Some are more positive than others and training needs differ, for example, between new and experienced or between technical and non-technical personnel. Some salespeople will be more adaptable and receptive than others but training cannot help those who cannot or will not learn and adapt.

What do you think?

Evaluating training options

Imagine a particular sales context and decide which options you feel would be most appropriate. Be prepared to defend your choices

	WHO		WHERE	
Criterion	**Inside vs. Outside**		**Central vs. Decentral**	
Time	−	+	−	+
Cost	−	+	+	−
Realism	+	−	−	+
Market orientation	−	+	−	+
Creativity	−	+	+	−
Security	+	−	−	+
Focus	+	−	−	+

+ = good; − = poor.

Neither is what has been said so far the complete picture. Policies, programmes and techniques can be taught but only up to a point. The key to most sales situations is a continuing dialogue, trust and respect between two parties. The personal rating that the sales manager gives his salespeople is important, but the rating the customer gives the salesperson is more important. The customer is the focal point. Being afraid or ignorant of your customer is fatal. Understanding customer needs, problems and situations is fundamental to the selling job. The essence of this cannot be easily taught: it must be felt and appreciated and translated into interpersonal business relationships. Customer-centred sales training is in vogue. Today's new breed of salesperson is someone who needs

■ to respect the priorities of the customer, enhance the image of the firm and keep promises;

■ to be aware of the financial constraints and cost drivers of their customers so that they can 'surprise the customer' and help the customer win (whereby the sales organisation will also win);

- conceptual, managerial and strategic skills which enable them to understand their customers business so that customer goals, aims and needs are effectively identified and fulfilled;

- to orchestrate their firm's capabilities for matching a feasible offer with an objective which is mutually agreed with the customer;

- the ability to create a context in which the buying experience is enjoyable and enhances the self-esteem of the customer (Tzokas and Donaldson, 2000).

11.6   Evaluating sales training

At the outset of this chapter, it was claimed that the purpose of training was to improve performance. This being so, it is necessary to evaluate the effectiveness of sales training. The costs of training are measurable and specific but the results less so. Improvement can be measured on a variety of dimensions:

- *sales* – for example, value, volume, number of orders, average order size and new customers;

- *activity* – number of calls, journey time and distance reports submitted;

- *costs* – expenses, expense ratio and commission rates.

One possibility is to collect relevant and measurable data on these parameters prior to training and immediately thereafter. Results should show on both the quantity and quality of sales performance. The difficulty of other factors influencing the result is considerable. The use of control groups who receive no training should be considered as a comparison with other groups who have. An improved sales/expense ratio or lower staff turnover is a good indicator of whether training has had a positive affect. It has been suggested that sales training evaluation should encompass both the impact of training on trainees and the impact on the firm (Attia, Honeycutt and Leach, 2005).

The requirements for future training needs should also be assessed as part of this planned approach. Figure 11.3 shows a helpful appraisal form to assess training needs. Other benefits of training might include increased customer satisfaction, a superior competitive advantage, higher morale, lower turnover (and lower cost) and less supervision. These benefits are perhaps more difficult to assess.

While some companies set specific training objectives, many fail to do so in any systematic way. Their training objectives are often bland platitudes and simplistic (value or volume), and fail to involve experienced salespeople in the process (Honeycutt *et al.*, 1993). These pitfalls should be avoided. It is not the sales training course that should be evaluated but the training process including the pre-briefing by the line manager outlining the initial training objectives; the event itself; the debriefing by the line manager; the subsequent encouragement and coaching; the opportunity for the salesperson to implement change. This requires input effort by the trainer (orchestrator), the manager (coach) and the salesperson (effort to implement) to assess how well the training process has worked.

FACTOR	Good (knows this) (needs no training)	Above average (knows this) (tries to do it)	Below average (knows this) (does not do it)	Poor (does not know it) (does not do it)	Training Recommendations
NAME AREA					
Product knowledge application Market Customer Sales skills Probing Questions Demonstration Closing *Administration* Time Territory Reports Records Care of car and equipment					

Fig 11.3 Training appraisal form

11.7 Leadership

Effective leadership can be one of the most important discriminating factors in the successful business. By leadership, we refer not only to supervising and motivating subordinates but also to leadership in business vision, process innovation, quality and customer care (Donaldson, 1995). Leadership, involving planning, directing, motivating and control, may there-fore be equated with management, but it is both similar to it and different from it. Leadership is one aspect of management but is not equal to it. A person may be an effective manager yet a poor leader while others may be effective leaders yet poor managers. This may mean that the leadership factor is the discriminating factor in high-performing sales managers. Certainly, because of the nature of many salespeople and the selling job, sales supervisors and managers require high-level skills in human resource leadership and management.

One of the problems that first-line supervisors, or sales managers, face is that they are often promoted from the ranks. This is both understandable and desirable in most organisations to encourage good performers and develop personnel. Not all salespeople, nor even the best salespeople, in an organisation will make good sales managers. Managing is different from doing. Examples of the differences between selling and sales management were considered in Chapter 1 by separating doing from managing tasks and vice versa. The job of the salesperson is to sell; the job of the sales manager is to supervise the selling activities of their salespeople. While these 'doing' tasks may be an important, indeed a crucial, aspect of the total job, separating doing from managing is a key feature of effective leadership. The sales manager as a leader will have a significant effect on the performance of subordinates. Quality leadership in both technique and style is necessary and desirable yet no definition or formula as to what constitutes leadership per se is accurate or convincing. Studies by behavioural scientists help to identify possible discriminating factors but these fail to provide a profile of a leader in the abstract. Great leaders, generals, politicians, sportsmen and women and leaders of industry do not have one set of characteristics or skills which enables their leadership role to be effective. The concern here is with sales management, yet the leadership problem is common to all management jobs. A leader is a person who rules, guides or inspires others. Theories of leadership can help to identify the importance of this person in a sales context.

Theories of leadership

Trait theory – There has been much discussion and debate over what makes a leader 'great'. Historically, the emphasis was on the born leader, with attempts to identify differences between leaders and followers and between great leaders and others. These studies initially concentrated on the traits or characteristics which were associated or could be identified in a leader. Some of the factors considered were appearance, competence, confidence, intelligence, knowledge, experience, innovation, determination, articulateness, persuasiveness and so on, yet these factors were found in some leaders but not in others. The outcome was inconsistency and uncertainty, and the evidence therefore inconclusive.

Power theory – Power, or the ability to influence, is also seen as part of leadership since it gives the sales manager authority over salespeople. Power, according to French and Raven (1959), can arise in different ways:

- *legitimate power*, based on the individual's position in the organisation, for example, sales managers have this power;
- *reward power*, based on the manager's ability to reward subordinates, for example through pay increases, promotion or other recognition;
- *coercive power*, which comes from the capacity to withhold rewards or punish, such as by dismissal;
- *expert power*, based on the subordinate's acceptance of the leader's expertise, skills, knowledge or special abilities;
- *referent power*, originating in the leader's inspirational or charismatic qualities.

These sources of power affect the salesperson–sales manager relationship and help to explain job satisfaction and/or performance.

What do you think?

Fortune magazine (2005) asked seven top bosses how to become a great leader. Here are some indicators from their responses:

'I had to make sure we got rid of the saboteurs, built a strong cadre of disciples, and moved all the fence sitters to the positive side.'

'Leading is like parenting: its one long process of pulling back and letting it become its own organism.'

'Courage.'

'If you're not excited, how can you get others excited?'

'Surround yourself with the very best people.'

'Culture is key.'

'don't try to change their minds as much as you try to show it serves their own interests.' (Fortune, 2005)

Discuss these responses and try to prioritise them in terms of perceived importance to you. To extend the debate see also 'Leading by Feel' in the Harvard Business Review, January 2004.

Behavioural theory – Studies of people in their work situation have provided new and alternative ways in which leadership style can affect subordinates. This has given rise to behavioural theories of leadership which have sound theoretical concepts to aid understanding, but again the empirical evidence questions its validity. Evidence in sales situations is weak and spasmodic, but one of these intuitively appealing models is the managerial grid (Figure 11.4).

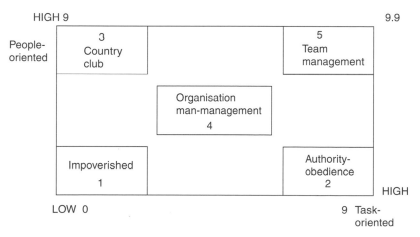

Fig 11.4 The managerial grid

The origins of the approach emanate from the Industrial Revolution. At that time, leadership styles were highly autocratic with rigid structures and defined hierarchies. Perhaps the emergence from production-orientation to sales-orientation encouraged a shift from autocratic to democratic leadership and a more people-based approach since effective selling is itself both task- and people-oriented. Whatever the cause, the idea of a 9.9 manager who is high on both people and task orientation has a certain intuitive appeal. While 81 possible positions may be identified, these can be differentiated into five distinct groups (Blake and Mouton, 1964, 1978):

Group 1: *Impoverished management*, low on both task achievement and concern for people, where there is minimum effort to get work done, just enough to sustain membership of the organisation.

Group 2: *Authority–obedience management*, which is highly task-centred. Getting results is top priority and systems and people must produce results, or else. This style may be regarded as somewhat of an anachronism, perhaps Victorian in attitude, but is not entirely inappropriate to some companies in Britain today. Its emphasis on results can make it effective as a style where 'carrot and stick' rewards and punishments are accepted.

Group 3: *Country-club management* directs attention to the needs of people, with the aim of organisations being effective if everyone is happy and contented, working together and not pressurised. It is therefore high in people concern but low in task concern. It assumes that job satisfaction leads to higher job performance – does it?

Group 4: *Organisation man-management*, where effective performance and job satisfaction are balanced in an effort to achieve a satisfactory outcome for both organisation and its employees.

Group 5: *Team management*, where 100 per cent commitment is coupled with care and concern for the welfare of employees. This is an ideal, combining maximum task orientation with concern for people. In reality, commonality in the corporate culture, its ethos and its objectives is difficult to achieve although most would acknowledge the desirability of this position.

Situational/contingency theory

Leadership seems to provide an analogous problem to that of seeking an ideal sales type. The lack of convincing evidence on the one-best type concentrates attention on the situational factors which affect leader–subordinate relationships. Again, a plausible explanation could be that situational factors themselves create the leaders. Such leaders are people who can help the individual, the group and the organisation reach its goals. Three factors – the leader, the subordinate and the situation – impinge on job performance (Figure 11.5).

Neither the theoretical constructs of the behaviourists nor the empirical evidence provide sufficient explanation of the myriad relationships thrown up by this diagram. The implications for sales management are important. It is not a case of whether sales managers are leaders – they are; rather, it concerns how this leadership can be exercised.

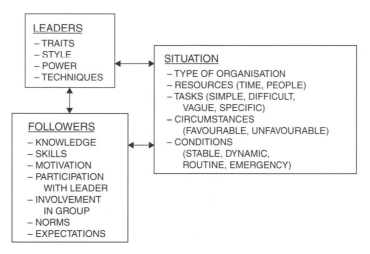

Fig 11.5 Contingency theory

11.8   Leadership styles in sales management

The contingency theory demonstrates the complexity of the leadership problem. The appropriateness of the sales manager's leadership behaviour will in turn depend on the subordinate, the situation and the manager's own behaviour. It can also depend on the personality and history of the organisation. A young and aggressive organisation may attract more freedom-loving sales personnel whereas a well-established, conservative organisation tends to attract more regimentation-loving personnel (Moriya and Gockley, 1985). Sales managers can control some but not all of these variables. They can modify their style of leadership and their means of supervision and improve performance by identifying problems and providing solutions. Just as the onus is on salespeople to modify or adapt their behaviour to the needs of the buyer, so sales managers should adapt their style to the needs of subordinates. As salespeople have to reconcile the interests of their paymasters with customer satisfaction, so sales managers must reconcile individual aims and aspirations with the objectives of the organisation.

Did you know?

Daniel Goleman is credited with being the first to use the term 'emotional intelligence'. His research at 200 large, global companies suggested that while intelligence, toughness, determination and vision are necessary attributes they are not enough to be successful. He found that five components create emotional intelligence at work. These are self-awareness, self-regulation, motivation, empathy and social skill. People with those qualities make the best leaders in the workplace (Goleman, 2004).

Leadership styles can be identified in different ways. One approach is to distinguish between democratic and autocratic leaders. McGregor (1960) drew a distinction between theory X and theory Y. Theory X holds that individuals naturally dislike work and must be coerced into putting forth adequate effort on the job (eight calls per day/earning a living salespeople). Such people avoid responsibility yet want security. Theory Y suggests the following:

- Work may be a source of satisfaction.

- A person will exercise self-direction and self-control in the service of objectives to which they are committed.

- Commitment to objectives is a function of the rewards associated with their achievement.

- With suitable circumstances, people will not only accept but also seek responsibility.

- The capacity to exercise a relatively high degree of imagination, ingenuity and creativity in the solution of organisational problems is widely rather than narrowly distributed in the population.

- The intellectual potential of people in work is only partially utilised.

McGregor was later to concede that 'The democratic/adviser type boss wasn't sufficient (human relations school), that it was also necessary to make difficult decisions, show leadership and exercise authority' (McGregor, 1960). Nevertheless, getting salespeople to work at higher levels of commitment and involvement needs to be encouraged rather than prescribed by doctrine.

Stroh (1978) has modified this dichotomy of managerial style into theory H, as shown in Figure 11.6.

This H style implies a gear-shift operation where leadership style can be changed according to the needs of subordinates, the responsibilities of the position and the situational circumstances. For example, an autocratic style may be appropriate where the job is routine, the salespeople young or inexperienced, in conditioned response selling or where unfavourable trading conditions necessitate a result or else! A paternalistic approach may be more relevant where the manager has a young team and the authority to reward or punish. A unified sense of approach, a shared culture, may take time to nurture and encourage. A consultative approach may work better in industrial,

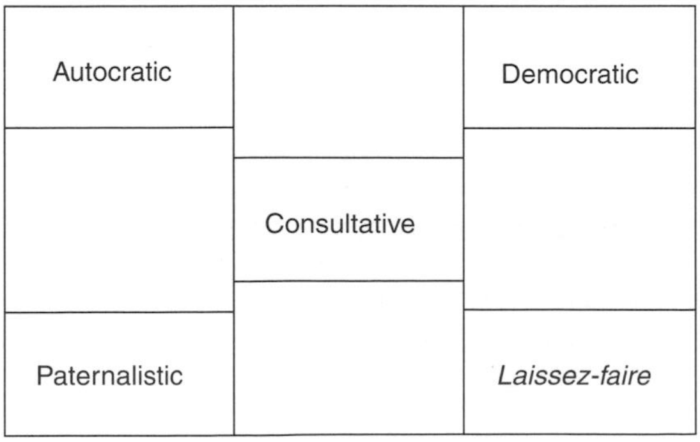

Autocratic		Democratic
	Consultative	
Paternalistic		*Laissez-faire*

Fig 11.6   Leadership styles

particularly technical, selling. Salespeople on a fixed salary with a service dimension seek advice and guidance rather than reward or retribution. A democratic style may work with a sales team who have strong group identity, such as a geographical region. Involvement, participation, self-improvement and joint determination are encouraged. Finally, highly motivated individuals may function most effectively if left to their own devices (laissez-faire). Direct salespeople on high-commission earnings or development salespeople in large-scale capital goods may respond favourably to this approach.

These leadership styles confirm that no one approach is suitable for all. Based on studies of the satisfaction–performance relationship, the paternalistic, laissez-faire and autocratic leadership styles were found to be less suitable for achieving satisfactory results from salespeople. This is the result of individuals not being allowed to have any influence on performance standards. There is no room for self-improvement, self-evaluation or two-way communication between subordinate and manager. The democratic or consultative styles are more likely to be motivators and to increase job satisfaction.

Care should also be taken by sales managers not to exhibit inconsistency. Subordinates will be uncertain and unable to respond to dramatic changes in a sales manager's leadership style from a previous norm. Since the role of the sales manager is to manage the sales force rather than sales, being a leader is a crucial aspect of their effectiveness. A few managers have charisma (a divinely conferred power or talent, a capacity to inspire followers with devotion and enthusiasm). Most managers must develop leadership by promoting a common purpose, through teamwork and through a variety of technical and human relations skills. Effective leaders exhibit their skills and modify their behaviour depending on the situation. The skills required in emergency crisis situations will be different from those required in stable, routine circumstances. With these provisos in mind, various means of supervision can be considered.

Means of supervision

Direct

With new or inexperienced salespeople, particularly in larger, more bureaucratic structures, the salesperson is looking for guidance in their job, in their relationships and on performance evaluation. The sales manager leads using a direct instructional approach, telling salespeople what to do, how to do it and the means of evaluating performance. This approach will reduce role ambiguity, role conflict and increase job satisfaction (Churchill *et al.*, 1976). With more experienced salespeople, a direct approach can also be appropriate but a more persuasive communicating style will be required.

Consultative

Leadership in sales management also works as part of a group activity. Fostering and promoting teamwork is a leadership skill whether in a regional sales team, a national sales team or an overall company context. By presenting problems, situations or options to salespeople, by discussion and consultation and by taking decisive and appropriate action, the manager exhibits leadership. In some cases, first-line supervisors can achieve the required result by participating in group or joint decision-making. The conflict between satisfying superiors and subordinates can be a problem but one at which an effective leader will show their true worth.

Delegation

A third approach is for the sales manager to present the problem or objective to the individual salesperson and leave the method and decision to the individual. This is not necessarily an abdication of leadership, as might be implied. An effective style is one where individual sales performance is improved. Delegation of managerial responsibility to the salesperson can encourage self-improvement and self-motivation but only in certain circumstances and with certain types of subordinate. This approach implies management confidence in a subordinate.

Indirect

Leadership does not imply control of manager over subordinate yet sales management problems are concerned with action and results. There is a danger of managers failing to strike a balance between too little and too much control. Furthermore, effective leadership should focus on control of activity and capability rather than on output controls (Challagalla and Shervani, 1996). This enables salespeople to enhance their performance rather than assessing results which are then used in a critical way. Good leaders do not do the work themselves, do not supervise too closely but do discuss with and involve their subordinates. This can be achieved face to face, by indirect means such as telephone consultation and sales meetings or through reporting procedures and controls.

11.9   Coaching

Somewhere between formal training and inspired leadership lies the importance of coaching. In his literature review on the topic of sales coaching, Rich (1998) concluded that sales coaching is a multidimensional activity that consists of three constructs: (1) supervisory feedback, (2) role modelling and (3) salesperson's trust in his or her manager. Guidance is also quoted by Ingram *et al.* (2001) as a major construct of the sales coaching. Cocoran *et al.* (1995, p. 118) define sales coaching as 'A sequence of conversations and activities that provides ongoing feedback and encouragement to a salesperson or sales team member with the goal of improving that person's performance.'

Doyle and Roth (1992) argue that the process of building relationships with customer is long and complex and requires more learning, making the once a month coaching schedule insufficient. On this basis they argue that coaching by joining the salesperson to a single sales call cannot work because only the sales person is able to place the call in context of past conversations with all the unique personalities of that account. Therefore, coaching in relationship selling requires frequent interactions to jointly discuss account relationships, potentials and projected economic returns aiming at developing insight rather than evaluate sales call behaviour. They argue that the salesperson must keep a diary of the interactions held with his or her customers. This diary should be well structured in terms of the information that will be kept and how it will be analysed to prevent coaching discussions deteriorating in a series of fuzzy blue-sky monologues. These coaching discussions are led by the salesperson who analyses data for every call and describes the progress and problems encountered in the accounts. The sales manager should encourage insight by asking self-reflective

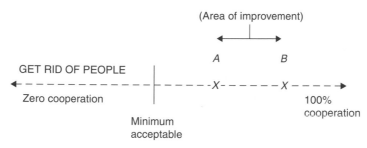

Fig 11.7　Sales force cooperation

questions such as 'Why do you think the customer did that?', 'What could you have done to prevent that?', 'Any early warning signals that could have alerted you?', 'What have you learned as a result of this call?' According to Doyle and Roth (1992) the result of the discussion and the self-reflecting questions should be new insight that the salesperson commits to apply on future sales calls. Many authors have argued that relationship selling requires more analytical and management skills, hence the title of 'account manager'. A recent article by Gosling and Mintzberg (2003) argue that everything a manager does is sandwiched between action on the ground and reflection in the abstract. Action without reflection is thoughtless, and reflection without action is passive. They argue that events become experience only after they have been reflected upon whereby most people go through life undergoing happenings that are undigested into experience. On this basis, we can conclude that the role of the coach is no longer that of a teacher who tells the salesperson what and how to do his job. The role of the coach is to facilitate the digestion or interpretations of events that happened during a customer interaction so that the salesperson continuously enhances his or her knowledge about how to manage customer relationships.

If managers are ineffective as leaders of their sales subordinates, there will be a lack of cooperation between the two and inevitably between the salesperson and the organisation.

Salespeople who do not or cannot cooperate must be released, while 100 per cent cooperation is equally remote (Figure 11.7). Effective leadership and supervision enhances cooperation and performance.

In Figure 11.7, salespeople operating at point A are operating below optimum. The result is lost business, lower customer satisfaction, late or inadequate reports, higher expenses, higher absenteeism and a higher turnover of sales personnel. Keusel (1971) identifies six deadly diseases that can afflict a sales force:

1 *Complacency*, especially among older or longer-serving salespeople. The senior person on first name terms with the managing director who knows the business but is not developing new business, new product sales or new accounts is a problem. Leadership skills to rekindle interest, special incentives and job enhancement are needed to break the mould.

2 *Staleness*. Like complacency, repetitive actions are habit-forming so that sales presentations can be routine and stale. Sales managers can motivate by coaching, training and information bulletins to enable salespeople to take alternative approaches with their prospects.

3 *Gun-shyness*. Salespeople calling on regular customers (service selling) or calling on non-customers can suffer from an inability to get orders or obtain commitment from buyers. Sometimes negative responses act as a deterrent rather than a spur. Specific sales objectives or ways of pioneer selling, for example at an exhibition, may rekindle dormant selling skills. Remember that successful salespeople want advances and not just continuations.

4 *Scepticism*. Salespeople quickly learn of customer dissatisfaction and competitive superiority yet, to be effective, they have to believe in themselves, their product and their company. While basic inadequacies must be corrected, the sales force can be reassured (constantly) by R&D bulletins, improvements in products, service, distribution and so on. To extend the cliché, they can only fire guns if given the ammunition.

5 *Indecision*. Role conflict and ambiguity are part of the selling job. Management can reduce these problems by giving clear and consistent decisions. Salespeople respond to strong decision-taking by managers. Procrastination, on the other hand, is the enemy of progress in sales and a sign of weak leadership.

6 *Competition*, especially the low-price variety. The weak salesperson always blames price, yet it is seldom the only feature in a buyer's decision. If it were, salespeople would not be necessary anyway. Salespeople should sell benefits rather than features, they should be customer problem-solving, for example, on quality, reliability, image and so on. The customer who asks why the price is so high is really asking the salesperson to explain why the product is so good.

Leadership skills are exhibited when different situations require management solutions. Sometimes, under normal, routine conditions, business operates efficiently and smoothly. At other times, such as in a recession or during competitor price-cutting activity, exceptional conditions may arise. The way in which different situations are handled, or perceived to be handled, inspires confidence in subordinates. Some people thrive on emergencies and firefighting but most tire of this if it is more than a temporary situation. Crisis management is OK but not for long. Anyone can cut costs and reduce the workforce by 10 per cent. True leaders, who can motivate salespeople to work hard in November and December when the annual target is reached by October, are usually harder to find. The positive leader is harder to find than the ruthless cost-cutter, but no one style of leadership can be prescribed for all situations.

Sales managers must learn to recognise frustration, identify its source and take remedial action to help the individual overcome this frustration. This can be achieved by improved techniques, selling skills, training and other means, including leadership skills.

What do you think?

Job-related sales problems.

The following have been identified as some of the problems faced by salespeople:

- failure to consummate a sale;
- failing to achieve quotas;
- failing to obtain new prospects;

- inability to grant a prospect's request;
- failure to achieve promotion;
- failure to circumvent closed-door tactics.

As a sales manager what remedies would you suggest for these problems?

Several leadership roles, not merely a single individual role, require to be played. These roles are

- the *effective performer*, the competence dimension of leadership, guiding salespeople to more effective action, for example, how to improve sales technique, asking questions, what to add to a sales presentation, solving customers' problems and so on;
- the *inspirational leader*, who can overcome bureaucracy, enhance team effort and obtain subordinates' commitment to the cause (sales objectives);
- the *innovator*, who can develop, suggest new ideas and new approaches and helps salespeople to achieve their objectives by sales support, better organisation and training;
- the *parent or guardian*, who will rule, respect, judge, discipline and recognise subordinates in a fair, objective and involved way;
- the *guardian of the status quo*, someone who represents company policy, accepts behaviour norms and provides trust and respect.

These multi-roles require adaptation to different situations yet demand consistency. The role must be played with sincerity rather than hypocrisy. Since the various roles (for example, innovator and guardian) do not come naturally to all, managers must work hard at developing effective leadership skills. To increase the sales manager's job satisfaction, role clarity has to be improved. Better communication and feedback between supervisor and senior manager will increase job satisfaction. There appears to be a delicate balance in 'creative tension' between constructive or destructive elements of the job.

The supervision element in managing is that aspect of leadership which directs sales subordinates in the daily performance of the selling job. This responsibility means providing salespeople with the necessary resources, including training, to be effective. In return, salespeople need to cooperate in achieving their objectives. Specific tasks in sales supervision include

- interpreting and enforcing company policy;
- acting as a two-way communicator between the salesperson and top management;
- establishing standards of performance;
- creating a favourable work environment.

To do these supervisory tasks requires the development of basic human relations skills. First is perception or the ability to look, see and hear. This can be done formally or informally, directly or indirectly, with individuals or in groups. Managers must be careful to assess behaviour accurately and objectively. Rumours, mistakes and careless asides can be interpreted differently and often mistakenly. Second, managers require conceptual ability to understand the way in which messages are communicated and received. For example, do individuals and supervisors both understand and interpret communication in the same way – is it accurate, is it realistic? Salespeople may not know what to do, in which case they can be trained, or they may be doing the wrong things, which must be corrected. Salespeople who do not want to improve cannot be helped. Third, sales managers can improve their communication skills with subordinates. The way in which messages are transmitted and received has different effects. For example, memos, faxes, e-mail and the telephone can stress different levels of urgency. The essence of good communication is that it should be consistent, reinforcing and strengthening the link between superior and subordinate. Finally, managers must develop self-awareness. Leadership should not be separated from self. Accept it, manage it, change weakness into strength and inaction into decisiveness. Most people attribute their own success to the help that others gave them, especially mentors at some point in time. Successful salespeople credit sales leaders while unsuccessful salespeople will blame their leaders.

11.10　Summary

How to get the best out of the people you employ is the management challenge. One way is through training to improve individual sales force productivity. Good training has a specific purpose, is planned and is aimed at the individual. Various people, locations and content can be used. To be effective, training requires behavioural aspects of buyer–seller interaction to be developed. Another way is through effective leadership but this quality is difficult to define and operationalise. Effective sales managers require leadership skills to guide, coach and develop salespeople to perform better. Various theories of leadership – trait theory, power theory, behavioural theory and contingency theory – help our understanding but do not adequately explain how leadership works or is most effective. Different styles, democratic, autocratic, consultative, paternalistic and laissez-faire, seem to work more effectively in some situations than in others. A combination of conceptual, human relation and technical skills are important in sales leaders. The ability to coach individuals to perform to their best in a coherent way is part of this mystique. More evidence is required to explain the causes and linkages in this process.

Questions

1　Evidence suggests that sales managers and trainers leave the customer out of training programmes, preferring to concentrate on product tasks. Make a case for incorporating alternative training content for new and experienced salespeople.

2　The training requirements of salespeople should reflect changing market conditions. Using your own examples, indicate which areas of training might be necessary because of changes in today's environment.

3 The sales training programme varies from company to company because of differences in products, markets, company policies, organisational size and trainees' experience and ability. Discuss.

4 It is often postulated that top sales performers do not make the most effective sales managers. Explain why this may be the case.

5 As a first-line supervisor (regional manager), several of the salespeople under your control are considering leaving the company. How would you deal with this situation?

6 A company selling industrial products to business clients has a sales force of 15 people. Five of these are aged over 55, some of whom have been passed over for promotion and appear to have negative views about the company and senior management. Explain how a more positive attitude might be encouraged. What do you recommend?

Case study

Edmunson Electrical Distributors

Edmunson Electrical Distributors (www.edmundson-electrical.co.uk) is a leading distributor of electrical equipment and components with over two hundred and thirty branches in the United Kingdom. The company is an electrical wholesaler acting as an intermediary between manufacturers and customers. Accounts are classified according to turnover and margins achieved. The 'bread and butter' of the business is the electrical contractor, who provides high turnover but low margins. The more significant the purchases, the higher are the rebates and discounts awarded to these customers. A second important group of customers are hotels, hospitals and other institutional customers who provide less volume but better margins. It is company policy to maximise the turnover of each customer so that Edmunson can, in turn, command a better price from the manufacturers. With such a wide range of product lines and items, the company cannot afford to stock every product so their own competence is measured not only in price but also by their service, especially delivery reliability.

The structure of the company is adapted from a US management style that uses a SPI (standard practice of initiation) to give similar accounting procedures for stocks, invoicing, ledger entry and so on. Branches in all other respects compete with each other in terms of orders, charges and revenues, which are the sole responsibility of the branch manager. Each branch is a separate profit centre and operates more like a franchise since the capital is given directly to the branch, although 19 per cent of annual profits go to the parent company. Although the branches compete with each other, the sales representatives feel that the system is fair and motivating. The manager is usually supported in each branch by an accountant and at least one representative as well as buyers, telesales and store personnel and van drivers.

Branch A is one of the most successful in the group. There are several major accounts but relatively few electrical contractors and competition is not well represented in the area. Turnover is higher and costs are lower than in many other areas. The branch manager is well respected and highly successful, the youngest within the group, and last year steered his branch to a £3 million turnover with a profit share between the eight employees of £160,000. This success, combined with the hunger created by the profit share, has produced a highly motivated team. This team spirit is encouraged by the manager with open plan offices and an easy communication style. People are allocated to tasks according to their suitability – one salesperson actively seeking new accounts, another servicing existing accounts. All staff are aware of the 19 per cent profit levy so they aim to beat this on all business negotiated. However, because these figures are based on previous year's targets, sales are in some months held back if the increase was too great, in the knowledge this will raise next year's figure. Salespeople have been sent on training courses, but no qualitative targets are set for them.

▶

Branch B is currently in financial trouble and operates in stark contrast to Branch A. In the past two years, turnover fell by almost one-half, a stock deficit was recorded and, since 19 per cent of profit was to be paid, no profit sharing to staff was achieved. Competition is fierce in this area, with 30 other wholesalers operating, but no involvement of salespeople in setting targets is allowed. For example, a new recruit with 2 weeks experience was given the task of opening 40 new accounts in 12 months. He failed and left the company. No sales forecast is set and people are encouraged to get business wherever they can. The result is that several people left and, after two years of disastrous results, the manager was asked to resign.

- From the information given, what factors contributed to the diverse performances of the two branches.
- Analyse the leadership styles of the two managers.
- From a company perspective, what would you recommend to senior management about their branch operation management.

Key terms

- autocratic style
- behavioural theory (of leadership)
- behavioural sales training
- coercive power
- cognitive maps
- consultative approach
- contingency theory
- delegation
- democratic style
- expert power
- first-line supervisor
- job satisfaction

- laissez-faire style
- leadership
- legitimate power
- paternalistic style
- programmed learning
- power theory
- referent power
- reward power
- role-playing
- subordinate
- supervision
- trait theory

References

Attia, A.M., Honeycutt, E.D. and Leach, M.P. (2005) 'A three-stage model for assessing and improving sales force training and development' *Journal of Personal Selling and Sales Management* **25** (3): 253–68

Blake, R.R. and Mouton, J.S. (1964) *The Managerial Grid* Gulf Publishing: Houston, TX

Blake, R.R. and Mouton, J.S. (1978) *The New Managerial Grid* Gulf Publishing: Houston, TX

Challagalla, G.N. and Shervani, T.A. (1996) 'Dimensions and types of supervisory control: effects on salesperson performance and satisfaction' *Journal of Marketing* **60** (Jan): 89–105

Churchill, G.A., Ford, N.M. and Walker, O.C. (1976) 'Organisational climate and job and satisfaction in the sales force' *Journal of Marketing Research* **XIII** (Nov): 323–32

Corcoran, K.J., Petersen, L.K., Baitch, D.B. and Barrett, M.F. (1995) *High Performance Sales Organisations: creating competitive advantage in the global marketplace* McGraw-Hill: New York

Donaldson, B. (1995) 'Customer Care' in Baker, M.J. (ed.) *Marketing Theory and Practice* 3rd edition Macmillan: Houndmills

Doyle, S.X. and Roth, G.T. (1992) 'Selling and sales management in action: the use of insight coaching to improve relationship selling' *Journal of Personal Selling and Sales Management* **12** (1): 59–65

Fortune (2005) 'Follow these Leaders' 19 December, pp. 43–46

French, J.R.R. and Raven, B. (1959) The bases of social power in Cartwright, D. (ed.) *Studies in Social Power* University of Michigan Press: Ann Arbor, MI

Goleman, D. (2004) 'What makes a leader?' *Harvard Business Review* (**Jan**): 82–91

Gosling, J. and Mintzberg, H. (2003) 'The five managerial mind sets' *Harvard Business Review* (**Nov**): 54–63

Harvard Business Review (2004) 'Leading by feel' (**Jan**): 27–37

Honeycutt Jr, E.D., Howe, V. and Ingram, T.N. (1993) 'Shortcomings of sales training programs' *Industrial Marketing Management* **22** (2): 117–23

Honeycutt Jr, E.D., Ford, J.B. and Tanner, J.F. (1994) 'Who trains salespeople?: the role of sales trainers and sales managers' *Industrial Marketing Management* **23** (1): 65–70

Ingram, T. et al. (2001) *Sales Management: Analysis and Decision Making* 4th edition Harcourt Inc.: Orlando, FL

Keusel, H.N. (1971) Six deadly diseases that can affect your sales force in Kurtz, D.L. and Hubbard, C.W. (eds) *The Sales Function and its Management: selected readings* General Learning Press: Morristown, NJ, 148–53

Lidstone, J. (1986) *Training Salesmen on the Job* 2nd edition Gower: Aldershot

McGregor, D.M. (1960) *The Human Side of Enterprise* Harper & Row: New York

Moriya, F.E. and Gockley, J.C. (1985) 'Grid analysis for sales supervision' *Industrial Marketing Management* **14** (4): 235–8

Rich, G. (1998) 'The constructus of coaching: supervisory feedback, role modelling and trust' *Journal of Personal Selling and Sales Management* **18** (Winter): 53–64

Roman, S. and Ruiz, S. (2003) 'A comparative analysis of sales training in Europe: implications for international sales negotiations' *International Marketing Review* **20** (3): 304–27

Stanton, W.J., Buskirk, R.H. and Spiro, R.L. (1991) *Management of a Sales Force* 8th edition Irwin: Homewood, IL

Stroh, T.F. (1978) *Managing the Sales Function* McGraw-Hill: New York

Tzokas, N. and Donaldson, B. (2000) 'A research agenda for personal selling and sales management in the context of relationship marketing' *Journal of Selling and Major Account Management* **2** (2): 13–30

12 Motivation and rewards

12.1 Overview

Ability and technique may make the difference to whether a sale is won or lost, but a key factor in sales performance over time is motivation. The motivation problem is how to get salespeople who operate on their own, in a hostile environment, at a relatively high cost and geographically spread, to do their job well in the way management wants it done. Part of this is monetary reward. Everyone likes to be rewarded for doing their job well. While rewards are not exclusively monetary, people will be affected in their job and their attitude to work by how much money they can earn. Salespeople who earn only on commission in direct selling jobs may be motivated solely by earning potential. Most people, and most salespeople, weigh up potential monetary gains against the cost in time/effort/difficulty of the job and the opportunity of doing what they like and enjoy. Individuals' needs vary, but money is an important factor in most cases. Likewise, for the company, there is a dilemma between higher levels of pay and keeping costs down. Therefore, to tackle the problems of motivation and rewards integration and synthesis of material from many disciplines – management science, behavioural theory, psychology – with recent empirical evidence from the sales management literature is required.

12.2 Learning objectives

In this chapter, the aim is

- to consider appropriate levels, methods of payment and the role of financial incentives;
- to assess the trade-offs in higher levels of pay against the control of personal selling costs and their effect on performance;
- to understand what motivation is;
- to consider various theories of motivation and their relevance to selling jobs;
- to identify the link between motivation and job performance.

12.3 Definitions

Motivation is the amount of effort that a salesperson expends on each activity or task associated with the job.

Job satisfaction is the extent to which the individual salesperson finds the job fulfilling and rewarding.

12.4 Remuneration

For the individual, there are different incentives to work and to exert effort in their job. These incentives can be grouped into financial and non-financial categories. Non-financial incentives would include opportunities for advancement, recognition, self-esteem and other intangible factors. These will be considered later. Financial incentives include direct payments in salary, commission and bonuses and indirect payments such as expenses, a company car, private health care and so on. For most people, after a certain basic level of pay is reached, money may no longer be a sufficient motivator to work harder or longer. Yet where that point is, and how individuals react to monetary incentive, is not easily determined. The methods of payment are not surprisingly varied by type of business and type of selling. It is to be expected that capital goods (long lead time, organisational buying, service- and technical-related) and basic consumer goods (high service-related, central buying) tend to favour salary only, sometimes with bonuses and performance-related pay. Direct selling tends to favour commission or salary plus commission reward schemes. Most people would probably concede that, while remuneration is by no means the only motivation, it is by far the strongest force in promoting job effort, at least at a basic level. Money is seldom the only factor and definite conclusions on the effect of money on effort and performance require wider consideration of what constitutes motivation.

There will inevitably be a conflict of interest between the company and the individual regarding pay levels. The company would like, and need, to keep wage costs down whereas individuals naturally prefer as high an income as possible. Even in the most committed individual, and the most enlightened organisation, this underlying difference must exist. Companies must pay attention to pay to stimulate effort, reward achievement, control staff or be able to recruit and retain staff. Individuals need money to live, but remuneration may also be an incentive to work harder and better. In deciding the remuneration package, the following factors are to be considered (Tosdal, 1953a):

- *Fairness*. To overcome the basic dilemma of paying too little or too much, the first issue to resolve is fairness, to both the employee and the company. Wage levels can be a morale builder in a job where other role demands create problems.
- *Income and security*. Those companies who are tempted to pay on results, through commission only, overlook an individual's need for a liveable wage and the security of at least some earnings regardless of circumstances.
- *Incentives*. Above a minimum level of pay for security, there is an added incentive for individuals to work harder for more money. Sales performance does respond to sales effort, so offering a reward produces results.
- *Flexibility*. Salary levels should be relatively stable, avoiding high/low fluctuations. For this reason alone, combination methods are to be recommended but excesses in one period cannot be redressed by scarcity in another. For example, some firms operate retrospective commission payments above a target level. In a subsequent

period, if target is not reached, the previous surplus is claimed back. This avoids salespeople artificially pulling sales into a period to make a bonus at the expense of next period's sales. This kind of approach therefore satisfies neither salespeople nor the company.

■ *Economic.* Systems of pay, including expenses, should be economic in operating terms. Salespeople are a significant overhead cost and must justify their existence in cost/revenue terms. Complex payment schemes which are difficult, time consuming and costly to operate should be avoided.

There is inevitably an inherent conflict in these desirable objectives. A trade-off between security and flexibility, incentives and fairness, is required. To achieve a suitable compromise, the methods of payment, rather than just the level of pay, have to be considered.

Methods of payment

Salary is a regular fixed sum which is time- rather than output-related. The job that salespeople are expected to perform includes tasks which are not volume-related or even quantifiable, for example, providing market information, technical advice and handling complaints. Salary compensates for these tasks and can also be increased for levels of experience, length of service and other reasons. Where effort relates to time, as in protracted negotiations or development selling, salary may be the only basis for payment. New staff in training will also need to be salary-related rather than performance-related. Salary enables the firm to know in advance their wage bill; it is economic to administer and easy to control. These advantages may be at the expense of a more results-oriented method and may reduce an individual's drive and initiative.

Salary can be 'a floor which many salespeople desire and a ceiling which many dislike' (Tosdal, 1953b). Salary levels should be set at a level sufficient to attract, retain and stimulate the type of salesperson desired. Cognisance has to be taken of going rates for similar jobs by competing firms. Pay has to be attractive enough to appeal to sales recruits and retain good salespeople yet not out of line with other employees. If managers are paid less than subordinates, it is bad practice in the long term but should not be viewed negatively, especially by the manager! Underpaying on salary attracts poor-quality salespeople. Low pay increases staff turnover, adding to recruitment costs and possibly lost sales.

Advantages of salary are

■ a basic level of pay is assured, providing security for the salesperson;
■ a known cost – easy to administer for the company;
■ it encourages loyalty and commitment of the salesperson;
■ it enables transfer of individuals from one area to another;
■ control can be exercised on activities.

Problems with salary only, include

■ no direct incentive to greater effort;
■ costs being fixed regardless of sales levels;
■ that it will result in below-par performers being overpaid and high performers underpaid.

Commission is a payment for a unit of work related to volume, value or profits. An individual, or team, earns directly, related to sales performance, so that in extreme cases, salespeople become almost self-employed agents. The incentive for strong performers is the high, in some cases very high, earning potential. The attraction for the company is that weak performers eliminate themselves. The risk is that misrepresentation affects service and reputation, with negative public relations. Commission can, of course, be varied by time, products and markets. Its effect on a fixed cost business may be highly profitable. In this case, a sliding scale may be appropriate. Where costs may be more volume-related, a regressive scale might operate. For example, a third option is to pay a fixed rate, for example, 2 per cent on all sales.

In some types of selling, for example, Tupperware, Avon cosmetics catalogues and so on, salespeople work on a semi-voluntary basis with friends or door to door. The individual chooses to work as hard and long, or as little, as they like. For smaller companies with no resources, commission-only payment protects cash flow by relating sales costs directly to sales made. With commission schemes, the sales manager has to decide the basis of the commission (volume, value or profit), the starting point (minimum order level), the time it is to be paid (e.g. when customer places order or settles the account) and the rate (usually a percentage of sales).

Advantages of commission-only are that

■ payment is related to results for both individual and company;

■ it is easy to calculate once the scheme has become established;

■ there is no ceiling;

■ costs relate to sales;

■ no other evaluation method is required;

■ individuals can be virtually self-employed.

Problems might include

■ a lack of loyalty, commitment and time from salespeople;

■ a lack of service, customer-building and non-selling activities;

■ a large turnover of people (recruitment and training costs may rise);

■ other sales activities being ignored;

■ cost control being at the expense of area coverage, quality of presentation and company image.

Bonus is a more normal payment for achievement which is not strictly volume- or individual performance-related. A company which achieves a satisfactory profit performance may reward every employee's contribution to the overall effort. Individuals can achieve a bonus for reaching their individual target or for other achievement, for example, the number of new outlets or forecasting accuracy. A bonus can sometimes be paid as a commission to a sales team. In this case, if the area target is achieved, each member receives the bonus despite different individual contributions. In recent years, performance-related pay in the United Kingdom has enjoyed tax advantages for both company and employees and has proved popular as a result. This method should be closely linked to agreed dimensions of the job, as discussed in the section on targets.

Most firms pay employees on some form of *combination* basis. This disguises a multitude of variations, reflecting diverse corporate and sales objectives and the variety of selling situations and sales tasks. This is understandable since the factors which affect the method of pay might include such variables as the buying process complexity or the number of influences in a purchase decision. Where there is a high-risk or large-value purchase, the time lag in the sales process may be prolonged. Selling is a continuing dialogue rather than a one-off presentation. The need for pay reward could encourage individual salespeople in an overaggressive (dominant/hostile) approach detrimental to the company image. Payment plans of this type, like any other marketing variable, require careful evaluation and testing before implementation. Combination schemes can be varied by the size of the salary, the starting point of commissions, the type of commission scale and the methods of calculating expenses. No plan will accommodate all situations. Combination plans provide greater flexibility and control for sales managers over subordinates and encourage reward for effort. They provide both security and incentive for the individual. Problems with combination schemes usually relate to the expense of administering them. As with tax systems – if it's fair, it won't be simple; if it's simple, it won't be fair!

Financial incentives

Some of the problems in remuneration apply in greater degree to the financial incentive element of pay and reward. In particular,

- the more that is paid out, the more it costs the company, so a basic conflict persists;
- the incentive has to be sufficiently lucrative to be continuing and ongoing over time;
- the incentive must not be so insignificant that it ceases to function in a trade downturn or unfavourable economic conditions;
- incentives must be easily understood and economical to operate.

Did you know?

Not all incentives are introduced to improve performance. The use of incentives for reasons such as quasi-pay increases, avoiding pay disputes and so on is a sign of weak management and should be avoided. There is also the implication that if no incentive is paid, performance will suffer, yet in a survey of salespeople's motivation, it was found that 'doing a good job' was the most highly rated of 11 motivators, 'more money' being rated only sixth (Donaldson, 1997). Incentives may temporarily change what salespeople do, but they do not alter the attitudes that underlie behaviour (Kohn, 1993).

Many sales managers, ever alert to stimulating interest and improving sales performance in the sales force, like sales contests. They encourage competitiveness and entrepreneurship among salespeople and are generally thought to be positive in effect. The popularity of contests suggests that they have a part to play in achieving sales objectives. This seems particularly relevant to increase volume with specific targets. Examples of this would be new customers, the promotion of special items, seasonal offers or new product introductions. Sales contests, like sales promotions, have legal constraints since benefits won will be liable for tax. Care has to be taken over how long the contest will run and how valuable the prize will be perceived by participants. Evidence suggests that contests work as motivators because they provide recognition (status and enhanced self-esteem), excitement (risk and a change from routine) and reward. Contests often backfire because of poor management. Weak prizes, or too difficult targets, are common failures. Some of the common problems are

- failing to set clear objectives for the contest;
- bad timing;
- the contest being too complicated;
- quotas being too high;
- the wrong type of prize;
- a lack of promotion;
- no manager or customer involvement;
- being too slow in assessment and reward.

What do you think?

Some of the objections raised against contests include the following:

- Salespeople are paid to do a job. Further reward or incentive should not be necessary.
- High-calibre, experienced salespeople consider contests to be juvenile and silly.
- Contests have undesirable results, for example, greater returns, credit problems and stock losses.
- Contests distort 'natural' sales trends by bunching sales during the contest, with slumps before and after.
- Losers in the contest suffer loss of morale.
- Too frequent contests become obsessive.
- Competition can mean conflict, weakening team spirit.

Do you agree?

Contests must be assessed on their individual merits in terms of the objectives set. They cannot overcome basic management deficiencies but, properly conducted, do provide incentives. They are short term rather than long term in duration. The effect must be evaluated in total business over the longer period and on sales force morale. Care has to be taken on the basis for a contest so that everyone has an equal and fair chance of success. If, early on, two-thirds of the sales force opt out, it may be self-defeating. Competition for reward and recognition can be a great motivator.

Companies may offer a range of fringe benefits to encourage greater commitment by their staff. The worth of these may differ, especially between company and individual, but more evidence is required on their effect on job performance. The car and an expense account (telephone, meals and so on) are the most obvious. Other fringe benefits include share options, private health care, club membership and travel perks. The approach that sales managers take to handling expenses incurred by sales-people in the course of their job has an effect on the individual's earnings, their morale and their performance. From the company point of view, especially with a large sales force, the cost of expenses is significant. At the same time, it is unwise to look at expenses as a necessary evil when they are in fact a legitimate expense. The difficulty is to determine what is and is not legitimate, that is, lunch, a night out, the postman's Christmas tip and so on. One approach is to classify expenses into

- essential, such as petrol, car and telephone;
- reasonable, for example, lunch allowances;
- borderline, including personal use of the car, membership of the Chartered Institute of Marketing and so on;
- definite 'no's.

The responsibility for design and execution of the expense budget rests with the sales manager. The principles on which it is designed need to include the following:

- It should be fair in that expenses actually incurred are fully reimbursed but earnings are not through 'hidden' expenses. As well as being a weak method of remuneration, this is likely to incur the wrath of the tax inspector.
- The expense plan should also be flexible to take account of regional and customer variations. In particular, legitimate long-run customer-building expenses or costs of prospecting should be encouraged and reimbursed.
- Expenses should also be assessed and paid with minimum time and administration costs.
- Expense plan rules should be simple and unambiguous.

12.5   Assessment of pay and performance

Like any management activity, the remuneration package should be planned and coordinated. The first step in deciding reward is carefully to review the job specification and job description. This will indicate what the company must pay to get the people required. For example, graduates' technical expertise or sales experience require a premium on standard wage rates. Similarly, salary levels will be on average less for companies who recruit young, inexperienced people than for those companies who hire experienced salespeople. The job review should indicate the importance of non-financial aspects in the job from the individual's point of view. These may include a desire for personal recognition in the company, a desire for status, a desire to excel and the need for job satisfaction. These needs cannot be met exclusively by financial incentives and rewards. Objectives motivate individuals to plan ahead and use time effectively. They encourage salespeople to do what management wants done in the way they want it done. The result is higher sales, lower costs and more profit.

Company objectives might include the following:

- Increasing volume. Sales increases, in real volume terms, have a positive effect as long-term cost curves fall, improving market share and profitability. Commissions on the sliding scale are more effective than bonuses in achieving such an objective.

- Increasing profits. Again, increased sales normally lead to increased profits but different product and customer mix can have different effects. Too much volume on low contribution may be at the expense of profit. Profit-sharing schemes would be beneficial in achieving this objective.

- Increasing sales of specific products, especially new products. In this case, special commissions or bonuses can work but the complexity of the plan may be such that it results in demotivation or excessively high administrative costs.

- Achieving a predetermined sales level. In this case, it is appropriate to pay on a regressive scale of commission.

- Increasing sales to particular classes of customers, for example, large buyers, new types of outlets or specific market segments. Selected groups of customers such as government departments may not respond in a similar way and a selective commission is more appropriate.

- Achieving adequate across-the-range stocking policies. Here the emphasis is on obtaining and retaining distributor loyalty. Incentives are paid on all product lines or a product mix. A bonus would be appropriate.

- Adding new customers. Again, a bonus would be preferable or a contest can be set up.

- Increasing goodwill, sustain long-term customer benefits or provide advice is more salary-related.

- Encouraging missionary selling. A fixed salary, contract or payment per call is more appropriate. Commissions on indirect sales through wholesalers can be added if sales areas are reasonably self-contained.

- Doing a good job – salary with annual merit awards.

Personal sales objectives emerge from a different perspective. Individuals are concerned with achieving adequate income as represented by

- ensuring a minimum income (salary);

- achieving a regular income – frequent commission or bonus;

- removing excessive fluctuations, especially downwards.

Salespeople, like other workers, are also motivated by non-financial incentives. It is important with remuneration to consider non-financial incentives. While money is never not important, it may not be the prime motivator, but other pecuniary rewards can stimulate extra effort. A sound remuneration plan takes account of financial as well as non-financial incentives. It may be that non-financial incentives take precedence at higher levels of pay.

> ## Did you know?
>
> Doyle and Shapiro (1980) found from their research that the determinants of motivation, in order of importance, are
>
> - the nature of the task, depending on the time span of performance feedback, the accuracy with which individual results can be determined and role clarity
> - the salesperson's need for achievement, related to task clarity and personality
> - the type of remuneration plan, incentive pay was a more effective motivator than straight salary but the ability of incentive pay to act as a motivator depended on the sales task
> - the quality of management; for example, goal-setting, evaluation, coaching, empathy and know-how were important.

The sales plan will have, as a major component, a sound remuneration plan to cover

- what the job is and specific individual and company objectives;
- an assessment of the appropriate level of pay which is neither too high nor too low; the plan should determine minimum, average and maximum desirable levels of pay, taking cognisance of new and existing staff, competitive pay levels and individual company needs;
- the method of payment, which could include a fixed element, an incentive element, a reimbursement of expenses element and any appropriate or desirable fringe benefits;
- a means of involving, consulting, communicating and testing the remuneration package prior to and during implementation;
- a follow-up to check that objectives are being met.

Problems in the assessment of pay and performance

The methods and levels of pay are important tasks which management must decide and administer. Ambiguity, inconsistency and errors with pay create special problems for individuals. For example, bonus or commission related to performance creates problems if the target level set, and its parity with previous periods or other salespeople, does not seem equitable. Some of the problem areas may include the following:

- Most salespeople use value as a measure of performance comparing against a previous time period. As the basis for evaluation, however, real increases in sales can only relate to volume- or price/inflation-corrected values.
- Payment by results has to relate to invoiced sales rather than orders received. The problems with goods returned or orders cancelled can be a source of frustration to salespeople who feel they won the order only to be let down by quality, delivery or service problems.
- In certain types of selling, the problem of bad debts and poor credit risks may mean that business won is of poor value to the organisation. Salespeople incorrectly assume that this is not their problem.

- Salespeople paid on performance may benefit or be handicapped by dual contribution sales situations where sales are generated by more than one person. For example, distributors or intermediaries may operate in several sales areas. Since these purchase decisions may involve a number of personnel at different locations, the origins of who won the sale may be in dispute and uncertain. Another example would be where an order has been won yet sales are administered elsewhere. For example, suppose Wimpey decide to adopt a particular product, for example, doors, for their house building programme in the north-east. The credit for this may be due to the salesperson for the door company in that area yet the product may be supplied through a builders merchant group whose headquarters may be in a different area, for example, Yorkshire, a region serviced by a different salesperson. The actual number of units supplied by this merchant may be impossible to separate from the Wimpey contract.

- A related problem is the credit for house accounts. Many companies have subsidiaries which trade with each other. Sales in these situations may require extensive sales support but are not considered a basis for remuneration to individual salespeople.

- Key accounts are also a bone of contention with many salespeople. Although orders may be attributed to a central head office location, the size of these orders may owe much to the efforts of individual salespeople at branch level. Conversely, if no credit is attributed, certain necessary merchandising and service tasks, vital to support major accounts, may be neglected by individual salespeople.

- The problem of identifying sales performance as the result of sales effort may also be greater if the size of business is significant. Let us use the Wimpey example again. A medium-sized joinery firm winning such a contract from a large house builder would perhaps see this as the result of product quality, price, service and other customer-related benefits. To pay one person high commission as a result of this 'windfall gain' may be seen as inappropriate – although not by the salesperson who won the contract.

- In other sales situations, such as direct selling of, for example, cars, the value given to trade-ins may affect the real value of the sales, which in turn affects the commission paid.

- A related problem may be the treatment of instalment sales and credit agreements. For example, sales of many investment plans only become profitable for the company after year 1. Early payments only cover the salesperson's commission.

- The problem of telephone sales and posted orders has always been difficult to attribute to the individual. The developments in eCommerce will exacerbate this problem. Fairness and flexibility are needed in these situations but are difficult to resolve.

12.6   Motivation theory

Motivation is the amount of effort that a salesperson expends on each of the activities or tasks associated with their job. Underlying motivation are the 'why's of behaviour': Why do people work? Why do they put in the effort they do? Why do some work

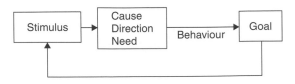

Fig 12.1 The basis of motivation

harder than others? Why do individuals respond differently to attempts to increase their motivation? As a starting point, the sales manager has to understand the why of salespeople's behaviour. Figure 12.1 shows conceptually how this process may work.

Individuals respond to stimuli. These stimuli have many, diverse origins but three factors underlie behaviour. First, behaviour is caused by such factors as hereditary or environmental conditions. Second, behaviour can be directed by specific objectives or desires. Third, behaviour can be motivated, by need or incentive, to act in a particular way.

If a sales manager is to motivate subordinates, it is necessary to have some underlying theory of motivation that can identify factors which influence motivation yet still incorporate the uniqueness of the individual and the situation. Two popular theories which achieve this are Maslow's hierarchy of needs (Figure 12.2) and Herzberg's motivation–hygiene theory (Figure 12.3 below).

Maslow's needs theory

Maslow suggests that an individual has an hierarchy of needs which vary in order of importance from the basic physiological level (hunger and thirst) through various other levels – safety and security, a desire for love and belonging, a need for status and enhanced self-esteem – and culminating in the highest-order needs of self-actualisation. These needs are structured from the bottom upwards, hence the pyramid. The lowest level must be satisfied before the next level needs become a motivating factor. When each level of needs is satisfied, it is no longer effective as a motivator. For example, work may initially be undertaken to acquire money to feed oneself and one's family. Later, money may provide some of the symbols of status. At the highest level, work is a means of achieving maximum personal satisfaction or self-actualisation. In this way, the model is robust enough to apply to every individual in work and to salespeople in their particular context. The implication for sales managers is that, for some, money soon loses its power as a motivator and other incentives or goals, such as opportunity for promotion and status-enhancing benefits, better meet an individual's needs. These higher-order factors have a greater effect on motivation. While this concept is undoubtedly true, the individuality of the human psyche makes it somewhat difficult to translate the effects of this theory in a managerial and organisational way. Individuals' expectations inevitably differ. The outcome is to concentrate on dimensions of job satisfaction but the lack of attention given to job performance dimensions may be a problem.

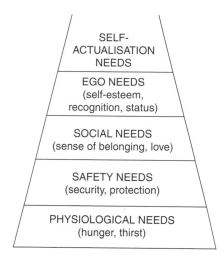

SELF-
ACTUALISATION
NEEDS

EGO NEEDS
(self-esteem,
recognition, status)

SOCIAL NEEDS
(sense of belonging, love)

SAFETY NEEDS
(security, protection)

PHYSIOLOGICAL NEEDS
(hunger, thirst)

Fig 12.2   Maslow's hierarchy of needs

Herzberg's motivation–hygiene theory

Herzberg's theory distinguishes between factors which cause dissatisfaction (hygiene factors), such as working conditions, salary, company policies and supervision, and those factors creating job satisfaction (motivators), for example, achievement, recognition, responsibility and opportunity for growth and advancement. The underlying premise is that the hygiene factors do not motivate and do not improve performance but can cause a decrease in performance if they are absent. Sales managers must maintain hygiene factors while providing motivators to improve performance.

This theory has certain managerial implications. The nature of the job, in terms of delegating responsibility and enhancing status, works more effectively as a motivator than do factors such as job security and salary. Sales managers must provide adequate levels of hygiene factors but attention to job enhancement works better as a motivator. This method includes providing new challenges, giving respect for expertise, providing good communication and performance feedback. These factors will be significant motivators and more effective determinants of performance. Many companies and most sales managers do not realise this fact and do not put sufficient emphasis on these motivators.

The proviso to this argument is that individual needs and reactions are different. Greater rewards and non-financial incentives work on individuals' behaviour and motives in different ways. Solutions which are individualised rather than generalised offer better results. If individual solutions become too complex and unmanageable, some compromise solutions may be both workable and effective. One approach is to segment the sales force into types of salespeople who are similar in some key respects yet different from other identifiable groups.

Ingram and Bellenger (1982) identified three styles of salesperson who may respond differently to motivators. First are the 'comfort-seekers', who are likely to be older, less

```
┌─────────────────────────────────────────────┐
│  MOTIVATION FACTORS                          │
│                                              │
│    1  Achievement                            │
│    2  Recognition for achievement            │
│    3  Work itself                            │
│    4  Responsibility                         │
│    5  Advancement                            │
│    6  Possibility of growth                  │
├─────────────────────────────────────────────┤
│  HYGIENE FACTORS                             │
│                                              │
│     1  Supervision                           │
│     2  Company policy and administration     │
│     3  Working conditions                    │
│   4–6  Interpersonal relations with peers,   │
│          subordinates, superiors             │
│     7  Status                                │
│     8  Job security                          │
│     9  Salary                                │
│    10  Personal life                         │
└─────────────────────────────────────────────┘
```

Fig 12.3   Herzberg's motivation–hygiene theory (*adapted from Herzberg, 1987*)

educated and with higher incomes, a proportion of which is concentrated on commission. This person seeks greater value in job security and in liking and respect from colleagues and managers. Second, also an older group, are the 'spotlight-seekers', who favour highly visible pay and rewards. This group has lower incomes than the first group but is more concerned with extrinsic rewards. They are more likely to respond to promotion opportunities and incentives such as contests. Third, salespeople who are more highly educated, younger, with good incomes and small families are 'the developers'. These people seek opportunities for personal growth although not necessarily status through promotion. As a group, they are most likely to benefit from training and career development.

Expectancy theory

The theories by Maslow and Herzberg have general appeal but seem only partial explanations of sales force motivation. The link between effort and performance requires further explanation of salespeople's behaviour. Vroom's expectancy model (Vroom, 1964) forms the basis of much work in sales-related motivation (Walker *et al.*, 1977). People are motivated to work by choosing between different behaviours if they believe that their efforts will be rewarded and they attach value to these rewards. Three factors underlie their behaviour – choice, expectancy and preference. Motivation is a key factor in sales performance, perhaps the key factor, but it is not the only factor. Aptitude, rewards and organisational and managerial factors also will be important and this is shown diagrammatically in Figure 12.4.

Walker *et al.* (1977) contend that motivation responds to a variety of personal and organisational variables (experience, training and closeness of supervision influence on standards), is related to the nature of the job itself and is influenced by the individual's

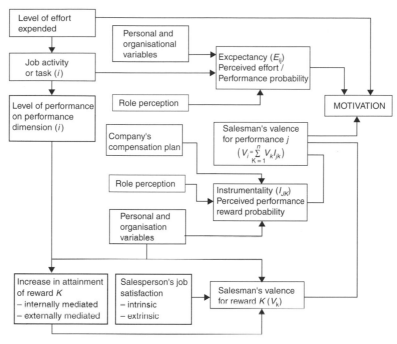

Fig 12.4 The motivation component (*Walker et al., 1977*)

role perceptions. Motivation is also goal-directed behaviour and has two dimensions: the direct goal of improved performance and the indirect goal which stems from achievement of the direct goal. For example, increased sales achieves the direct goal but may also result in promotion, an indirect goal. An individual may choose between different goals. Salesperson A may be given a target to meet which is higher than any previous sales objectives. That person may decide that the target is way above their capability and may not aim for it. Salesperson B, given a similar target, may decide to put in extra effort, intending that this will be enough to reach the target expected and the resultant gain will be worth the effort. This is expectancy theory.

Motivation and behaviour are affected by the perceived value or worth of attaining the goal. This perception is itself based on the expectancy of the individual that performance is the result of particular actions (e.g. more calls) and is profitable and desirable. The link between effort and performance can be expressed in terms of expectancy, particularly the magnitude of expectancies and their accuracy. For example, magnitude will be influenced positively by a belief in one's own ability, by higher levels of self-esteem and by experience. Environmental factors such as competition and trading conditions may have a negative effect. Accuracy of expectancy will relate to role perception. Another major factor in role perception is experience, which then becomes a common antecedent. It can be hypothesised that salespeople will have greater accuracy of expectancies the longer they are in the job, the greater their role accuracy, the lower their role ambiguity and role conflict, and the more closely they are supervised. Motivation, in terms of expectancy, will also be affected by rewards and the desirability of higher rewards. These rewards can be externally mediated (pay incentives) or internally mediated (self-fulfilment and career growth), which provide different levels of satisfaction for the individual.

The link between expectancies and performance requires understanding of two further concepts from the model in Figure 12.4: instrumentality and the salesperson's valence for reward. Instrumentality is the salesperson's perception that their individual actions will result in the required performance and that this performance will lead to other desired goals. Valence for rewards is the expected value placed on the goals/desired results. This has either a positive or a negative effect depending on the value placed on achievement. Expectancy theory suggests that the effort expended on the job depends on the valence (anticipated satisfaction) in accomplishing it and the expectancy of a result (probability of achievement).

What do you think?

According to Vroom, 1964 effort = expectancy (probability of achievement) $\times$ valence (anticipated satisfaction). Therefore, motivation can be measured by the individual's perception that various performance dimensions will lead to specific outcomes (probability 0–1) multiplied by the value placed on each outcome (on a scale -1 to $+1$). This being so, it is possible for salespeople to give explicit answers to the subjective question 'Is it worth it?'

Assess the worth of this formula.

12.7 Motivation and job performance

The link between job satisfaction and job performance is not a straight forward positive relationship. As Bagozzi has suggested (1980), four possibilities exist:

1 Satisfaction causes performance.
2 Performance causes satisfaction.
3 The two variables are reciprocally related.
4 The variables are not causally related at all, and any empirical association must be a spurious one owing to common antecedents.

Job satisfaction is related to performance, but differences in performance can also be attributed to individual differences, for example, skills, aptitude and self-esteem. Furthermore, longitudinal studies are required to assess the true nature of the satisfaction–performance–satisfaction sequence. Bagozzi tentatively suggests that enhancement of self-esteem through personal recognition, monetary rewards or visible acknowledgement of good performance would be a better means of management style than job enhancement per se. Salespeople can perhaps be motivated more by challenging targets, by achieving these targets, by receiving accurate and complete feedback and by appropriate visible rewards than by job enhancement or job enrichment. These increase job satisfaction, leading to lower recruitment costs and lower staff turnover but are not the prime movers in higher job performance.

The motivation of salespeople is neither easy nor straightforward. There is no doubt that it has great significance on sales performance. Part of the complexity of this problem is the multiplicative nature of the variables which impact on performance, such as aptitude, role perception and the components of motivation itself. The problem is compounded by the individuality of the selling job since the nature of the task and the individual's perception of each element, and their reaction to them, will vary. The problem of industry-specific contexts, the type of selling and the characteristics of individuals all hamper the search for definitive solutions and create unique problems. To prescribe a management solution requires that a selection of factors or influences be considered which can then be adapted to the particular circumstances.

Some of these factors which affect motivation include the following:

■ *The job itself.* If a salesperson does not find the job challenging or interesting, there will be a motivation problem. Compared with many jobs, this problem will be less for salespeople than, for example, assembly-line workers. Sales managers should be careful that excessive routines, job simplification or too strict a discipline do not demotivate. Part of the attraction to the job is the freedom of action which is permitted. This autonomy combines with the variety of tasks and their perceived importance. A quantification of these job characteristics as motivators has been incorporated in a motivating potential score (MPS) (Hackman and Oldham, 1975; Becherer *et al.*, 1982): MPS = (Skill variety + task identity + task significance)/3 × autonomy × feedback.

■ *Accuracy and feedback.* A problem already identified is that sales tasks and sales effort have an indirect rather than a direct effect on sales performance. Missionary selling is particularly prone to this difficulty. For others, organisational complexity or dual effort may confuse the sales process and its effect on performance. Nevertheless, accurate and timely feedback for salespeople has a positive effect on job performance and job satisfaction (Bagozzi, 1980).

■ *Motivated people.* Salespeople who have drive and a need for achievement will have a higher sales performance. Demirdjian (1984) suggests that this motivation can be expressed as a function of a salesperson's economic, social and self-actualising needs: M = f [(+ En) + (Sn) + (+ SAn)] where M = Motivation; En = economic needs of the salesperson; S = social needs of the salesperson; SAn = self-actualising needs of the salesperson.

■ *Participation.* As discussed in target-setting, there is greater commitment and involvement when salespeople take an active part in decision-making. The use of management by objectives, or similar schemes, has a positive effect on sales force motivation.

■ *Being part of the company.* As for participation, so is involvement increased by salespeople who are committed to their company, colleagues and supervisors. This belief extends to the products being sold (task importance) and that the sales effort will make a contribution to the company's prosperity and the prosperity of other employees.

■ *Morale.* Motivation is affected by morale. Morale is itself a difficult thing to define but is a mix or sum of a person's feelings towards their job, pay, other employees, conditions of work, competitors and other factors. Good morale is by itself not sufficient to motivate but poor morale can be a demotivating factor.

■ *Discipline.* Views on the correct amount and type of discipline vary, but it is a factor to be taken into account. Too strict a discipline can alienate people but no, or weak, discipline leads to a situation of anarchy. A fair code of behaviour not allowed (e.g. dishonesty), of areas requiring improvement (e.g. late reports and poor appearance) and of areas of freedom (e.g. call patterns) should be established. Negative factors are generally weak motivators since more people are convinced by the attractiveness of heaven than by the horrors of hell!

■ *Monetary rewards*. Remuneration is the most important reward used to motivate salespeople. The variety of payment plans in operation, even within similar industry and sales situations, suggests that management do not understand the effect of payment on their employee's motivation. The factors which determine the method of remuneration were outlined earlier in this chapter.

■ *Good management*. Although Doyle and Shapiro (1980) were unable to measure management practices with the necessary degree of precision to make conclusions on sales motivation and performance, it was recognised that they do have a combined impact. Factors such as goal-setting, evaluation, control, coaching, understanding and know-how contribute to individual salespeople's motivation. Furthermore, sales managers' own performance and satisfaction could be significant (Comer, 1985).

The importance and complexity of motivation and its effect on performance has led to the idea of the motivational mix, as shown in Figure 12.5. These factors, individually and collectively, influence an individual's motivation to work and ultimately their job performance. The individual may respond positively or negatively to the different factors which management can deploy to motivate the sales force. Solving the problems of individual salespeople and providing definite solutions will resolve some of the motivational problems in the sales force.

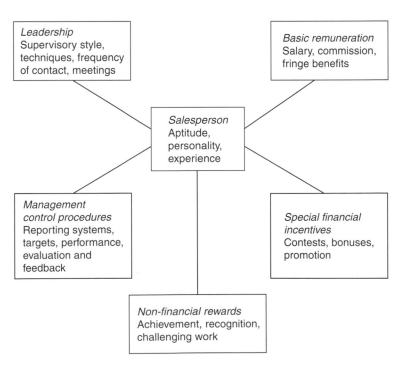

Fig 12.5   The motivational mix

The management of motivation

The quest for understanding the components of motivation and its impact on performance should lead to some tentative formulae for improving sales force motivation. First, it is necessary to restate and highlight the problems created by a lack of motivation. One problem is that sales will be lower. Enthusiasm, drive and hours worked will be less if individuals are not fully motivated. These directly affect sales performance. A related problem is that sales staff turnover will be higher, especially among the better performing salespeople, more able (and motivated) to find work elsewhere. A lack of motivation results not only in fewer hours being worked but also often in higher expenses relative to sales. Indeed, salespeople who feel underpaid or badly treated may be highly motivated to redress the balance through expense claims, more give-aways to customers, higher mileage or other expenses. Lower motivation often coincides with indiscipline or 'bad-mouthing' to other colleagues or customers. As in most occupations, the importance of minor complaints becomes magnified, diverting management time to peripheral issues.

Things to avoid which may exacerbate the problem include

- poor working conditions;
- poor reporting procedures;
- unfairness in rewards;
- a lack of promotion opportunity;
- a lack of individual involvement and participation;
- a lack of incentives;
- a disproportionate number of older salespeople;
- poor communication between subordinates, supervisors and top management.

A more positive approach is to take action which will increase motivation. Such action involves the elements in the motivational mix previously described. Among the most vital are likely to be the following:

Status enhancement. Acknowledgement of a job well done, a more prestigious title, a management training course or an above-average pay increase are important not only in themselves but also as recognition of effort and a stimulus to greater effort.

Positive communication. People are less motivated if they have negative views about the job, the company or their performance. If these views are accurate, the cause of dissatisfaction must be corrected through product, price and distribution policies or organisational and managerial changes. If the views are inaccurate, management must improve their communication message. This can be done by measuring existing levels of satisfaction, by a complaints procedure, suggestion box, formal survey or exit interviews (for leavers) or by keeping close to employees. Whatever the technique or approach, good two-way communication is vital for effective management of the sales force.

Individual recognition. Salespeople exist in an environment of relative isolation. It follows that they will be sensitive to the distance between themselves and control of the operation. They require not only rewards for work done but also frequent and positive acknowledgement of their performance.

Ability to handle rejection. In doing the job, salespeople will inevitably get many rejections, rebuffs and lost sales. To overcome these negatives, especially in newer recruits, management must train salespeople to handle and expect rejection. These problems relate to role perceptions, particularly role conflict and ambiguity.

Group involvement. Since salespeople operate on their own, fostering team spirit, camaraderie and group involvement are part of the management task.

Be available and understanding. As with any employee, individuality is important. At any one time, salespeople may face personal problems such as health, finance, marital difficulties and so on. These can only be treated on an individual basis.

Engagement. Sales managers who interact with their salespeople on an individual and on a team basis to further their organisation's objectives are likely to be more productive in their sales effort and performance.

The formula for the management of motivation is as follows. First, give status rewards. Second, pay particular attention to role problems and handling rejection, especially for new recruits. Third, arrange frequent communication individually and through regional or team meetings. Fourth, provide coaching and training for sales staff, including special assignments for older, more experienced staff. Finally, stay close to subordinates – be available and understanding.

12.8 Summary

One of the most important factors in sales performance is the motivation of salespeople. Motivation is the amount of effort that a salesperson expends on each of the activities or tasks associated with their job. Theories of motivation such as Maslow's hierarchy of needs, Herzberg's motivation–hygiene theory and Vroom's expectancy theory help our understanding of why people work and behave the way they do. Pay is important to individuals and companies alike. Both the level and method of payment can affect salespeople's performance. This relationship is not an easy one to evaluate since people react differently to pay and incentives. As expected, monetary rewards and good management practices seem to be important. Emphasis should not be placed on job satisfaction at the expense of job performance. An integrated managerial approach to the motivational mix, taking cognisance of individual and situational factors, is recommended.

Questions

1 To what extent do you agree that, after a certain level, monetary rewards lose their power as motivators for salespeople?

2 Explain how and in what ways salespeople may differ in their motivations from workers in other occupations?

3 A toy manufacturer whose sales are highly seasonal is thinking of introducing a new remuneration package for her sales force. What alternative remuneration packages should be considered?

4 What potential problems and advantages are there in using sales contests? Is this form of remuneration appropriate for all sales situations? What are the critical considerations in designing a successful sales contest?

5 A company are about to launch a new product range on the UK market. What are the probable effects of low sales force morale on this venture? Outline steps which could be taken to increase sales force commitment to the new range.

6 Discuss the link between a salesperson's motivation and job performance.

Case study **Denham pharmaceuticals**

Ian Renton is the newly appointed sales manager at Denham Pharmaceuticals (name disguised), a medium-sized company (small by comparison to competitors) in the area of over-the-counter drugs and proprietary medicines on prescription. In its early years, the company grew rapidly, marketing several related drugs developed by the founders of the business and a highly motivated and innovative research team. Selling by five or six representatives concentrated on wholesalers and larger chemist outlets. The importance of specifiers, namely general practitioners and hospitals, had always been recognised, but the company did not have the resources to call personally on all UK doctors and pharmacists. The current sales force is 18 in number, some of whom have been seeking out specifiers in response to leads and inquiries. These calls have been proving very effective in sales terms, although the link between specifying, stocking, and end-users has been hard to identify. Ian wants to encourage more detail calling as well as improving sales effort on existing accounts. A new remuneration package seems to be required to achieve these objectives.

■ Design a suitable remuneration package.

■ Point out the possible advantages and disadvantages in your own plan.

Key terms

- behaviour
- bonus
- comfort-seekers
- commission
- contests
- developers
- expenses
- expectancy theory
- goals
- Herzberg's motivation–hygiene theory
- incentives
- instrumentality
- Maslow's hierarchy of needs
- morale
- motivation
- motivational mix
- motivating potential score
- performance-related pay
- remuneration
- salary
- spotlight-seekers
- stimulus-response
- task clarity
- valence

References

Bagozzi, R.P. (1980) 'Performance and satisfaction in an industrial sales force: an examination of their antecedents and simultaneity' *Journal of Marketing* 44 (Spring): 65–77

Becherer, R.C., Morgan, F.W. and Richard, L.M. (1982) 'The job characteristics of industrial salespersons: relationship to motivation and satisfaction' *Journal of Marketing* 46 (Fall): 125–35

Comer, J.M. (1985) 'Industrial sales managers: satisfaction and performance' *Industrial Marketing Management* **14** (4): 239–44

Demirdjian, Z.S. (1984) 'A multidimensional approach to motivating salespeople' *Industrial Marketing Management* **13** (1): 25–32

Donaldson, B. (1997) 'The importance of financial incentives in motivating salespeople' *Proceedings of the 1st International Symposium on Selling and Major Account Management* Southampton Institute: Southampton

Doyle, S.X. and Shapiro, B.P. (1980) 'What counts most in motivating your salesforce?' *Harvard Business Review* **May–Jun**: 134–9

Hackman, R.J. and Oldham, G.R. (1975) 'Development of the job diagnostic survey' *Journal of Applied Psychology* **60**: 159–70

Herzberg, F. (1987) 'One more time: how do you motivate employees?' *Harvard Business Review* **Sep–Oct**: 109–20

Ingram, T.N. and Bellenger, D.N. (1982) 'Motivational segments in the sales force' *California Management Review* **24** (3): 81–8

Kohn, A. (1993) 'Why incentive plans cannot work' *Harvard Business Review* **Sep–Oct**: 54–62

Maslow, A.H. (1970) *Motivation and Personality* 2nd edition Harper & Row: New York

Tosdal, H.R. (1953a) 'Administering salesmen's compensation' *Harvard Business Review* **Mar–Apr**: 70–83

Tosdal, H.R. (1953b) 'How to design the salesman's compensation plan' *Harvard Business Review* **Sep–Oct**: 61–70

Vroom, V.H. (1964) *Work and Motivation* John Wiley: New York

Walker, O.C., Churchill, G.A. and Ford, N.M. (1977) 'Motivation and performance in industrial selling: present knowledge and needed research' *Journal of Marketing Research* **XIV** (May): 156–68

13 Monitoring and measurement

13.1 Overview

At one level, the evaluation of salespeople is easy – they either make target or they don't. The problem with the link between sales effort and sales response is that it is neither simple nor direct. Most companies conduct some form of monitoring but few do this in a formal way which evaluates the causes as well as outcomes. Part of the problem is that to do evaluation properly is time consuming, costly and difficult, yet evaluation is part of the control element in management. Control implies setting standards, comparing results achieved with these standards and taking any corrective action. However, sales managers must be careful not to link evaluation solely to the salesperson or the sales team. Evaluation is also required of management policies and systems and of the specific tasks that salespeople are expected to perform.

Hence, principles of total quality management (TQM) can be applied to the sales process. It is one thing to monitor performance but requires another level of performance to be 'best in class'. Similarly, benchmarking can be used to assist sales managers in assessing and improving performance.

13.2 Learning objectives

The aim in this chapter is

- to identify the most appropriate measures which can be used to evaluate salespeople and control sales force operations;
- to consider how evaluation can best be conducted and by whom;
- to understand how TQM and benchmarking can be applied to the sales process;
- to review the key determinants of sales force performance.

13.3 Definitions

Total quality Management (TQM) is an organisational approach whereby everyone is concerned with and about quality in all activities throughout the organisation to better serve customer needs.

Benchmarking is a management process whereby an organisation compares its performance with that of its competitors and with others in the same or related industries with the objective of establishing best practice. It applies learning from the best performers and applying those lessons in your own organisation.

13.4   Evaluation of salespeople

At the individual salesperson level, evaluation is necessary to identify above- and below-average performers or to identify possible candidates for promotion or dismissal. Areas of weakness in salespeople and the effectiveness of salespeople in carrying out their tasks must also be assessed. For management, evaluation is necessary to assess the efficacy of sales management practices such as territory deployment, recruitment, training and remuneration policies. Finally, evaluation is necessary to modify the sales tasks in line with customer and company needs so that sales plans are compared with the most appropriate criteria for improved sales performance.

A good sales force evaluation programme should be realistic and fair. It should be positive and contribute to motivation and improved job performance. It should be objective, involve salespeople and be economic in cost and time to administer. These aims inevitably conflict. Accountants, operational researchers, behaviourists, management scientists, economists and many other disciplines have tried to find better and more accurate measures of sales performance with varying degrees of success. It appears that evaluating salespeople is still something of an art struggling to be a science. Evaluation of salespeople is not easy. For example, eight calls per day may be better than six calls but what about the quality of each call? A higher sales value in one area may appear better than a lower value in another but what are the prevailing market and competitive conditions?

As with any management task, a planned approach is recommended for the evaluation task. This approach is typified by the following:

1 *Clarifying sales objectives.* These objectives normally mean sales volume levels but should relate to corporate and marketing strategy as well as sales objectives. The type of business, the type of customer, the sales, distribution and pricing policies and the level of service and support all need to be predetermined.

2 *Specifying sales tasks to achieve sales objectives.* Objectives must be translated into tasks. For example, to achieve certain types of customer requires lead generation, prospecting, account development and a range of service and support tasks. Sales force productivity relies on other support from marketing, production, distribution, sales administration and service support functions. Task clarity enables a more objective evaluation which relates output measures to particular inputs.

3 *Writing, or rewriting, a job description with key and secondary tasks.* Evaluation is only possible on written preset criteria. This removes much ambiguity about performance dimensions.

4 *Establishing suitable evaluation measures.* For various reasons, sales do not directly result from sales effort. Furthermore, improved sales productivity can be achieved by increased sales volume, reduced costs, a change in the mix of products and customers or a combination of these methods.

5 *Involving salespeople*. The most significant gains in sales force productivity will come from self-evaluation and self-improvement by salespeople themselves. Where management feels a need for greater control, a joint approach is recommended which at least involves salespeople in the process.

6 *Taking action*. As suggested earlier, the process is incomplete unless corrective action is implemented.

A six-stage, planned approach to evaluation implies a rather matter-of-fact situation. Before considering how information can be collected for evaluation purposes, it is worthwhile reconsidering the unique problems of the selling job:

■ Salespeople have inadequate or incomplete information about their job, especially concerning the needs and preferences of customers and customer organisations.

■ Salespeople mostly work alone and independently without direct supervision. Although considered by many to be an advantage, this independence creates other problems of role clarity.

■ Salespeople operate in an interorganisational boundary position which creates role conflicts.

■ The sales job is demanding in terms of the degree of innovation and creativity required. There is no one right approach.

■ The job requires adaptability and sensitivity by salespeople to the needs of customers yet is frequently met by different degrees of antagonism, hostility and aggression.

■ Sales decisions may have to be made quickly, requiring decisiveness and mental alertness.

■ Individual sales performance evaluation lacks direct observation of inputs – only outcomes are assessed.

■ Evaluation is often inferred and subjective, people biased.

■ Salespeople have little control over the conditions in which they operate.

13.5 Sources of information for evaluation

To conduct appropriate evaluation requires an adequate quantity and quality of information. Plans without evaluation are useless. Likewise, only by assessing variations against plan can the real reasons for performance be identified and corrected. Types of information are many and varied, from formal market research surveys, sales reports and management appraisal to internal records. These can all be used for sales force evaluation but each technique offers different benefits to the sales manager. It is good policy for information to be collected and assessed at the individual level where most use can be made of the data. With electronic capability now available through CRM and SFA the problem may well be too much data, some of which are not directly relevant to the particular person or situation. This may result in information overload. The temptation to exert excessive control needs to be resisted by new approaches in leadership and coaching to get the best from salespeople. Before considering the range and type of information that sales management can use, the main sources of information for evaluation of the sales force should be reviewed. These include the following:

- *Company records.* Sales orders, invoices and customer records form part of the marketing information system and can all be used to assess sales performance. The advantages of using internal records is that the source of the data is known and available. It should be quick, low cost and consistent. It would normally be accurate and relevant. Disadvantages might be the absence of knowledge on relevant market conditions and the possibility of too much information being available for an individual's needs.

- *Sales reports.* Formal records can be time savers and helpful to management for evaluation. Salespeople are closest to the customers, their own records provide a high level of involvement and information can be collected regularly. The disadvantages may be that reports show the truth, but not the whole truth; for example, call content may be disguised. Since peer evaluation of these reports is likely, salespeople may distort the content to gain favour, for example, reporting favourably on new orders and new customers but omitting lost customers.

- *Managers' field visits.* This provides a useful comparison between different salespeople. If conducted well, it would entail joint involvement, which should also improve with practice, reinforcing the supervisor–subordinate relationship. The disadvantages with this method concern the people-to-people bias, the subjective views of managers, perhaps bias by salespeople in preselecting calls and the lack of quantification.

- *Customer contact.* Sales evaluation using customers provides first-hand, up-to-date information. It should be more independent and objective. It can also provide new insights into customer needs. The problems may be the random nature of the response or the lack of representativeness, for example, small and big customers' views being given equal merit. The main disadvantage may be that this type of contact undermines the salesperson–customer relationship. It is, however, possible to use a combination of these methods in conjunction with other external hard data such as retail audit information to gain a more complete picture.

Did you know?

One of the fastest growing businesses in recent years has been sales force.com. The company offer on-demand solutions that meet the needs of a variety of businesses from SMEs to global organisations. Unlike expensive customised software and IT providers, they aim to provide sales teams and managers with a complete customer view in real time to make full use of existing and new opportunities and to track and monitor sales force activity and sales pipelines. The difference is that you only sign up for what you use, the on-demand model. Its success testifies that its immediate deployment and up-front costs are a popular choice for many sales managers (www.salesforce.com).

These sources have been at the disposal of sales managers for many years but using software to integrate information should give a more complete picture of performance. The danger is that data without a sound theoretical basis can tell what happened but not always why. Part of the problem is the lack of a theory which is comprehensive, accurate and testable. As a result, many sales managers still use traditional, obvious but inappropriate and inadequate measures of sales performance. Like other marketing problems, the dynamics of business plague accurate measurement. Not only are the goal posts moving, but the location of the pitch is also shifting. Another feature of the game is that any identified weaknesses are designed out as soon as practical. For example, if poor performers are observed to have lower call rates, this problem could be addressed rapidly by management dictum. Those with low call rates (and low performance) are immediately asked to increase call rates. Finally, the impact of other variables such as market conditions or competitive activity varies in importance, not only with the company but also between different sales areas and individual salespeople.

Weaknesses in traditional evaluation systems include the following:

■ *An inadequate definition of the necessary inputs to achieve the desired outputs.* That is, the use of sales, call rates or other easily assessed measures is preferred to the more difficult quality dimensions of the job. The quality measures are often the most important. Anderson and Oliver (1987) call for more behaviour-based than output-based control. In a subsequent test of their propositions, they found support for the view that salespeople pursued organisation objectives more readily when control was behaviour-based whereas those using output-based control generated more self-interest behaviour in salespeople and less commitment.

■ *Over-reliance on subjective factors.* Seemingly contrary to the first point, many managers seem to evaluate salespeople on selected personality traits or qualities. These characteristics are seldom proven measures of quality in sales performance. They are more probably factors that managers consider made themselves successful when they were selling.

■ *Bias.* Managers themselves have particular personality traits, styles or techniques which affect their performance appraisal. These include the 'hire and fire' school, the overprotective 'mother-hen' syndrome and the 'wait and see' type. As well as being a management-type, bias can also result from at least four causes. First is the halo effect, where performance on one or more characteristics is equated with performance on all dimensions of the job. For example, the salesperson who submits reports on time, has a high call rate, is punctual and has a good appearance may achieve higher performance scores than others who achieve higher sales in adverse market conditions. Second, there is the bias of central tendency. Managers may avoid assessing performance at the extreme ends (very poor and excellent) and play it safe, for example, with 'Please try harder' or 'Well done'. Since opportunity for observation is limited and the consequences of actions may be severe on pay or holding down the job, managers abdicate their responsibility for evaluation and play it safe. Third, an opposite form of bias is that to exercise, or be seen to exercise managerial power, sales managers may be too lenient or too harsh. These decisions can have counterproductive effects on morale and motivation. Finally, bias arises for interpersonal reasons. Inevitably, managers may like some people more than others. DeCarlo and Leigh (1996) found that sales managers who like their salespeople as work partners (task attraction) and as friends (social attraction) were influenced in their performance appraisal. In particular, these managers were more likely to put weak performance down to external or other circumstances. Such bias is impossible to eliminate but should be acknowledged and guarded against.

- *The use to which performance evaluation is applied in the firm*. Evaluation without control is ineffective. A corresponding danger is that the performance evaluation is seen as more important than the performance. Evaluation used in a positive rather than a negative way will be a greater motivation.

- *A failure to relate evaluation to the tasks*. For example, higher sales in one time period may be at the expense of customer service and long-term business relationships.

These weaknesses relate to the management of evaluation rather than to the person being evaluated. It is incumbent upon sales managers to improve these evaluation procedures.

Performance evaluation

According to Anderson and Oliver (1987) sales control systems can be classified into three categories: (1) outcome, (2) hybrid and (3)behaviour-based. Outcome-based control systems focus on results and use objective measures to evaluate the performance of a salesperson. This involves little sales management interaction and is focused on the ends rather than the means. Behaviour-based control systems focus on how salespeople are selling and tend to use more subjective measures.

The conceptual model of outcome- and behaviour-based control systems developed by Anderson and Oliver (1987) treats behaviour control as a single construct. Challagalla and Shervani (1996) argue that behaviour control is not a single construct but consists of two types of control, activity and capability control. Activity control refers to the specification of the activities a person is expected to perform on a regular basis, the monitoring of actual behaviour and the administering of rewards and punishments on the basis of the performance of specified activities. Capability control refers to the development of individual skills and abilities.

How organisations evaluate sales performance has been categorised into five classes of sales performance evaluation methods (Boles, Donthu and Lohtia, 1995). Class one evaluation methods (output only) rely on results as the criteria for evaluation and can include objective measures such as sales volume or subjective measures such as 'achieving sales objectives'. The main advantage of this evaluation method is that most measures can be directly related to the organisation's bottom-line results. The disadvantage is that it does not provide information regarding requirements in coaching, training or career improvement for salespeople.

Class two evaluation methods (input only) rely on input and output measures such as number of calls made and sales skills which are evaluated against performance goals. Porter, Lawler and Hackman (1975) argue that these measure may motivate activities rather than accomplishment. Rankings of the input and the output measures may be used but they are independent from each other. Class three evaluation methods (individual evaluation) rely on both input and output measures combining both objective and subjective measures. These methods are described as supervisory methods incorporating both input and output into an overall assessment but with no explicit standards. Ratios can be developed and used for rank-order and may be particularly useful for assessing capabilities and further training needs.

Class four evaluation methods rely on the use of both input and output evaluation methods with explicit standards to compare salespeople with their peers. The comparison is performed either through supervisor evaluation or through statistical evaluation methods. Class five evaluation methods is similar to class four with the exception that it relies only on statistical evaluation and compares the performance not against the average but the best performers in the sales team. Boles, Donthu and Lohtia (1995) argue that comparing salespeople's performance against that of the best performers is an important step towards achieving sales force excellence.

<hr>

What do you think?

Given that you have been asked to assess the performance of individual salespeople would you favour outcome-based measures such as call rates, sales revenues and so on or behaviour-based measures such as relationship quality and opportunity management? Does your response to this problem correct any of the weaknesses in the traditional evaluation systems given earlier in the chapter?

<hr>

13.6 Total quality management in the sales process

This pursuit of excellence is strongly compatible with the TQM philosophy which advocates measuring process outcomes to evaluate performance. According to Plank and Blackshear (1997) most sales processes can benefit from the integration of TQM philosophies. They base their claim on a study performed by Cortada (1993) who analysed the efforts of a sales group at IBM applying TQM concepts to the sales process. The implementation at IBM was reported to be successful as it enabled the group to become more responsive and customer driven. The main tool in their effort was the use of process mapping. Process mapping involves the study of flows of behaviour, people, power, information and activities as they occur in an organisation and appears to be one of the main challenges when introducing TQM to the sales process itself (Plank and Blackshear, 1997).

When mapping the sales process it has to be done from the customer perspective and it has to demonstrate how each step adds and delivers value to the customer (Adair and Murray, 1994; Rackham and De Vincentis, 1999; Web, 2003). The danger is that too many internal process details are mapped losing track of the bigger picture and how each of these steps is actually going to be measured. From a TQM perspective, the processes need to be mapped into a series of relevant sales activities and need to be measured through a method called statistical process control (SPC). By having identified all activities as part of a process, one is able, through the use of SPC, to control output by checking its quality while the work is still in progress. Some of the reported advantages of using SPC are, increased efficiency, greater ease of pinpointing the cause of problems, a more consistent output, clearer communication of objectives, improved customer relationships (Chaudry and Higbie, 1990; Welch and Geisslet, 1992). On these bases, it is argued that the application of SPC to the sales process could be used to combine behaviour- and outcome-based control methods into a performance evaluation system that is both comprehensive and easy to understand.

Lemmens and Donaldson (2004) identified that while organisations with a simple sales process where able to implement sophisticated sale control systems, others, dealing with relationship selling involving more complex sales processes, were still dealing with the problem of mapping out correctly their internal sales processes. Cravens *et al.* (1993) researched how the TQM philosophy and more specifically statistical control charts can be used for the evaluation of sales performance. Their results showed that the TQM approach results in much less disparity between the performance of salespeople when compared with the judgemental evaluation method. The difference in the results between the evaluation methods is attributed to the fact that TQM assumes that all salespeople perform equally well and that most differences in results can be attributed to the process (Cravens *et al.*, 1993). They concluded that the principle whereby all salespeople perform equally well was in direct conflict with sales management beliefs and practices.

The idea of measuring the sales process is one that is also spoken of in the commercial literature and it is often referred to as a sales funnel (Heiman *et al.*, 1998; Bosworth, 1995). According to Heiman *et al.* (1998), the sales funnel enables evaluation of the current sales situation and the sales strategy. They claim that the use of sales funnel or process to report sales opportunities provides

- more clarity in terms of where each opportunity really stands;
- better communication as it provides a common way to view opportunities;
- more perspective as it enables to see how different opportunities are linked together;
- better forecasting as it provides a detailed view of how far each opportunity really is from being closed.

They also argue that the overall process ratios would enable a sales manager to detect problems related to sales skills and to time and territory management.

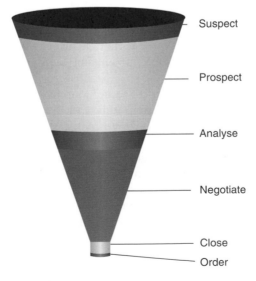

Status	Revenue	Adj. Revenue
S	889540	97189
P	1489508	505521
A	283458	94877
N	928735	508911
C	83680	75312
O	21913	19722
	3696834	1301532

Fig 13.1   Pipeline report

Low conversion ratios would reflect sales skills problems and unbalanced amounts of opportunities at each stage would reflect time and territory management problems.

Bosworth (1995) shares these views and extends it by arguing that statistical analysis should be used to measure and manage the sales process. In Bosworth's view, historical process measures, combined with average sales cycle duration and average order value enables the development of process objectives needed to accomplish the sales targets. Both Heiman *et al.* (1998) and Boswoth (1995) claim that process or funnel measures are best used during coaching sessions or sales review meetings. Figure 13.1 shows a funnel for a salesperson in a delivery service business. Expected revenue at each stage is adjusted and updated based on performance which can be used for comparison purposes and for subsequent coaching and evaluation. Software programmes are available to simplify and automate the process. See, for example, www.dundas.com

13.7 Benchmarking and best practices

Understanding the cause and effect relationship between activities and their outcomes based on quantitative measures is part of a process known as benchmarking. In essence, Benchmarking is the process of finding the best practice that leads to superior performance and implementing it. According to Zoltners *et al.* (2004) in order to improve sales operations a company needs to develop a set of best practices based on benchmarking methods that enables it to measure the cause and effect relationship between its sales activities and their outcomes.

Benchmarking has revitalised the old concept of performance comparison. It also involves a goal-setting process and in the achievement of these goals encourages empowerment of employees to effectively integrate the responsibilities, work processes and reward systems (Camp, 1989). Internal benchmarking is about comparing business units or processes within a single organisation which overcomes the problem of finding an external organisation to measure against. However, only by external comparisons can an organisation hope to achieve 'best-in-class' performance.

Fong *et al.* (1998) argue that benchmarking can be very expensive and top management must include instructing middle management and lower levels of management to use these techniques and provide adequate training to induce a planned transfer of knowledge. This is essential as findings must be adopted by both operational and management personnel. Employee commitment to the benchmarking project is essential as they are the people who will carry out the benchmarking practices. In order to gain support, the findings must be able to convince those requiring the data that it is from reliable sources and correctly analysed with clear and presentable findings (Fong *et al.* 1998). According to Biesada (1991) the toughest part of benchmarking is to get people out of their routine way and to get them to think about the underlying process. Benchmarking will scare people if they think it is a device to get rid of them. Communication between management and employees is essential in order to avoid misinterpretation.

Chonko *et al.* (2000) argues that the sales manager must identify the relevant sales activities and for each of these activities define its goals, objectives, performance standards, what behaviours are needed to complete the activity and the relevant importance of each behaviour. Developing benchmarks for selling activities may not be suitable for all types of selling environments. Rackham and De Vincentis (1998) argue

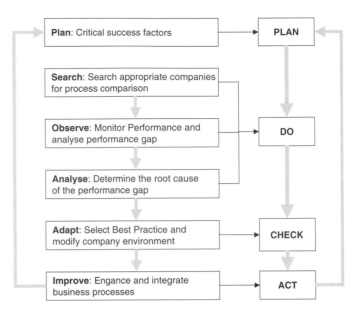

Fig 13.2   Benchmarking the Sales Process

that within a transactional sales environment selling costs are critical and non-selling time should be kept to a minimum. This selling environment is characterised by a simple sales process where one sales call is often sufficient to result in an order. Their advice is to assess activities that are easily measurable without going into too much detail. In a consultative selling environment, they argue, that several process- and opportunity-related key performance indicators (KPI) should be measured. These selling environments are characterised by longer and more complex sales cycles, which include several individual sales calls to complete a sales process. Measuring the result of each sale call offers the ability to measure and track the individual sales process itself. Unlike transactional selling, consultative selling offers the ability to analyse and adapt the sales approach throughout the process. Figure 13.2 shows the stages in benchmarking the sales process.

This leads us to conclude that benchmarking systems, in order to be successful, need to be based on reliable data, correct analysis methods and clear presentation of the results. The employees need to be trained and management must obtain their commitment in order to implement and share best practices identified through the benchmarking process.

13.8 Dimensions and determinants of sales performance

The sales manager must be concerned with certain key dimensions of sales and company performance, including

1   *Sales volume.* This refers not only to the absolute volume or value level but also to sales against budget and sales related to market potential. Loss of competitiveness,

or sales below levels which reduce profitability, must be identified immediately and corrective action taken as soon as possible.

2 *Profit.* The key performance dimension in management is profitability. Management analysis has to focus on ways of increasing profits, although the difference between immediate realisable profit and long-run growth in profits can involve significant trade-offs. Those customers, products, salespeople and regions with relatively higher costs and lower revenues must be examined to improve performance in terms of overall company profitability.

3 *Number and size of orders.* Related to the profit factor, but more readily controlled, are the number and type of orders obtained. Total sales volume may be achieved by a high proportion of relatively uneconomic sales per customer or by a disproportionate level of sales from selected customers (the 80/20 principle) or selected sales areas. Sales managers must carefully appraise the worth of low-volume customers with high service costs and the high-cost, low-volume regions with higher-volume, lower-cost regions. Most companies operate from a basis of strength in their own locality. The worth of current low-volume territories and customers must therefore be assessed not only in current sales terms but also for their future potential or perhaps for reasons of competitiveness.

4 *Call rates, orders to calls, hours worked.* Most sales managers cannot afford too laissez-faire an approach to calling schedules, especially with larger, younger sales teams. Performance dimensions on these activities are important measures of motivation and performance.

5 *Expense control.* Records have to be kept of salespeople's expenses for accountancy as well as for disciplinary reasons. Again, part of this can be delegated to individual salespeople to assess their own performance, but total expense levels, variances and comparative assessments are a management responsibility.

6 *Time and territory management.* Returning again to identifying ways of improving sales productivity necessitates management appraisal of comparative sales performance dimensions such as face-to-face selling time, time spent prospecting and other related sales activities.

7 *Customer satisfaction and relationship building.* This is ultimately the most crucial dimension of all.

In their review of the many studies which have been conducted on the evaluation of salesperson performance, Churchill and others uncovered 116 separate studies listing 1653 possible associations (Churchill *et al.*, 1985). The only certain conclusion of this meta-analysis is that there is no one variable which has a significant influence on salesperson performance. In these studies, with few exceptions, only on average 4 per cent of variation in salesperson performance could be explained by a single predictor variable. The answer must therefore be sought from multiple predictor relationships and causes.

To make any assessment meaningful, variables need to be categorised in groups. Churchill *et al.* utilise six categories:

1 *Aptitude* is a frequently used independent variable which has many components. It is, however, the most frequently used predictor since a priori, inherent or acquired ability, empathy and so on have long been advocated as essential ingredients in above-average sales performers.

2 *Skill* has received less attention (fewer studies and harder to define) but seems to correlate well with performance. Again, since it is a composite variable (listening, presentation, persuasive and perceptual), this result could be expected.

3 *Motivation* is also a factor which has been linked to performance. Unfortunately, the ability to measure this variable is relatively recent but it does seem to provide a better predictor of performance than aptitude, although somewhat less than the skill factor.

4 *Role perception* is even more recent as a measurable independent variable. While the evidence of a few studies suggests the relationship to be strong, measurement problems, such as common antecedents with motivation, present peculiar measurement difficulties.

5 *Personal variables* have long been suggested and measured for their effect on sales performance. Results do exhibit some strong and consistent relationships.

6 *Organisational and environmental factors.* Such is the range and complexity of these factors that, as expected, they do not provide strong or consistent relationships to performance. Very few studies in fact attempt this measurement problem.

The findings of this meta-analysis suggest that the largest relationships could be found, in order, by

- role variables;
- skill;
- motivation;
- personal factors;
- aptitude;
- organisational/environmental factors.

However, when real variations, with the sampling error removed, were assessed, the most significant factors were

- personal factors;
- skill;
- role variables;
- aptitude;
- motivation;
- organisational/environmental factors.

These results are, of course, subject to severe constraints. The limitations of the approach are many. It adopts a static view of studies ranging over 50 years and fails to measure interpersonal relationships and longitudinal effects. The variables themselves are grouped according to the preferences of the researchers for these factors. Strong influence is exerted by the sales situations, for example, direct life insurance or industrial situations. The definition of what constitutes performance is by no means unambiguous. In particular, the distinction between behaviour and performance outcomes is important. Sales by regional variation and potential and competitive activity mean that similar behaviours yield quite different performance outcomes which are not the result of salesperson variables.

The worth of these studies provides some help for the enlightened manager. First, solutions must be sought within the relevant context of the sales job. Service calling and development selling, organisational and individual customers and industrial, consumer or service selling can be so varied as to require separate, perhaps unique, analysis. In the complex trading situations now encountered, the use of sales volume or value is itself incomplete if not inadequate. Furthermore, the mix of hard and soft, quantitative and subjective data, causes real assessment problems. The search goes on. Multiple determinants of sales performance are a better explanation but no single factor, or single set of factors, provide adequate and satisfying explanation of salesperson performance. Personal characteristics, aptitude and skill will be important but sales managers need to concentrate not only on improving these attributes through training but also on relating them to the buyers and needs of the market. The right people, experience, skill and role clarity do matter but only when matched to the prospect. This confirms what successful salespeople and sales managers already know but few seem able to achieve.

Future researchers in selling and sales management should be encouraged away from trying to predict performance across salespeople in different kinds of sales jobs and in different firms and industries using the same set of performance criteria, to a more focused company- and industry-specific analysis.

13.9 Summary

Monitoring and measurement of what is really important in sales and sales force effectiveness is difficult, time consuming and costly. The differences in personal, regional and company characteristics make measurement problems fraught with difficulty. This in turn makes evaluation and control more complex. Information can be collected by salespeople themselves or by management through sales reports, company data, customer surveys or management observation and field visits, normally part of the customer information system. Traditional methods of evaluation, such as sales against target, are simple and direct but neither fair nor accurate. Sales and cost analysis is an important element in management control as is a quality focus and best in class aspirations. Determinants of salesperson performance have to take account of situational factors. While personal characteristics, skill, role clarity, aptitude and motivation are important to all sales jobs, the company-focused solution will help management to deploy the right person more effectively.

Questions

1 Compare the adequacy of the different sources of information which can be used to evaluate salespeople.

2 What are the implications for sales force productivity of low-volume customers and small orders?

3 The easy part of evaluation is measuring output. The difficult part is to assess the relevant inputs and measure them effectively. Discuss.

4   What differences would you expect to observe in a sales organisation that follows the TQM process from one that does not?

5   Some managers suggest that benchmarking is too expensive in both time and resources to be of real value to the sales organisation. Discuss.

Case study   **A G Barr**

Barr's Soft Drinks Ltd (www.agbarr.co.uk) is one of the significant companies in the booming UK carbonated soft drinks market and is best known for its brand IRN BRU. They have manufacturing plants and offices located in the north of England and Scotland, with distribution depots in all parts of the United Kingdom. In terms of market share Barr is number three in the United Kingdom, a long way behind Coca-Cola and Britvic (Pepsi) who dominate the market, although in Scotland Barr is number one with 52 per cent market share. In terms of competition, there are also many strong regional companies and literally hundreds of small localised concerns. Sales have a significant seasonal bias and the market is split into colas, other carbonated and mixer drinks. Barr's have traditionally been strong in the other carbonated sectors with its Irn Bru brand and to a lesser extent Tizer. In distribution terms, they are also popular with smaller types of outlets (cafes, fish and chip shops, confectionery, tobacco, newsagents [CTNs] and independents).

In their traditional areas, particularly Scotland, distribution has not been a problem. In England, penetration into new areas has been with low unit sales per outlet and relatively high selling and distribution costs. Penetration of south-east-based chains has been difficult and somewhat costly – low margins and service problems. Management have adopted this policy in an effort to gain wider recognition as a national rather than a regional company. Sales, relative to market share, are high in some English regions ($> 20\%$) but low in others ($< 2\%$), averaging 5 per cent across the United Kingdom. Customers are split into key accounts handled by senior salespeople or otherwise into an ABC classification by size. A are usually wholesalers or retail chains; B and C customers are varying sizes of outlet. Salespeople are paid a salary plus commission, with a new accounts bonus scheme.

1   Outline the problems of assessing individual salesperson performance in this company.

2   What approach to evaluation would you recommend sales management to adopt in this situation?

Key terms

- activity measures
- behaviourally anchored rating scales
- control
- cost analysis
- customer record

- daily report evaluation
- meta-analysis
- sales analysis
- sales management audit

References

Adair, C. and Murray, B. (1994) *Breakthrough Process Design* AMACOM: New York

Anderson, E. and Oliver, R.L. (1987) 'Perspectives on behavior-based versus outcome-based salesforce control systems' *Journal of Marketing* **51** (Oct): 76–88

Biesada, A. (1991) 'Benchmarking' *Financial World* **17** (Sep): 28–47

Boles, J.S., Donthu, N. and Lothia, R. (1995) 'Salesperson evaluation using relative performance efficiency: the application of data envelopment analysis' *Journal of Personal Selling & Sales Management* **XV** (3): 31–49

Bosworh, M. (1995) *Solution Selling* McGraw-Hill: New York

Camp, R.C. (1989) *Benchmarking: the search for industry best practices that lead to superior performance* ASQC Quality Research: Milwaukee, WI

Challagalla, G.N. and Shervani, T.A. (1996) 'Dimensions and types of supervisory control: effects on salesperson performance and satisfaction' *Journal of Marketing* **60** (Jan): 89–105

Chaudry, S. and Higbie, J.R. (1990) 'Quality improvement through statistical process control' *Quality Engineering* **2** (4) April: 411–19

Chonko, L.B., Low, T.W., Roberts, J.A. and Tanner, J.F. (2000) 'Sales performance: timing and type of measurement make a difference' *Journal of Personal Selling and Sales Management* **20** (Winter): 23–36

Churchill, G.A., Ford, N.M., Hartley, S.W. and Walker, O.C. (1985) 'The determinants of salesperson performance: a meta-analysis' *Journal of Marketing Research* **XXII** (May): 103–18

Cortada, J. (1993) 'Implementing quality in a sales organisation' *Quality Progress* **Sep**: 67–70

Cravens, D.W., LaForge, R., Pickett, G.M. and Young, C.E. (1993) 'Incorporating a quality improvement perspective into measures of salesperson's performance' *Journal of Personal Selling and Sales Management* **13** (Winter): 1–14

DeCarlo, T.E. and Leigh, T.W. (1996) 'Impact of salesperson attraction on sales managers' attributions and feedback' *Journal of Marketing* **60** (Apr): 47–66

Fong, S.W., Chong, E.W.L. and Ho, D.C.K. (1998) 'Benchmarking: a general reading for management practitioners' *Management Decision* **36** (6): 407–18

Heiman, S., Sanchez, D. and Tuleja, T. (1998) *The New Strategic Selling* Warner Books: London

Lemmens, R. and Donaldson, B. (2004) 'Relationship selling – implications for the evaluation of sales force performance' *Proceedings of the Academy of Marketing* University of Gloucestershire, Cheltenham, UK

Plank, R.E. and Blackshear, T. (1997) 'Standardising the sales process: applying TQM to the industrial selling function' *American Business Review* **15** (2): 52–58

Porter, L., Lawler, E. and Hackman, R. (1975) *Behavior in Organisations* McGraw-Hill: New York

Rackham, N. and De Vincentis, J. (1998) *Re-thinking the Sales Force: re-defining selling to create and capture customer value* McGraw-Hill: New York

Web, M. (2003) 'How to avoid the four most common mistakes of sales process mapping?' www.sixsigma.com [Accessed 16 June 2005]

Welch, C. and Geisslet, P. (1992) 'Measuring the total quality of the sales function' *National Productivity Review* **11**: 517–31

Zoltners, A.A., Sinha, P. and Lorimer, S.E. (2004) *Sales Force Design for Strategic Advantage* Palgrave Macmillan: Basingstoke

Ethical issues in sales

14.1   Overview

Ethical issues affect everyone. The difficulty for most of us is that while there may be an official company code, ethical issues are dilemmas, the answers to which, in a business context, may depend on conditions and circumstances as well as moral positions. Furthermore, what may be seen as unethical to one person may be considered normal practice to another. For example, if your firm has a sales contest, do you try to get the customer to order more than they require or reschedule orders to improve your chances of winning? Do you go further and suggest an imminent price increase to achieve your objective? The answer, for some, will be that any such action is unethical but others may see this as part of the 'game' and within their normal remit as salespeople and 'winners'. Individual and business ethics are a complex area and, in this chapter, the focus is on ethical issues affecting sales operations. This concerns the moral problems and rights and wrongs of sales practices.

14.2   Learning objectives

In this chapter the aim is

- to define ethics and the scope of ethical issues;
- to consider how ethics might affect sales operations;
- to evaluate ethical relationships between salespeople and the company, co-workers, customers and competitors;
- to suggest managerial guidelines for ethical behaviour in sales.

14.3   Definitions

Caveat emptor from the Latin means let the buyer beware. In commercial terms it means the buyer must carry the risk for the quality of the goods purchased.

Ethics are the moral values held by a group or profession that result in a code of behaviour considered to be correct.

Multilevel marketing is a sales system incorporating several layers of distribution each of which adds a mark-up to the cost from the previous one.

Network selling refers to a sales system using a network of agents each of whom receives a commission on value of sales.

14.4 Scope of ethical issues

For some people, ethical issues are not a problem. It is either right or wrong and, if there are grey areas, they tend to have their own unofficial code of conduct to resolve these. For others, the sales job creates a number of ethical dilemmas which create role stress. Individuals and management have to decide how to approach these ethical issues. Being ethical includes being fair, truthful and impartial and not profiting unjustly at someone else's expense. Some managers seem to regard ethics as 'soft' and operating against the profit maximisation ethos which drives many firms. This view is naïve and firms must acknowledge that their prosperity depends upon their interdependence with a variety of groups of people. This idea of the stakeholder economy is important and firms need to accommodate the interests of different role partners affected by their business dealings, as shown in Figure 14.1.

For example, firms operating in a financially driven mode might conduct personnel matters in a 'hire and fire' way, abide by laws but only as a minimum, be late payers to creditors, see customers as a means to an end but be highly focused on the needs of shareholders. It could be expected that salespeople in these firms would be results-oriented and prepared to bend the rules to make a sale or achieve targets. The Shell executive who said that they did care about the environment but that it was not a priority since nobody had found a way to make money from being environmentally friendly may have been reflecting this approach. Perhaps the way to confront this issue is to ask Shell shareholders if they would prefer to be perceived as more environmentally friendly rather than receiving increased dividends. An attempt by some shareholders to encourage the company to conduct an ethical audit was blocked by Shell directors with the backing of one of their largest shareholders, Prudential, Britain's largest life assurance company. The interests of stakeholders in a company often conflict with each other, thus increasing the difficulty in resolving ethical dilemmas.

From a personal and company perspective, ethical issues can be viewed in different ways. This is shown as Figure 14.2.

At one level, there are the basic right and wrong issues, which, as a minimum, means keeping within the law and abiding by rules and regulations – this is the legal

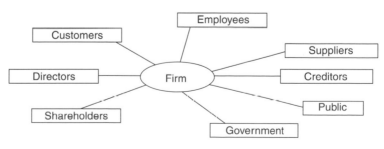

Fig 14.1   Stakeholding in the firm

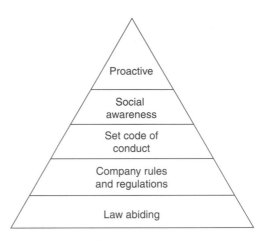

Fig 14.2 Hierarchy of ethical standards

minimum level of ethical behaviour. A second level is setting ethical standards, with company rules and procedures written as part of a job description or contract of employment. This implies the ethical standards expected of an employee which are reciprocated by the company. A higher ethical level is to establish a code of conduct which raises ethical standards in the way you do business. Rather than pay a minimum wage, the company pays above this level and also treats staff well in terms of benefits and allowances. At this level, the company will also be totally open and honest with their customers. A further level is that of social awareness, where every effort is made to increase benefits to a wider public than just your customers, perhaps including the local and wider communities and other groups who can benefit from your business success. At this level, the ethical standard is raised because a social responsibility is acknowledged. Finally, firms can be pioneers who set the ethical agenda and standards for others.

Kuhlman (1994) derived a list of six basic duties of sellers derived from various consumer rights. These were as follows:

1 Manufactured and offered products must provide a minimum level of security.

2 Supplier communication must not contain any deceiving or misleading information but rather educate the consumer with regard to important product qualities.

3 Contracts must not be drawn up at the consumer's disadvantage but must enable both parties equally to attain their interests. Furthermore, they should provide the consumer with the right to demand redress for damages.

4 Suppliers should be open to customers' complaints and attend to their problems as well as to the reasons for satisfaction and dissatisfaction concerning products and services.

5 The environmental pollution caused by the production, distribution, use and waste disposal of goods should be minimised.

6 Suppliers of goods can help to educate the consumer. Companies offering high-quality products and services at reasonable prices have nothing to fear from a well-informed customer.

14.5 Ethics and sales operations

Sales operate at the boundary between organisations and customers. To achieve sales objectives, ethical issues come into play, particularly at a personal level but also with the company, competitors and customers. In a survey of ethical issues in marketing, Chonko and Hunt (1985) listed the most important concerns of marketing practitioners, in order of frequency of mentions, as

1 *bribery* – gifts from outside vendors, money under the table, questionable commissions and rebates;

2 *fairness* – manipulation of others, conflict between company and family, inducing customers to use services not needed;

3 *honesty* – misrepresenting services and capabilities, lying to customers to obtain orders;

4 *price* – differential pricing, meeting competitors' prices, charging higher prices than firms with similar products while claiming superiority;

5 *product* – products that do not benefit consumers, copyright infringements, product safety, exaggerated performance claims;

6 *personnel* – hiring, firing, employee evaluation;

7 *confidentiality* – temptation to use or obtain classified, secret or competitive information;

8 *advertising* – misleading customers, crossing the line between puffery and the misleading;

9 *manipulation of data* – distortion, falsifying figures or misusing statistics or information;

10 *purchasing* – reciprocity in supplier selection.

At the personal level, salespeople are faced with several ethical dilemmas. The most obvious, and probably the most frequently encountered, ethical conflict is the sales-person trying to obtain the highest possible price from a buyer seeking as much value from the deal as possible. Another frequently occurring, yet grey, area concerns expenses incurred while carrying out the sales job: what is legitimate and what is not? Some sales managers, unable to award a performance bonus or salary increase because of company or other pay restraints, in an effort to motivate and retain their 'best' staff, may feel that a generous expense account is a surrogate for a salary increase. This is an ethical dilemma. With a large sales force, high sales expenses will, unless there is strict control, be a problem. Entertaining customers is a particu-larly grey area, where lunch expenses will probably be approved for a valued customer, but some salespeople might prefer to lunch with a friendly customer whose turnover is small than a larger customer whose company they do not like as much. Does the lunch cover drinks? Similarly, a sales manager may be involved in recruiting staff. If you are asked to fly to London, do you fly your air miles carrier or the cheapest or the best?

Did you know?

A UN inquiry into bribes paid to the Saddam Hussain regime in Iraq under the oil-for-food programme reported that the Glasgow-based Weir Group paid £2.5 million in bribes. They were not alone. The report stated that half the 4500 companies in the programme had paid £1 billion in kickbacks and illicit surcharges including companies such as Volvo and Daimler Chrysler. The Weir salesperson involved claimed, 'I work for the company and I did as I was told'. Weir chief executive, Mark Selway stated, 'We are the only ones who have put their hand up and said we did wrong and apologised'.

(Source: The Herald, 28 October 2005)

With customers, some issues are particularly difficult to solve. Withholding information about a price reduction or a new product introduction to a customer is an ethical dilemma with, very often, no 'right' answer. Suppose that a distributor requires help to create a trade show but your company also supplies a nearby competitor. This help requires merchandising support and much salesperson's time in promotion. How do you reconcile this with regard to your other supplier? Offer no help to anyone, offer help in proportion to the business they do or help anyone who asks for it? Also, building close relationships directly with customers may affect relationships built up over many years with distributors. The point at which sales growth is sacrificed in the name of established relationships, and vice versa, has to be very carefully drawn. In a different context, the trend to more relationship-based selling creates ethical problems of openness between companies and individuals. The factors important in human relationships are listed as friendship, care, support, loyalty, honesty, trust, openness and self-sacrifice (Duck, 1991). In business, they are cooperation, trust and commitment (Morgan and Hunt, 1994). Thus difficulties can and do arise, particularly for the salesperson where there are conflicts in their role. For example, suppose that you found some interesting information about a competitor while working with a distributor. Would you feel obliged, or not, to relate this information to your superiors?

From a buyer's perspective, some firms move their purchase staff around to avoid close personal relationships developing with salespeople. This implies that commercial judgement might be affected by close personal relationships so different standards are being applied. In recommending the skills and techniques required for negotiation, the problem of ethical behaviour can arise. Indeed, in describing the art of negotiation, this can be misconstrued as bending the rules, involving deception and replacing honesty with guile and being cute. For example, when doing your homework for a major contract, you are negotiating and receive inside information. Do you hide this or reveal it to your customer, adversary or friend? There is no evidence to suggest that salespeople are less ethical or more Machiavellian than other groups, although many sales staff perceive that they are expected to bend the rules by their senior managers in order to make a sale.

For a company, discounts and rebates create ethical dilemmas. Published quantity discounts are clearly unambiguous, but hidden loyalty rebates based on retrospective sales may be earned by the customer and paid retrospectively. Do all customers know of these rebates? Are they the same for all customers or biased for one customer over another? Should sales representatives for tobacco companies try to maximise sales? Should Nestlé sell powdered baby-milk to Third World countries that do not have adequate hygiene and water purification systems? While individuals may have a personal position on these issues, which may or may not come into conflict with the company's stance, there is seldom a right answer for most of the dilemmas where ethics come into play. It depends . . .

Salespeople may also find that ethical issues arise with co-workers. A common problem here concerns who makes the sale. Many customer accounts may have several branches which operate across different sales territories. The initial contact may be made at one branch, a subsequent order placed at another while the ultimate level of business may be determined by company performance on a range of product, service and information issues. Team-selling is popular currently but has anyone told the sales force? Another dilemma between co-workers might involve whether a manager should tell a prospective recruit that they are planning to leave the company to join a competitor? These are just a sample of the ethical issues affecting co-workers. Finally, dealing with competitors is another area that particularly affects the sales force. Do you meet with competitor salespeople and have a gentleman's agreement not to poach from each other's customers? Should you socialise with competitors at all or do you treat competition as the enemy and customers as the battleground on which the fight takes place?

14.6 The sales manager and salespeople

The foundation for an ethical relationship in business is based on honesty and trust, plus doing the right thing. If a salesperson is not performing, one approach is to kick up the backside by putting pressure on salespeople with the threat of the sack. Stories are legendary of people being called to the head office for their periodic review, told they are being made redundant and asked to leave their car keys. Such an approach is level one or two on the hierarchy of dealing with unethical behaviour. A more productive approach, in the long term, is for managers to be involved and to participate with salespeople in the performance of their jobs. Coaching and training subordinates, offering advice and guidance, may be more time consuming and difficult but are more humane and should lead to a more ethical approach. A different type of dilemma can arise with a highly successful salesperson. Do you split their territory in two, offering improved service for customers but reducing valuable bonuses or commission for the successful salesperson? While performance-related pay, profit-sharing and team bonuses are all conducive to greater job satisfaction and performance, individual rewards may be divisive and lead to lower job satisfaction. In one study (Donaldson, 1997), it was found that the prime motivation in industrial salespeople was 'doing a good job'. Doing a good job is in line with the objectives and preset criteria that the manager has agreed with their salespeople.

Very little research has been done in the area of anti-citizenship behaviour in the sales force (Jelinek and Ahearne, 2006). One study suggests that 60 per cent of sales managers have caught their salespeople cheating on expenses (Strout, 2001). Customer may force a change in ethical behaviour. For example, Gilbert asserts that

70 per cent of customers consider a salesperson's ethics when making purchasing decisions (Gilbert, 2003). For the sales manager, the problem of how to discipline salespeople and what is or is not permitted can be difficult to manage fairly and consistently. The manager's ethical approach will be closely observed by staff who take their lead from, and sometimes set their standards against, what the boss says and does (Schwepker *et al.*, 1997). Falsifying sales reports and concocting expenses are the most commonly reported unethical practices (Smith, 1995). Control of expenses has already been discussed but other possible grey areas include the misuse of company equipment, the improper use of, especially, company cars, cheating on time and expenses and moonlighting. You may feel the salesperson caught by their manager on television watching test-match cricket to have been unlucky but this is a serious discipline issue. What was the sales manager doing watching television in the first place? Similarly, salespeople may enjoy the freedom of their sales job but they may also be involved in running a family business which you may or may not know about. Moonlighting of this type needs to be managed and controlled.

What do you think?

Sam is an averagely performing salesperson with 20 years' service for the firm, who becomes quite seriously ill and is away from work for several months. On his return, there is a noticeable decline in performance and most people agree that Sam, although only 52, can no longer perform as expected. The long hours, the travelling and the increasingly difficult job in a changing environment all take their toll. The sales manager has to decide how to handle this situation. Does she offer Sam another job, sack him or offer some form of redundancy/retirement package? What is appropriate, ethical and also in the best interests of Sam and the company?

Another issue where ethical behaviour is noted concerns discrimination on religious, racial or sexual criteria. In the United Kingdom and the European Community (EC), this now applies to age discrimination. There are laws which demand equality and should influence behaviour, but there can be no doubt that discrimination has been widely practised. Many managers practise positive discrimination in that they recruit people they think will do the job best, looking for similarities between salespeople and buyers, or people who traditionally fit the profile of the company. These are invariably white, male and of Anglo-Saxon origin. While this is, thankfully, rapidly changing in many walks of business life, there are ethical issues involved here. Worse still, the number of industrial tribunals reporting sexual harassment is high, and this is often in sales-related areas. While the cynical may say that this is inspired by tabloid journalism or is the most successful way for a tribunal lawyer to build a case for the defence in dismissal cases, it should represent a real concern in sales management. Managers must be ethical in dealing with all staff, set the standards and abide by a code of conduct to reinforce the message.

14.7 Managing ethics

In most countries, there are legal constraints on how business is conducted in order to avoid exploitation and unethical practices. Some of the restrictions affecting salespeople and sales managers were considered in chapter nine but companies who are innovative, progressive and enlightened will be operating at standards well above those required as a minimum in law. There are ethical problems in sales jobs that are not found in other professions, some of which have been suggested in this chapter. However, sales' ethical problems are possibly less than those experienced by accountants and lawyers and much less life-threatening than those experienced by doctors. Nevertheless, some ground rules for dealing ethically in sales need to be set.

Leadership

Society's expectations of business are now much higher, which puts pressure on managers to behave in a more responsible and ethical way. Kwik-Fit used to reward their branch managers on sales performance. The result was higher sales of tyres, shock absorbers and related products, Unfortunately, unsuspecting customers did not realise that these replacements were not always required and the company began to get a reputation as a 'rip-off merchant'. To be fair, the company quickly rectified this and rewards are today related to overall performance and customer satisfaction. Tom Farmer, founder and former chief executive and chairman of the company set his own standards and exhibited what was expected by his qualities of leadership and example. As a result the company set as its mantra 100 per cent customer satisfaction every time a customer visited a Kwik-Fit outlet.

Code of conduct

Again, it is difficult to give rules which could govern ethical leadership. Some people base their moral position on religious or humanitarian grounds while others base their ethical position on the own personal value system. To class someone who works on a Sunday as unethical might seem strange. Therefore, to draw up an ethical code is difficult. Smith (1995) suggests a number of maxims to decide whether or not actions are ethical. First, the golden rule is to do unto others as you would have them do unto you. Second is the media test – would I be embarrassed in front of colleagues/family/friends, if my decision were publicised in the media? The third item is the invoice test – are payments being requested that could not be fully disclosed in the company accounts? Fourth, good ethics is good business, the belief that the best interests of the firm are served by good ethics. Fifth comes the professional ethic – would the action be viewed as proper by an objective panel of professional colleagues? Finally, when in doubt, don't.

Climate and structure

To implement ethical practices does not necessarily imply the need for a democratic process but certainly one of consultation and participation. A firm should have some form of group or committee with ethical responsibilities such as a staff group or committee. This should not be a peripheral company activity but an important part of the firm's strategic purpose. A necessary part of creating an adequate ethical position is fostering the correct climate within a company. This forms part of the corporate image conveyed to other stakeholders, particularly customers. Firms new to a market, in an effort to compete, may adopt alternative, radical ways of meeting the needs of customers and their own corporate objectives. For example, one firm which manufactures and supplies respected skin-care products use network marketing or multi-level selling to obtain orders and supply their customers. The existing market and conventional distribution channels would be difficult to penetrate and they have chosen to use alternative means of achieving their aims. While products, and other aspects of their business, are of a high and respectable standard, the sales techniques are presented as part of a get-rich-quick scheme. Some of their sales agents have been highly successful. These people are well organised, hardworking and determined to succeed. They have a good product, company support and a form of competitive advantage in their direct sales approach. For a low investment, if successful, generous returns can be earned, but it works on the principle that the more people that are recruited to sell the product and, in turn, the more people they recruit and sell, the richer you get. Margins do not therefore reflect the costs of distributing the product but the costs of recruiting additional salespeople to expand the business. Instead of paid advertising and retailers' margins, the commission goes to the sales force but not for the sales; it goes for sales recruitment. It is legal (although there are limits to the number of levels of recruitment), but those recruited early in the chain and who are able to recruit further salespeople do very well financially – but is it ethical? The latest recruit earns a low commission, part of which goes to the salesperson who recruited them but is not directly involved in the sale. Again, legal restrictions have been placed on this type of operation because, ultimately, it cannot be sustained.

14.8 Summary

Today's customers have greater choice and freedom to purchase what they want from where they want but customers are still conned, cheated and misled. Social causes, the environment and other issues have moved up the agenda and companies that do not acknowledge these realities, although possibly making short-run profits, will struggle in the longer term. Management involves not only profit and return on investment but also with human and moral issues that concern employees, customers and the public at large, and these issues will gain in importance. These ethical issues will have to be built into the company's audit procedure now and in the future. Management is not merely arithmetic but involves human and moral issues.

Questions

1   Are some stakeholders more important than others? If so, which ones and why?

2   Can a staff committee deal with ethical issues more effectively than individual leadership from senior management?

3   Outline some of the ways in which a firm operating at the top of the ethical standard hierarchy can set the agenda for others to follow.

4   List some of the key ethical issues faced by sales management and suggest how they can be resolved.

5   Owing to changing conditions in one of your overseas markets, outside the EC, you are encountering increased requests for special commissions to government officials. Discuss how to approach and deal with this issue.

Case study

Grampian Leasing

Grampian Leasing (name disguised) is part of a large international group with substantial interests in financing and real estate. Grampian's main business is in the market for supplying finance to companies who sell office equipment. Basically, they facilitate businesses to purchase the benefits of office machinery without having the risks of ownership associated with purchasing the machinery outright. Grampian's customers are primarily the equipment supplier, although deals are done with the individual consumer or business firm. A typical transaction is for the supplier to contact Grampian with a proposed new client who typically wants to lease some type of office equipment. Grampian underwrites this proposal before accepting the contract. Effectively, Grampian buys the equipment from the supplier and leases it to the end user. This process is shown in Figure 14.3.

Grampian typically uses a telephone prospecting system, contacts the account and grades them by size. The salesperson will then call to evaluate the supplier, who is likely to be in reprographics, telephone communications, computers and information technology or vending. Many customers are loyal and known, and use Grampian because of previous experience and service. These customers will be offered a more competitive rate than a new customer since less work is required because of the previous trading history. Grampian is very aware of competitors' prices and each salesperson is expected to work around a different rate sheet for the end user. The sales approach is to deal not only with the company but also with the employee. Grampian prefers to allocate the same salesperson to the same dealer, thus building up the relationship. Part of their relationship-building is an extensive programme of corporate entertainment, sports events in particular are popular. The sales force are appraised every six months and training and refresher courses are periodically held. The regional sales team meets on a Friday, once a fortnight, for an open exchange of ideas and information and to encourage team building. Schemes that are run include longer holidays for longer service and bonus schemes, for both individuals and groups, if targets are met. A normal bonus is of the order of 10 per cent of salary, paid quarterly.

Ian has worked for the company for several years and has three particular contracts in the pipeline as he begins his week on Monday. First is a potentially lucrative deal with a computer company, but he knows that his major competitors will also be bidding. Ian has built up a good relationship with the marketing director of the computer firm, who use a supplier evaluation form to grade the bids. This director has informed Ian that Grampian is behind on their performance evaluation against one of their competitors. On a number of performance dimensions Ian knows Grampian to be the better offer, and he is sure that this competitor has falsified the return.

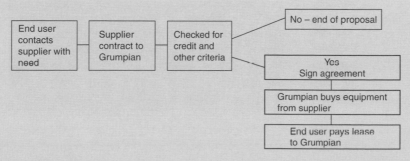

Fig 14.3 The proposal process

MISSION STATEMENT

"We will strive to solve customer needs by being a world-class company through the excellence of our workforce, support for the community and by operating to the highest ethical standards"

THIS ENTAILS

Teamwork – We can only achieve our mission if employees work together effectively.

Commitment from everyone, throughout the organisation, in order to meet our goals.

Excelling in everything we do to ensure that we continue to delight our customers and offer a better service than our competitors.

Providing superior financial services is what we do best. We must build our strengths in order to offer our marketplace the products and services they need.

OUR RATIONALE

Customer satisfaction is a fundamental source of sustainable competitive advantage

Striving for total quality by seeking continuous improvement in the cost and quality of our service

Enabling our employees to give of their best.

HOW WE WILL ACHIEVE OUR MISSION:

Integrity
Give business ethics and customer satisfaction the highest priority at all times.

Quality
Concentrate on the core business by continuously improving quality and cost effectiveness.

Customers
Ensure our customers constantly receive excellence and good value for money in all the services we provide.

Employees
Provide a fulfilling and meaningful career experience which attracts and retains committed employees. Through a mix of on-the-job experience, formal training and professional development, allow them to fulfil their potential and contribute directly to the success of the company.

Shareholders
To encourage the company and its shareholders to perpetuate and profitably grow the business and to consistently generate above average returns.

Fig 14.4 A mission statement

A second potential contract is with a smaller company with limited potential. As part of relationship-building, Ian had entertained this client to dinner. He is being specifically asked by the customer to repeat the event but Ian knows that the expense cannot really be justified. Furthermore, the buyer is fond of 'a little libation', and Ian knows that there will be a long evening of drinking without much work being discussed and that he personally will be seriously out of pocket on expenses.

Finally, Ian has good prospects of interesting a major company in a deal but he knows that, if the deal goes through, it will be from their head office and the credit for the contract will go not only to another salesperson but to the region where the head office is located. He is undecided whether it is worth the effort.

1 Discuss the ethical issues involved in all three situations that Ian faces.

2 Evaluate the mission statement (Figure 14.4) and specifically identify how it might be implemented by a sales force in a company such as Grampian.

Key terms

- *caveat emptor*
- consumer protection
- ethics
- hierarchy of ethical standards
- misrepresentation

- multilevel marketing
- network selling
- overselling
- stakeholders

References

Chonko, L.B. and Hunt, S.D. (1985) 'Ethics and marketing management: an empirical investigation' *Journal of Business Research* 13: 339–59

Donaldson, B. (1997) 'The importance of financial incentives in motivating industrial salespeople' *The Journal of Selling and Major Account Management* 1 (1): 4–16

Duck, S. (1991) *Understanding Relationships* Guildford Press: New York

Gilbert, J. (2003) 'A matter of trust' *Sales and Marketing Management* 155 (3): 30

Herald (2005) 'UN rules that Weir bribed Saddam' 28 October: 1,2,5

Jelinek, R. and Ahearne, M. (2006) 'The ABC's of ACB: unveiling a clear and present danger in the sales force' *Industrial Marketing Management* 35: 457–67

Kuhlmam, E. (1994) 'Customers' in Harvey, B. (ed.) *Business Ethics: a European approach* Prentice-Hall: Trowbridge, Chapter 5

Morgan, R.M. and Hunt, S.D. (1994) 'The commitment–trust theory of relationship marketing' *Journal of Marketing* 58 (Jul): 20–38

Schwepker, C.H., Ferrell, O.C. and Ingram, T.N. (1997) 'The influence of ethical climate and ethical conflict on role stress in the sales force' *Journal of the Academy of Marketing Science* 25 (2): 99–108

Smith, N.C. (1995) 'Marketing ethics' in Baker, M.J. (ed.) *The Companion Encyclopedia of Marketing* London: Routledge, pp. 905–29

Strout, E. (2001) 'Are your salespeople ripping you off?' *Sales and Marketing Management* 153 (2): 56–62

Longfellow Office Supplies

Longfellow Office Supplies (www.longfellowsltd.co.uk) was originally a sole-trader formed some thirty years ago by the current managing director, Bill Sewell. A strong customer base in the Lancashire area was created and maintained primarily through his direction. The company name was chosen because Bill is a very tall man (long fellow) and an 'own-brand' product range of stationery items was created called Hiawatha (the legendary Indian, from the poem by H.W. Longfellow). Links between Bill himself, the name Longfellow's (as it became known) and these products formed a very strong focus for customers both current and prospective.

As with many small businesses the company relies on strong personal relationships with customers. It is interesting to note that Longfellow's still survives on this basis in the twenty-first century and until recently managed to retain a customer base which included the likes of British Aerospace.

There is a clear split in Longfellow's product ranges, namely between office machines and the service element of these, and other office products such as stationery, office sundries and furniture. The sales of office photocopiers have provided the majority of machine sales over the years and, having been sold on a 'cost per copy' maintenance basis, have provided the service department with a regular flow of work, albeit charged for by metered copy charges. The advent of cartridge based copiers, removing much of the need for routine service as parts were incorporated into replaceable cartridges has adversely affected the potential for profit within the service element of the operation.

Current Situation

The market for large scale office copiers is continuing to decline, with more and more companies using laser printers to create multiple originals rather than using traditional photocopiers. Whilst Longfellow's has made some small inroads into this market, there is little doubt that its traditional reliance on older copier technology is starting to have a severe impact in the revenue achieved through the 'cost per copy' metering arrangements. Although there has been an attempt to move into personal computers and related product, the skills required in terms of service backup for these items are substantially different from those available within the existing service engineer profile.

In terms of the general office products market, there is concern that consumer demand is slowing, and this is hitting the big suppliers. The increase in Small Office and Home Office (SOHO) markets means that a local presence, with shop facilities as an add-on to its main commercial distribution service still have a reasonably bright future. Interestingly, one of the very large office products distributors, Corporate

Express, recently handled its merger with other companies extremely well because of its strong customer relationship management (CRM) programme.

Longfellow's has some significant resources at their disposal – notably their computer system. Unfortunately much data which would be considered as 'must have' for marketers (e.g. overall sales, costs, profits; sales and profit breakdowns by market segment, channel, brand, account and customer type; customer relationship monitors, etc.) is not readily available to management, and indeed never has been. The business has always been run on very much an 'idea of what is happening' basis, which is now simply no longer viable.

Most of what would be considered 'must have' data is likely to be able to be extracted from the integrated computer system, which the company has been using to a certain extent for some years now. However, appropriate procedures had to be put in place to ensure that all relevant functions of the system were being used. The company is beginning to produce management accounts regularly which show, amongst other things, sales and profit breakdowns by product and account, which is a first step towards more meaningful planning.

Real benefits however will come from utilising the marketing database elements of the system and ensuring that the online updating features of this system will enable analysis to be treated as a continuous process. The marketing tools available allow information to be input in respect of many attributes of a customer, and allow tailoring to track, for example, sales orders by individual within a customer account. This data, combined with sensible promotional activity targeted towards specific groups will enable the company to hone in on the relationship marketing idea once again but from a different perspective. Instead of reliance on the memory of an individual, details stored electronically about customer accounts and order-placers within can be onscreen in front of an operator within seconds of a telephone call being answered. The system is sophisticated enough to store details right down to birthdays and anniversaries of the individual together with their likes and dislikes in terms of hobbies, although it is unlikely that Longfellow's will use such intricate reporting for the foreseeable future.

Real value will begin to accrue when the historical data within the integrated database is interrogated to provide insight into possible sales opportunities. Some examples of this would be where the software is asked to report on all those customers who have bought a fax machine within the last six months but who have not bought fax rolls for that machine. Such analysis is relatively easily carried out provided some sensible thought is given to the questions asked, and the results can be tailored to produce mailshot/faxshot/emailshot promotions for the items not bought.

Internet capabilities

There seems no doubt that more and more companies will wish to source product through the World Wide Web and that simply having a Web presence is no longer enough. The nature of buyer/seller interaction is changing such that electronic ordering can often account for 60 per cent of an office products dealer and some now place 90 per cent of their purchase orders electronically. Thankfully, Longfellow's has now invested in a website which has an electronic ordering catalogue facility, allowing customers to browse products or order from their paper catalogue by simply entering product code and quantity details.

Transparent ordering on to suppliers

The existing integrated system within the company will support recent developments in the industry to allow fully transparent ordering from customers straight through to Longfellow's computer and then, if a product is not in stock, straight through onto their preferred supplier's system. Such systems are now sophisticated enough to ensure that the customer is given an acknowledgement that the product is 'in stock' for next day delivery even if it has in fact to be ordered from Longfellow's preferred supplier. This type of facility, if developed properly can enable vastly increased consumer participation in the ordering and supply process. The trend towards just-in-time purchasing by firms places ever increasing demands on a company such as Longfellow's and their existing capability to place orders upon suppliers electronically for next day delivery to customers is important.

Branding

Unfortunately, it is difficult to see a sensible forward marketing strategy for the Longfellow 'own-brand' Hiawatha. In order to compensate for the relatively weak buying power of a small organisation, the company is now a member of the North East Marketing Organisation (NEMO) which forms an alliance between competitors, similar to that formed between global players like Motorola, IBM, Philips, Siemens, BT and Toshiba. With buying power combined with other dealers around the world through Europa Office and BPGI, over £7.5 billion worth of purchasing is combined. This allows exceptionally priced access to branded and unbranded product together with private-label mid-priced lines for general stationery sundries. The economics of sourcing Hiawatha branded product probably far outweigh the benefits gained by having this 'own brand' and its links to Bill Sewell through the company name. The strength of the brand connection with the company name however is such that perhaps new means of linking the two together should be sought.

There is great advantage in retaining the association of such a brand, particularly when there is a 'story' behind it that can be told briefly and capture the imagination. Office products are dull lifeless things, the big players such as Staples, Office International and the like, have no such 'story' to link to their names.

Questions

1. Your task is to analyse Longfellow's current market position, the segments in which it should operate and identify where the opportunities lie for the business.

2. Make recommendations on a suitable go-to-market strategy for 1–3 years.

Specifically, for the next year, prepare a sales planning document.

Score Ltd

Score (www.score-group.com) is a privately owned company with an annual turnover of approximately £75 million who are primarily contractors involved in engineering research, design, manufacture and repair for oil companies in the North Sea. The company was founded in 1982 by Charles Ritchie after he left one of the multinational companies, which he had joined in the early stages of North Sea development. A qualified mechanical engineer, Charles is entrepreneurial, enterprising and aggressive. His style is very much hands-on, and he has personally built up the business to the stage it is at now of almost 1000 employees, operating in five continents, and the company has diversified into aerospace and marine as well as energy technology. As the company has grown, it has been able to compete for larger contracts where they are seen as competent, cost-effective but still relatively small on the global map. Most of the managers in the organisation are also hands-on technical operators or highly skilled artisans with a limited knowledge and experience of sales and marketing. The basis on which Charles Ritchie has built the business has been mainly precision engineering with a focus on the service and maintenance of other people's equipment. The company consider themselves a quality supplier and are now operating in the big league of contractors to the oil industry, both in the North Sea and elsewhere in the world.

The UK oil and gas industry is in a mature stage of its development. Current estimates of oil and gas reserves can be found at http://www.og.dti.gov.uk/information/statistics. This maturity is characterised by the decline of the larger, earlier discoveries in the North Sea, increasing smaller field development, but renewed exploration activity with an increasing emphasis on cost-reduction strategies by operators in both capital expenditure and operating costs. These development phases in the UK continental shelf oil industry, along with an account of the nature of the activity, are summarised in the figures CS2.1 and CS2.2.

Despite fluctuations, business activity is still high in this sector. This can be explained by a combination of the high price of oil and high productivity, itself a result of two main variables, namely technology and efficiency. Advancements in technology, enabling the exploitation of smaller marginal satellite fields and innovative exploration techniques, indicate that the North Sea is only mature at certain geological levels. It is the increases in efficiency that are enhancing productivity rather than the price of oil itself. These increases are also inspiring a new-found confidence in the Grampian region, where most activity takes place. Furthermore, these efficiencies are reflected in operators' recent claims that their cost-cutting initiatives have yielded savings of up to 25–30 per cent in both capital expenditure and operating costs. Such productivity enhancement transforms the economic viability of older fields that were previously threatened by closure as exploration and production became uneconomic.

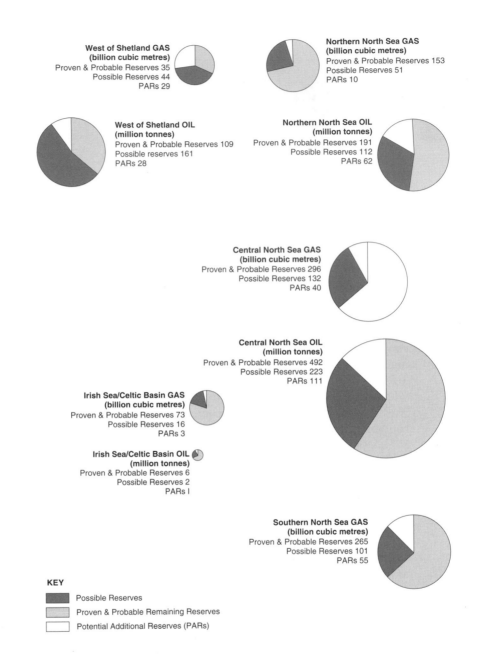

West of Shetland GAS
(billion cubic metres)
Proven & Probable Reserves 35
Possible Reserves 44
PARs 29

Northern North Sea GAS
(billion cubic metres)
Proven & Probable Reserves 153
Possible Reserves 51
PARs 10

West of Shetland OIL
(million tonnes)
Proven & Probable Reserves 109
Possible reserves 161
PARs 28

Northern North Sea OIL
(million tonnes)
Proven & Probable Reserves 191
Possible Reserves 112
PARs 62

Central North Sea GAS
(billion cubic metres)
Proven & Probable Reserves 296
Possible Reserves 132
PARs 40

Central North Sea OIL
(million tonnes)
Proven & Probable Reserves 492
Possible Reserves 223
PARs 111

Irish Sea/Celtic Basin GAS
(billion cubic metres)
Proven & Probable Reserves 73
Possible Reserves 16
PARs 3

Irish Sea/Celtic Basin OIL
(million tonnes)
Proven & Probable Reserves 6
Possible Reserves 2
PARs I

Southern North Sea GAS
(billion cubic metres)
Proven & Probable Reserves 265
Possible Reserves 101
PARs 55

KEY

Possible Reserves
Proven & Probable Remaining Reserves
Potential Additional Reserves (PARs)

Fig CS2.1   Pie charts showing potential for UK reserves growth

A pattern in North Sea exploration and production is emerging whereby, on the one hand, the established operators exercise cost-reduction initiatives to justify continued production from existing declining fields (Shell, BP, Exxon-Mobil), while, on the other, new operators are benefiting from technological advancements which enable them to develop and operate new smaller fields for the first time (Apache, Talisman, etc.).

	lower	central(2)	upper	
oil	73 [95] 545 [710]	208 [247] 1560 [1855]	453 [496] 3400 [3720]	million tonnes million barrels
gas	64 [74] 2255 [2610]	138 [153] 4870 [5405]	252 [276] 8885 [9760]	bcm(3) bcf(3)
Billion cubic metres (bcm), billion cubic feet (bcf)				

Fig CS2.2   Potential additional reserves(1) as at end-2004 – (figures in brackets are for end-2003)

Year	Total	Platform structures	Modules and equipment	Offshore loading systems	Pipelines	Terminals	Development wells	Other expenditure
1994	3,620	1,288	737	32	297	195	1,037	33
1995	4,309	1,334	1,063	142	163	144	1,429	36
1996	4,326	1,008	1,041	247	171	157	1,635	68
1997	4,229	908	807	316	133	160	1,841	65
1998	5,050	2,000 < included		154	208	85	2,327	158
1999	3,103	1,023		74	97	76	1,643	190
2000	2,783	1,099		14	79	91	1,320	180
2001	3,543	1,639		64	59	76	1,529	176
2002	3,637	1,472		98	17	82	1,809	159
2003	3,449	1,341		357	51	110	1,428	163
2004p	3,263						1,573	1,690
p Provisional								

Fig CS2.3   Development expenditure by operators and other production licensees (£million)

Either way, the industry is continuing to attract a substantial amount of risk capital which augurs well in terms of development expenditure.

As a result of these market trends, operators seek to reduce their costs further by divesting certain operational responsibilities. This increasing focus on cost reduction for both new developments and the maintenance of existing offshore production facilities is leading to opportunities for contractors in the oil industry. For the contractor, the bid process begins at a prequalification stage and involves the application to operators for contracts which, by European Union (EU) competition law, have to be advertised in the daily EU contracts publication for UK contracts. At this stage, operators will specify certain criteria to try to ensure that only the more suitable contractors apply.

Such criteria will include

- experience in maintenance and modification;
- a proven track record and sound reputation within the industry;
- satisfactory financial strength to perform the necessary work;
- evidence of a complementary corporate culture with the operator.

These criteria will be specified in more detail in the tender document for those companies invited to tender. At this next stage, the companies will be given the opportunity to demonstrate their technical capability in relation to the job in question in more detail, they will be advised of possible contractual liabilities and the framework for remuneration will be discussed. With respect to remuneration, and despite the close working relationship between contractor and supplier, many contracts have contentious clauses in them involving risks that some contractors may not be prepared to take. In such cases, the contractor will account for such risks in a higher bid price or will qualify the risks to the operator, who would be expected to bear them. Depending on the nature of the contract, in terms of value and longevity, a post-qualification stage bid could cost the contractor as much as £100,000 to compile. Much of the expense will be in management time and the preparation of costings and promotional material for presentation to the client (operator). The general consensus among contractors is that the minimum value of a contract needs to exceed £500,000 to make it worthwhile pursuing.

To recoup the considerable expense of unsuccessful bids and those won on the basis of a minimum cost tender, contractors attempt to increase their charges with each modification requested by the operator. This causes conflict, which is exacerbated by operators challenging contractors' estimates, both sides incurring further costs by employing additional personnel to assess claims and counter-claims. Contractors respond further by incorporating complex terms and conditions into their tender submissions along with extensive contingencies in cost estimates.

Research in the UK service and supply sector indicates that there are about ten companies that compete in the bidding for contracts put out for tender by the operators in the region. However, the picture is made more complex because of two particular factors. First, the range of services offered varies from contractor to contractor, each being recognised for particular areas of expertise. Second, some of the contractors are engaged in alliances or joint ventures with other contractors for certain projects where their own range of capabilities is not sufficient or adequately specialised. Of the ten or so contractors they include large players such as Kvaerner, Haliburton and Hughes Christensen and more indigenous players such as the Wood Group and Score. Turnover and profitability for each company will fluctuate from year to year depending on the number of projects and the stage of each project. Naturally, the financial strength and resources of the organisation are important considerations for the operator when choosing a supplier of services. It can reasonably be assumed that the competitors and Score, all possess the required depth of resources for the majority of the contracts for which they bid, by virtue of the fact that they are all members of multinational groups and have developed in recent years to the status of front-line contractors, preferred by the operators to the detriment of smaller contractors. The job of the salesperson, usually with the title 'business development manager' or similar,

Year	Total	Tariffs	Other	Maintenance Platform & equipment	Field	Wages & salaries	Insurance	Transport	Platform Hire	Miscell.
1994	3,860			592	233	406	260	496	10	1,863
1995	3,913			517	290	393	226	559	4	1,925
1996	3,978			476	287	382	176	368	0	2,291
1997	4,152			536	321	358	135	311	48	2,445
1998	4,190	1,189	3,001							
1999	4,249	1,293	2,956							
2000	4,360	1,365	2,995							
2001	4,347	1,528	2,819							
2002	4,595	1,371	3,224							
2003	4,496	1,549	2,947							
P2004	4,664									

Fig CS2.4 Operating expenditure by operators and other production licensees (£million)

is to assess which projects are more suitable for their company to bid, to prepare a solution following discussions with the client and to coordinate and present the proposal to the client at the tender stage. Each solution will be customised to that project and to the client's requirements. For example, maintenance work in the southern North Sea will demand a totally different approach from fabrication work in the northern fields. For this reason, issues concerning price and product will be dictated by the market requirements of the project in question and finalised during the later stages of contract negotiations. The role of sales in this instance will be to provide the decision-makers with the relevant information based on sound analysis of the situation and particular requirements of the specific contract. As their work is mainly in the maintenance and refurbishment sector, Score's revenues and profits are more predictable since they come under the category of 'operating expenditure' (as opposed to capital expenditure).

However, the trend for partnering and alliances between large contractors and the large oil companies is creating problems for smaller players unable to offer a full service facility (Figure CS2.5).

As with many of the contractors, the terms 'sales' and 'marketing' tend to be used interchangeably. Score puts little emphasis on formal marketing, publicity or PR activity. Their approach is for their technical managers to put on their sales/business development hat and negotiate face to face for contracts and bids which they feel are attractive and the company are capable of providing. Presentations are made to clients and are based on technical solutions.

All the contractors recognise the importance of personal relationships within the industry, which also serve as a network through which new opportunities are learned of and, where appropriate, exploited. The advent of EU competition rules, which

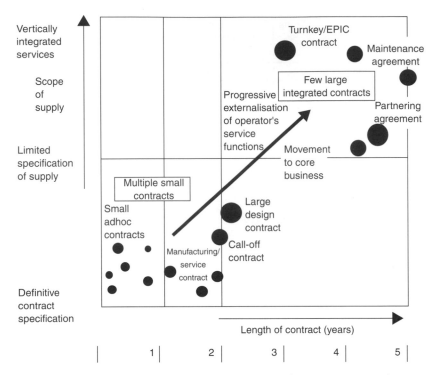

Fig CS2.5 The changing nature of North Sea oil industry contracts (*Drummond, 1993*)

demands that all new opportunities are documented, has created more bids for some of the contracts than was previously the case. Also, as the scale and variety of projects increases, so the number of personal relationships has also increased, requiring a more formal approach. The importance of personal relationships and contacts should not be underestimated, as the following quote from a manager of one of the contractors suggests:

> If you want to understand marketing in Aberdeen or North East Scotland the answer is simple. Befriend the chief buyers of the major companies, grease their palms, play golf with them and you will sell your product unless it is really bad, of course. If you want to put icing on the cake then the answer is simple. Join the correct golf club or, better still, the Freemasons. After almost 25 years of oil and gas Aberdeen is still just a service and maintenance centre. It is nothing more than a source of partially skilled labour for the rigs and production platforms. It is a retail outlet like an industrial equivalent of Tesco. Anything that is really high-tech comes from outside Aberdeen but all this talk of quality being the only name in town is nonsense. The only quality that matters in the oil patch is the quality of the back-handers and who one knows.

Although this may be seen as an extreme view, those contractors who appeared to place a low priority on such visible marketing activity were those who placed an emphasis on sales, relying heavily on the personal relationships network, which manifests itself in corporate entertainment at sports and social functions. More than one contractor have suggested that the expense involved in the bid process, plus the costs incurred with corporate entertainment, are a severe strain on their budgets. The nature and history of the industry and the methods perceived necessary to win business are responsible for such attitudes. The view in this industry is that marketing means little more than advertising and promotion. The benefits of a coordinated marketing strategy and a sound sales plan would suggest that there is considerable scope for a company such as Score to enhance their reputation and standing. Charles acknowledges that his marketing and sales operation needs to be on a more business-like and professional footing but is uncertain how to proceed. At the same time, he realises that the personal relationships in this industry are still vitally important.

Your tasks:

1 Draw up a strategic sales plan, with budgets, for Score Limited based on annual market potential of £500 million.

2 Draw up an organisational structure which incorporates marketing, sales and business development in this company.

3 Specifically, what development and training would you recommend for the existing sales/business development personnel in Score?

Fortis

Fortis (www.fortis.com) is a European business bank which is market leader in their home country, Belgium, and they are expanding their business banking network across Europe. They are one of the fastest growing companies in Europe (Fortune, 2006), and the group operates in different markets across Europe and Asia. This expansion has been mainly through various acquisitions over the past ten years which has resulted in different sales operations and practices in different markets. There are about hundred sales teams operating across Europe each with an average of eight sales people. In terms of their market growth, gross income and profit margins, they are a highly effective sales organisation.

In 2003, their net profit was 2247 million euro with a return on equity of 19 per cent. Their operations cover three distinct markets. In the Benelux countries, they operate retail and business banking and insurance where their market coverage is intensive. Elsewhere in Europe, they concentrate on business banking, factoring and leasing, asset management and offshore banking. Finally, in the global arena, their focus is on selective businesses covering Bancassurance, offshore private banking, export and trade finance.

In 1999, the company implemented a sales force automation system and a sales reporting system across the network to enable each sales organisation to measure and track their sales people's performance and activities. Until the beginning of 2004, sales performance measures were gathered through excel sheets and used between the salespeople and their sales managers. The evaluation method used corresponded with that of a class three 'supervisory' method as described by Boles, Donthu and Lohtia (1995); see Chapter 13. In 2003, the organisation decided to enhance their sales force automation system to record sales process measures to standardise the performance evaluation of their salespeople. This application enhancement was followed by the introduction of a sales reporting system providing all sales managers with the detailed performance measures of their sales people and enabling them to benchmark the results of each salesperson with the rest of the team. This system would enable sales managers to improve their sales performance evaluation methods from class three to class four using statistical methods as a basis for their comparison. The systems were implemented and have been used since January 2004. Figure CS3.1 gives an overview of this approach and Figure CS3.2 show the range of reporting tools being used at different levels of management.

Results to date indicate that the system has not achieved all of its objectives. In particular the problem of evaluation and reporting is not being fully utilised. Interviews

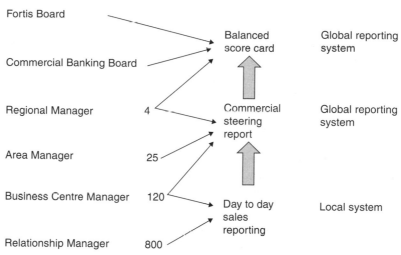

Fortis sales reporting systems in use

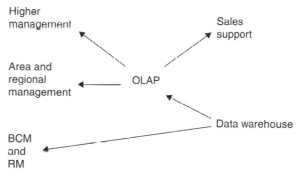

Sales reports must be available in SMS

with salespeople and sale managers revealed the following problems:

- The system of recording all the information required was excessively complex;
- Lack of training in the system;
- Existence of localised/customised sub-systems;
- Inaccurate or selective recording of data;
- Smaller teams did not use the system;
- Sales managers only want to follow the progress of larger deals.

The interviews revealed that the sales managers do not know how to link financial objectives with activity objectives. However the link between activities and financial result is assumed and objectives are given on both. The objective of introducing opportunity measures is a way for management to try and link activities, skills and results. These relationships are assumed but are not formally or statistically proven. The interviewees believe that given the quality of the data reported a large volume of data will be required for statistical analysis. In addition, they also believe that the analysis should be by country because the market conditions are so different. Others believe that the analysis will not be possible because the portfolios change too much and because the context in which each salesperson operates is too complex to measure.

At present, the information to be recorded includes calls made, conversion ratios, technical knowledge, customer portfolios, prospects and relationships. Basically there is evaluation of the process where the sales managers offer steering and coaching on activity and a yearly evaluation process linked to assessment and rewards.

This raises a number of questions:

1   Given that the information is not being fully completed to conduct class four type evaluation, benchmarking, are statistical relationships between sales effort and results going to be possible?
2   Assuming that relationships could be measured, is a causal relationship ever likely to be achieved?
3   How can salespeople and sales managers be encouraged to provide the data required?
4   How can the opportunity measures be identified and managed?

Report on these issues.

Author index

Subject index